International Praise for

The Retirement Plan Solution: The Reinvention of Defined Contribution

"With DBization as a core objective to strengthen the current DC design, but aware of the difficulties pure sponsor-guaranteed DB plans encounter as pension funds mature, the authors eloquently describe building blocks for a sustainable and satisfying retirement solution. These experienced writers have produced a work that is comprehensive yet accessible."

—THEO KOCKEN
CEO, Cardano, The Netherlands, and author of *Curious Contracts: Pension Fund Redesign of the Future*

"This is not just another retirement planning book. The authors turn sound theory, common sense, hands-on experience, and a friendly, conversational writing style into a transformative vision of how to design and implement strategies for financing retirement in the 21st century. Policy makers, employers, and employees alike will find much wisdom in this work."

—KEITH AMBACHTSHEER
Director of the Rotman International Centre for Pension Management, University of Toronto, Canada

"Ensuring a dignified retirement is an imperative for any society that dares call itself civilized. In *The Retirement Plan Solution* we finally have a roadmap that lays out how we get from here to there. This is a must-read for the retirement industry."

—CHARLES RUFFEL
Founder and Director of Asset International and Founder of PLANSPONSOR

"Improvements in DC plans are essential for us to meet tomorrow's demographic challenges. This book is really well thought through and makes a big contribution to this cause."

—ROGER URWIN
Global Head of Investment Content, Watson Wyatt, United Kingdom

"This book provides an invaluable roadmap from which to explore key characteristics of best-of-breed pension design. It contains important concepts and messages that will inevitably improve the evolution of pension products."

—DAVID ELIA
Chief Executive Officer, HOSTPLUS Superannuation
Fund, Australia

The Retirement Plan Solution

The Retirement Plan Solution

*The Reinvention of
Defined Contribution*

DON EZRA
BOB COLLIE
MATTHEW X. SMITH

WILEY

John Wiley & Sons, Inc.

Published by John Wiley & Sons, Inc., Hoboken, New Jersey.
Published simultaneously in Canada.

For general information on our other products and services or for technical support, please contact our Customer Care Department within the United States at (800) 762-2974, outside the United States at (317) 572-3993 or fax (317) 572-4002.

Wiley also publishes its books in a variety of electronic formats. Some content that appears in print may not be available in electronic books. For more information about Wiley products, visit our web site at www.wiley.com.

Library of Congress Cataloging-in-Publication Data:

Ezra, D. Don.
  The retirement plan solution : the reinvention of defined contribution / Don Ezra, Bob Collie, Matthew X. Smith.
      p. cm. – (Wiley finance series)
  Includes bibliographical references and index.
  ISBN 978-0-470-39885-2 (cloth)
     1. Defined contribution pension plans. 2. Retirement–Planning.
I. Collie, Bob, 1966– II. Smith, Matthew X., 1961– III. Title.
  HD7105.4.E97 2009
  331.25′20973–dc22   2008053368

Printed in the United States of America

10 9 8 7 6 5 4 3 2 1

This book is dedicated to:

My extended family
—Don

Corinne, Alex, and Kate
—Bob

Karen, Rachel, Emily, and Matthew
—Matt

Contents

CHAPTER 16
The Second Dial: Your Longevity Protection Policy

CHAPTER 17
The Third Dial: Investment Policy

CHAPTER 18
Product Innovation with Decumulation in Mind

Preface

The biggest pension system in the world is in the United States, where for decades the defined benefit (DB) plan ruled the roost. But since the 1980s the defined contribution (DC) plan has taken root, and as many corporations have shied away from the cost of a DB guarantee, DC now dominates the scene in the private sector. In fact, the trend from DB to DC is virtually universal, not just an American phenomenon. We have not devoted this book to a discussion of the sustainability of social security systems around the world, or bemoaning the triumph of DC over DB, or calling for new legislation that will miraculously solve all problems. Our approach is more pragmatic. We point out where the DC system, as it currently operates, is inefficient, and show how improvements in two areas can make it an extremely productive force for generating postretirement income.

The two inefficient areas are in accumulating assets, where investment returns are unnecessarily lower than they could be, and in the payout or decumulation phase, to which far too little attention is paid.

We use the United States as the basis for our arguments. But exactly the same principles apply to DC systems elsewhere, and, in fact, we use the experience of other countries to make our points, focusing on the DC system in Australia and on the "collective DC" approach in the Netherlands and Canada.

We are pleased that part of the solution is already coming into play. That makes us all the more eager to show that what is happening is part of a larger solution that requires a change in mindset, a different kind of education, and a new set of investment products. And all of these three things have started to show up. Improvement is achievable and likely. We are enthusiasts, not doom-and-gloom merchants.

We aim the book at five potential sets of readers, falling into two broad groups. One group looks at the world from the institutional point of view: plan sponsors, their consultants, and opinion leaders and policy makers. The other group looks at the same issues from a personal perspective: individual DC plan participants and financial planners.

In a sense, the main readership is the community of plan sponsors: typically employers, mainly in the private sector but increasingly in the public sector. There is one important section aimed at individuals; apart from that section, the rest of the book is directly addressed at sponsors. "Here's how your DC plans operate today. They're inefficient. You ought to get better value for the money you contribute to them. The solution is in your own hands." And a bit of: "This is now becoming part of public policy. Why not do it before it's done to you?"

We think that employers will also be interested in the section aimed at individuals, for two reasons. One is that it takes the shape of: "Here is what your participants face. Once you understand their problems, you will see why the solution improves their lives." The other is this angle: "You are a participant yourself; these are your personal issues, too." We know from experience that this angle is one that excites interest, because we have used it with our clients to great (and popular) effect.

Any book aimed at sponsors will inevitably interest the community of consultants to sponsors. This group is always interested in ideas, seeing what is new, what is in accord with their own thinking, what they disagree with, what they feel they can improve on.

An implicit group of readers is the community of opinion leaders and policy makers. We hope they will find this a short book, easy to read, with analysis and directions to follow—although we hope that the solutions will be adopted voluntarily by the sponsor community, after reading the book, discussing the issues and the solutions in industry conferences, and so on.

We address the average participant directly in one important section. "These are the issues you face and the choices you face. They are particularly difficult when your income from work ceases and you are left with your DC accumulation and you have a number of conflicting goals. Here is how to think your way through the issues and the conflicts." We are DC participants ourselves, and developed this perspective by thinking about our own situations. We believe participants will also be concerned to read a chapter that explains the studies that show how very inexpert they are as investors.

We think the financial planning community will also be interested in the chapters on individual postretirement issues and choices. We work with planners and have been told that our ideas are both original and useful. This is the first time that the ideas will have been widely published.

We aim the book directly at an American readership. But with extensive references to other countries, it will be easy for readers in other countries to identify with the issues and the solutions. That is our experience with literature in this field.

All the authors have spent a meaningful portion of their careers at Russell Investments. But this is not a "help Russell" book. Nothing in the book is aimed at favoring Russell's business or products. We came to Russell by different routes, in different countries, with different backgrounds; and we found a culture that encouraged us to think and debate and write and test our ideas in practice. We are grateful for that culture, but the book that has emerged is our own responsibility. Indeed, no one firm ever has a lock on excellence of thinking, and we have no doubt that our ideas have developed as much from discussions with clients, competitors, and other notables as they have from internal challenge. That is how our industry is, and it is all the better for it. Perhaps our only original contribution is to assemble all of these ideas and make a logical presentation of them.

We acknowledge separately many people who helped us. Their comments on our first draft made us realize two things. One is that our approach is to discuss ideas in principle and show how they can be applied in practice, but we do not prescribe a single solution as the only possible way to go. That leaves readers with the freedom to think about the issues themselves, and choose their own solutions. The second thing we realized is that we have not been driven by ideology. Our reviewers interpreted our text as supporting their own predilections, even when these pointed in opposite directions. Not, they told us, because we were not clear, but rather because we have left open the possibility of a range of different solutions—some favored by one set of experts, some by another. Our agenda is the improvement—the reinvention—of defined contribution, and our role in that is to set out the challenges as clearly as possible. There is more than one way to respond to those challenges.

Go ahead, then, and use this as a thought piece and reference book that should enhance your identification of the issues and your understanding of the possible solutions, as society strives to create the retirement plan solution. The job is crying out to be done. You can do your part.

THOUGHTS ON THE MARKET TURMOIL OF 2008–2009

We finished the body of our book just as the markets—equity markets, credit markets, currency markets—went crazy at the end of October 2008, and we felt we could not ignore the greatest financial panic our generation has seen. We write this addendum in mid-February 2009, not knowing whether the worst is behind us or still ahead of us. Logically, these observations should go after the book, which is itself written with a long-term perspective; but adding a chapter at the end diminishes the intensity of the experience. So we're placing this at the start.

What might otherwise have become a theoretical collection of ideas becomes very practical at a time when the whole financial system is being tested as it currently is. And looking at what we've written through the lens of these events sharpens the perspective. So we now touch on those ideas that appear to have grown in importance.

The first is the contrast in risk bearing between DB and DC. In a sense, the individual is always at risk, but in DB there are three buffers. The first is the pension fund itself; then there's the solvency of the sponsor; and finally (in the United States) there's the Pension Benefit Guaranty Corporation. Yes, after those buffers, the individual is still at risk, but the directness of the DC risk is in sharp contrast. In what we've called *collective DC,* that risk is shared by all the participants, whereas in the traditional individual-account DC there is no risk sharing. Plan design affects the incidence of risk enormously.

We devoted a chapter to the notion that retirement is expensive. This is not a new idea. But the uncertainty of how expensive it is arises from the uncertainty of investment returns (among other factors). This tie-in isn't often mentioned. We felt that it needed some elaboration, but because it's such an unusual concept we relegated some details to an appendix. The notion that markets might show no positive return over a 20-year period seemed outlandish to many of those we asked about it. It doesn't seem quite so outlandish now.

In the same chapter, we mention the choices available when you haven't accumulated enough money to support your desired postretirement standard of living. One is to postpone retirement. We suspect that it will now be the unhappy but necessary choice of many DC participants. In fact, when we discussed who would be affected by the stock market downturn, we knew that those close to retirement would feel it the most; but one of the many unfortunate impacts of a bear market is that a lot of people turn out to be further from retirement than they thought.

Wouldn't target date funds provide some protection? Yes, but the operative word is *some.* For the 12-month period ending December 31, 2008, the average return of the three largest target date fund families' 2010 funds (the fund for those nearest to retirement) was −24 percent.[1] This is less bad than the average return shown by global stock markets for the same period of −43 percent.[2] But "less bad" is all one can say. One ought to be at least partially grateful for whatever protection these funds provided. But the fact of risk exposure was undeniable.

The only way to avoid that risk exposure would have been to be completely out of the equity markets. You might have chosen to be out of the markets because you had low risk tolerance or because you indulged in market timing. Market timing is a dangerous tactic and very difficult to get right, because it requires you to be right twice: once in knowing when to get out of equities, and once more in knowing when to reenter the asset class.

That's a tall order, beyond the consistent capabilities of most investment professionals.

If you were out of equities because of low risk tolerance, this would have been one of those times when you could have slept more soundly than most. But then you would have denied yourself much upside opportunity over the years. Stocks rally from time to time; cash doesn't rally. The right time to decide how much exposure to the volatility of equity markets you can bear is the time you set your strategy. Once you've done so, it can be doubly damaging to get out in midstream. That's why "stay the course" has been the message of most experts.

Of course, this is not always the natural response of human beings, driven as we all are by emotional reaction. Risk tolerance itself comes into much sharper focus when you feel the downside of risk in your gut. We were reminded of our experience with DB clients in 2000–2002, when equities last tanked. Many representatives of sponsors hadn't personally experienced such a sharp down market before. Yes, they had read about the 1970s, and some remembered October 1987, but that one-day drama got lost in the calendar year charts. They looked at the standard projections of possible outcomes 10 to 15 years into the future and intellectually weighed up the pros and cons of taking different levels of risk. Then, when they lived through 2000–2002, many felt that they had overestimated their risk tolerance. We say this not to criticize them, but to remind us all that we are human and prone to overconfidence, and that not until the amygdala in our Stone Age brains triggers a feeling of panic do we really know what is the limit of our risk tolerance.[3]

The chapter on the behavioral tendencies we inherit along with our DNA seems more significant to us now.

There's one aspect of risk we simply shunted aside and ignored that now looms dramatically larger than when we were writing. It's too late for a re-treatment of the issue, but we can at least bring it to your attention here— counterparty risk. Yes, we mentioned it (well, of course—who wouldn't?). But with the serial collapses of firms that had been thought of as financial powerhouses, we now know that no financial institution is immortal, and the potential demise of any financial institution with whom you do business becomes a factor worth considering.

We don't know, as we write, the extent to which governments will feel obliged to offer blanket guarantees to restore confidence. But risk has a cost. In our everyday lives we call it a premium, and pay it year by year, whether or not the risk materializes. But governments traditionally don't take the cost into account. Few, if any, expense an annual premium in their budgets. They typically carry the risk with no reserve, and then cough up huge amounts if the risk materializes. Risk does not go away, even if its incidence is deflected or postponed. Government underwriting really means collective risk sharing for all taxpayers.

For those already in the decumulation phase of their lives, we think our ideas about the three dials they can turn, and how to prioritize them, would have been helpful if they had been adopted. Those we describe as being in the "essentials zone" wouldn't have had any exposure to stock markets. Those in the "lifestyle zone" should have had a large chunk of lifetime annuities, subject to counterparty risk (though as we write, no American life assurance company has yet collapsed) but not to equity market risk—unless these individuals or families deliberately took that risk in order to attempt to rise into the "bequest zone." Those already in the bequest zone can afford equity risk exposure, as long as they monitor (as we advise) whether they are in danger of falling into the lifestyle zone. And those in the "endowed zone" can afford a very large amount of risk exposure before their day-to-day lives are affected in any way.

We find it comforting that this approach seems every bit as sound now as it did when we wrote it up.

Somehow society manages to fill in whatever holes it finds itself in from time to time and rises again. When that happens, the ideas in this book can be considered more calmly again.

DON EZRA
BOB COLLIE
MATTHEW X. SMITH

Acknowledgments

This book reflects the collective experience of the three authors over many decades practicing in the fields of pensions and investments. No one learns in a vacuum, and we have certainly been blessed by our associations over the years. The people we have had the good fortune to interact with—plan sponsors, advisers, consultants, fellow researchers, colleagues, competitors, individuals planning for their own retirement, lawmakers, regulators—have all aided our knowledge along the way. This book, and our careers for that matter, would not be possible without such a rich association.

When you want something done, ask a busy person to do it. Over the years we have come to know a number of the leading lights in the pensions industry in many countries. We took the opportunity to send our manuscript to them and asked for their comments—at short notice, of course. Where they found the time we don't know. But they responded with insight and speed. We must have made a hundred changes as a result: some technical corrections, some clarifications, even some changes in direction. We didn't follow every piece of advice they offered, but we think the book is much better, thanks to their efforts, and we are very grateful to them.

Those who have given us permission to thank them publicly are: Michael Barry (President, Plan Advisory Services); Richard M. Ennis, CFA (Chairman, Ennis Knupp + Associates, and Editor, *Financial Analysts Journal*); Wichert Hoekert (Watson Wyatt in the Netherlands); Lori Lucas, CFA; Fred Reish, JD (Managing Partner, Reish Luftman Reicher & Cohen); Dallas L. Salisbury (CEO, Employee Benefit Research Institute); Steve Schubert, FIAA (Russell Investments–Australia); Roger Urwin (Watson Wyatt, Global Head of Investment Content); and Jack L. VanDerhei, PhD, CEBS (Research Director, Employee Benefit Research Institute).

We also want to thank the professionals at John Wiley & Sons for their help and guidance. The speed and professionalism they exhibited made this project smoother than it might have been otherwise. Thanks especially to Meg Freeborn and Laura Walsh.

Finally, thanks to those to whom this book is dedicated—our families. The time we spent writing this book is time we could have spent with them. Their patience and understanding during this project were invaluable.

DON, BOB, AND MATT

The Retirement Plan Solution

The Great American Retirement System?

The idea of an active retirement as a right is relatively modern. One of the earliest old-age pension programs was introduced in 1889 by Germany's "Iron Chancellor," Otto von Bismarck. This offered an income for life to workers who reached the age of 70. But since average life expectancy at the time was 45, this was not exactly a promise of a healthy and prolonged final phase of life, full of enjoyment.

Today, attitudes are completely different. We expect to retire from work rather than to die with our boots on. We expect to have several healthy years ahead of us when we retire. We want some fun before we go, and we expect the money to be available to pay for it. So retirement has become a phase of life to look forward to. But the longer we live, and the more we hope to do in our golden years, the more expensive a proposition it becomes.

This book is about how America—or any other country for that matter—can take steps to make that proposition affordable. We will address the background issues that make it so challenging: the fact that people are living longer, the need for regular saving throughout a working lifetime, and the demands and risks that come with putting those savings to work in the capital markets. We look at the inefficiencies built into the way in which the system operates today, and at how these inefficiencies might be overcome. We will set out a vision of how the system can be made better.

In America, "the system" is increasingly a defined contribution (DC) system, rather than a defined benefit (DB) system. America is not alone in this, although the pace of change is not the same around the world. Australia is probably furthest down the road toward DC, and among major developed economies, Japan appears to be the most committed to retaining DB. Whatever anyone's feelings about the relative merits of DB and DC, this trend means that to make the system better, DC must be made better. That's why the solution that the title of this book promises lies in the reinvention of DC.

Defined contribution plans started life as supplemental savings vehicles. Today, they have evolved into the primary retirement savings vehicle for the majority of private sector workers: the "retirement superpower" as we call it, with all of the increased attention and expectations that superpower status attracts. Despite this, it took many years for the plan's basic design to begin to change to reflect that new role. But that redesign is now well under way, and in Chapter 1 we will introduce a phenomenon that we call version 2.0 of the DC plan—a fundamentally different type of DC plan to play a fundamentally different role in the financial system.

DEFINED BENEFIT AND DEFINED CONTRIBUTION

DC is replacing DB in many places, and in a sense the difference between the two approaches is simpler—yet also subtler—than you might imagine. It is worth reminding ourselves of the basics of the two systems.

Both systems necessarily follow a fundamental pension equation:

$$\text{Contributions} + \text{Investment returns} = \text{Benefits}$$

This equation simply reflects the reality that there are only two ways to create and expand the fund from which benefits are paid. You can make contributions and you can earn investment returns. There is no magical third source of money.

Now, investment returns are uncertain. Everyone knows that in the context of the short term, stock markets can and do move 1 percent or 2 percent up or down, or even more, in a single day, and can gain or lose 10 percent, 20 percent, or more of their value over the course of a year. And that uncertainty is even greater over the long term.

The impact of that uncertainty is very different in DC than in DB. In a DB plan, the benefits are explicitly defined, so it follows that investment uncertainty is felt in the contributions required to support the benefits. It is the plan sponsor, as the ultimate contributor underwriting the benefits, that is affected by the uncertainty of the returns.

In a DC plan, the contributions are explicitly defined. So in a DC plan, investment uncertainty is felt in the benefits paid out. It is therefore the participants who are affected by the uncertainty of the returns.

Another, subtler difference lies in the management of each type of plan. The assets of a DB plan are pooled together and managed as a single portfolio. That's because each individual's expectation under the plan is defined in terms of their benefit; the assets don't need to be divided up until they are actually paid. In DC, each individual's pot of money needs to be tracked separately because that is what defines what they get from the plan.[1] Managing a single pool of assets is a different game than managing thousands of separate pools.

It should be clear, then, that the dynamics of a DC plan are different than those of its DB counterpart.

Having set this foundation in Chapter 1, the rest of this book is divided into six parts, each exploring a key component of the challenge that this change creates. These are: (1) the dynamics of a retirement plan; (2) the weaknesses and opportunities in the system as it currently works; (3) the type of education that participants need; (4) other ways in which DC plans can be run; (5) the retirement phase, from the perspective of the individual; and (6) the role of the employer in all of this. We will now provide a brief outline of each part.

THE DYNAMICS OF THE RETIREMENT PLAN

To lay the groundwork for the solutions that we will set out, Part One of this book will examine what makes DC plans tick. That begins with looking at the role of life expectancy, to which we have devoted Chapter 2. One challenge in retirement planning is that you don't know how long you are going to live. Nowadays, unlike in Bismarck's day, it could be a very long time. For the average 65-year-old American couple, there's a good chance—roughly 50 percent—that at least one of them will live to age 90 or beyond. That's a long time, long enough to indulge oneself in dreams that used to be blocked by the need to earn a living. It's worth planning for. And it's worth saving for.

The amount of saving required for retirement is large. The quality of retirement that we have come to expect is an expensive proposition, and we must steel ourselves to setting aside the necessary resources to finance it. Pension professionals around the world agree on this: Retirement expectations exceed the savings required to satisfy them, and saving more is the first essential element in an improved solution. That is a given. So in Chapter 3 we introduce a model of retirement saving that allows us to quantify just how much saving is needed to provide adequate levels of retirement income.

Starting with some base case assumptions, we see that for a typical worker to provide for a retirement income level at 80 percent of their working income, they'd need to save more than 16 percent of salary each year throughout their working life. Now, because this takes no account of Social Security, this overstates how much the typical American actually needs to contribute to their 401(k) plan, but it's still clear that this sort of savings regime is far from the norm.

Our model also allows us to vary our assumptions. Just as the fact that you don't know how long you will live presents a challenge in retirement planning, so too does the fact that you don't know how much investment return you will earn. We will see that varying the investment return makes a huge difference to the effectiveness of the system. This tells us that an inevitable feature of a DC system is that there will be cohorts of workers who happen to live through good markets in the key years and who will do very well out of DC—and there will be cohorts who are not so lucky.[2] Every individual is dependent on the markets they happen to experience, and that lies out of their control.

Of course, they are able to control some things, and we will list those. In the face of the uncertainty that is part and parcel of DC, workers must be prepared to vary their savings rate if they need to; they must be prepared to vary their retirement date; they must be prepared to adjust their expectations; and they must manage their investment program.

Investment returns are an all-important subject, and in Chapter 4, we explore this element of the dynamics of a retirement plan. We'll provide a brief overview of some of the most important principles that underpin the sound investment of any retirement program. This is also where we introduce the 10/30/60 rule, a somewhat surprising output of our savings model that shows that, in a sensibly structured lifetime investment program, every dollar drawn down in retirement is composed of roughly 10 cents originally contributed, 30 cents of investment return earned in the accumulation phase, and 60 cents of investment return earned in the decumulation phase.

The final part of our overview of the dynamics of a DC plan, in Chapter 5, is a look at sustainable spending rates. DC is not just about building up a pot of money during your working lifetime; it also needs to be managed properly on the other side of retirement, during the decumulation phase. One of the most challenging aspects of that is the question of how much income can safely be withdrawn each year. Too much, and you could run out of money. Too little, and your lifetime's effort and discipline in saving are providing you less than they could.

ROOM FOR IMPROVEMENT IN THE ACCUMULATION PHASE

In Part Two of this book, we will turn to the inefficiencies that currently exist in the accumulation phase of DC plans, and the opportunities for making this phase more effective. We will divide this up into four areas. The first (which we look at in Chapter 6) is to make sure that more goes into the system; if people do not participate in a plan, or do so at too low a savings rate, then the system cannot deliver a secure retirement. This means we need to ask questions like what to do with workers who do not have access to a DC plan, how to make sure people enroll in the plans that do exist, how to encourage adequate saving, and how to bridge the gaps in participation that occur when workers change jobs.

The second area of opportunity is to deal with the leakage that occurs when workers cash out of their plans or take loans or hardship withdrawals; this is the subject of Chapter 7.

Next, in Chapter 8, we begin to address the biggest and most complex part of the system: investment. Experience so far has been that DC plans earn lower investment returns than DB plans. That is a ball and chain around the ankle of the system. We will see that it does not have to be that way. We believe the best solution lies in creating the right type of default option. That means moving away from the emphasis on choice and on offering education to participants, and focusing instead on building prepackaged solutions based on the best practices of institutional investment.

The fourth and final area of room for improvement lies in the fees incurred by DC plans, which is the subject of Chapter 9. Administration and investment activity cost money, and it's worth paying for quality. But it's not hard to find ways in which the DC system may be paying more than it should at the moment. One way is through the use of hidden fee-sharing arrangements; the lack of disclosure can too easily lead to poor cost management. Another is the use of retail fee arrangements, such as are charged by mutual funds to individual investors; these fees tend to be higher than those paid by institutions (whose greater size allows economies of scale).

THE RIGHT SORT OF EDUCATION

In Part Three, we look in more detail at the role of the participant in a DC plan. We'll expand on the idea that the best solution to the investment flaws of the current system lies in a change of emphasis away from investment education and toward better default options. For reasons that we will explain in Chapter 10, we believe strongly that it is impossible to make the average plan participant an investment expert. It is not only futile to attempt to do so; it is actually counterproductive, and encourages behavior that results in huge amounts of waste in the system.

The problem lies in human nature. People are overconfident; they just are. They get confused by too much choice. They chase winners. The field of behavioral finance—the study of how natural human biases lead to investment mistakes—tells us a lot about why the odds are so strongly stacked against the nonexpert DC participant.

The current employee investment education model is implicitly based on the notion that, with pamphlets, communications, and seminars, any employee can be taught to develop sufficient expertise to make intelligent investment decisions and choices, down to the level of choosing specific investment funds once the broad characteristics of the fund manager's approach to investing is described. And the model is supported by the same premise that's implicit in TV networks and shows and other media that are aimed at the average participant.

In our view, this model is not only flawed, it's downright dangerous. Investing is a profession, not a hobby. The average person cannot fly an airplane, yet has no problem getting from Chicago to Atlanta whenever they want. It's a question of getting access to the people who *do* know how to fly a plane, without its costing an arm and a leg.

In fact, the education that is needed is not investment expertise. It is much more fundamental than that. It is basic financial literacy, which we consider an essential life skill. It is the ability to cope with everyday life: budgeting, banking, making simple choices, the notion of opportunity cost (every time you choose to do something, you are implicitly denying yourself the chance to do whatever your second choice is), using credit cards, and so on. This really ought to begin not in the workplace but in school. We'll look at the state of financial education in Chapter 11.

OTHER WAYS OF RUNNING DEFINED CONTRIBUTION PLANS

Part Four looks around the world for other lessons in how to make DC better. We start in Chapter 12 with a trip to Australia. We consider Australia to be the world's most advanced DC culture. It came to be that way because in 1992 the government introduced compulsion: Every employer had to have a plan that was at least as rich as a DC plan with an annual contribution of 3 percent of the worker's pay. Over time, the 3 percent figure was increased to 9 percent and, today, Australia has the largest total of DC assets in proportion to national GDP of any major country. From the Australian journey of the past 17 years, we can learn lessons about coverage, adequacy of savings, employer attitudes, and investment.

We will also describe in Chapter 13 three basic models of DC plan. These reflect different attitudes to what a DC plan is for, and may presage a future development of DC version 2.0 into version 3.0. The first model is the bank savings model, such as the earliest 401(k) plans in the United States, designed to supplement DB plans and allow tax-efficient saving. The second model is the fund supermarket model, based on choice and exemplified by Australia's DC system and the 401(k) system in the United States up to the present time. The third model is the retirement income model, explicitly aiming to replace the DB system and provide not just a savings vehicle, but a postretirement income stream designed to last a lifetime. Any DC system that aspires to being the best (rather than merely the biggest) must look to this model.

Our trip around the world is resumed in Chapter 14 with a look at the Dutch and Canadian "collective DC" approaches, which are of interest because they are the closest major systems in existence to the retirement income model we have described, while ignoring the accumulation of money in individual accounts. This chapter shows how imaginative design can go beyond the traditional concepts.

THE INDIVIDUAL'S ROLE IN DECUMULATION

In Part Five of the book, we will shift our perspective from that of the system to that of the individual and we concentrate here on the postretirement period. The financial problems faced by retirees are quite different from those faced in the accumulation phase, and the solutions too are different.

There are three basic reasons that a retirement account can run out of money: the participant could spend too much, live an unexpectedly long time, or experience poor investment returns. So we will frame this question in terms of three dials that can be turned: spending policy, longevity protection policy, and investment policy.

In Chapter 15 we describe how an individual can approach their spending policy, and how they can adjust that dial over time to balance spending power with security. In Chapter 16, we explore the concept of longevity risk, and look at how an annuity works. What is not at all well known is that the benefit from buying an annuity increases as you age—something that is difficult to explain simply in a sentence or two, but we tackle it in that chapter. Increasing benefit, declining cost: The conclusion is obvious. The later you buy a lifetime annuity, the better. In other words, self-insure as long as you can.

In Chapter 17, we jump back into the complicated world of investment. Here, we will describe the concept of wealth zones. If your preannuitized wealth (such as Social Security) is insufficient to meet basic living expenses, you are in the "essentials zone." At the point at which your wealth covers basics but is insufficient to cover your desired lifestyle (living in the style to which you are accustomed), then you enter the "lifestyle zone." Beyond that, wealth is built up to leave to others. Those who are managing their money not for spending (because that is comfortably covered) but for the wealth they will leave to others are in the "bequest zone." Finally, there is a zone above all of these, in which you are not decumulating at all—you can live your desired lifestyle out of investment returns alone, and do not need to tap into capital. That is the "endowed zone." The higher the zone you reach, the broader the range of wealth management choices that could make sense for you.

We end Part Five of the book with a look at the types of investment product that exist (or which may exist soon) for those facing the issues we have described. Annuities are not the only available product. There are variations, such as the advanced life deferred annuity. There are products that provide longevity protection but take more investment risk than traditional annuities do. There are pure decumulation products, which offer no longevity protection. Each of these—and some other variations we will mention—deals with some of the objections traditionally raised in connection with annuities. At this early stage, nobody knows which features are going to appeal most to the new generation of decumulators and thereby become the standard. But the whole scene means that there will be choice on a scale that simply was not possible even five years ago.

THE PLAN SPONSOR'S ROLE

In the final part of the book, we turn to yet another perspective on the challenge, that of the plan sponsor. We will start, in Chapter 19, with an examination of DC plan governance: how a DC plan ought to be run. Too often, the attention paid to DC plans has paled alongside that given to their DB counterparts. The challenges of running a good DC plan are just as great, however, and the right governance structure is a key to getting the rest right.

In Chapter 20 we will turn to the ways in which plan sponsors can measure the effectiveness of their DC plan. This will list nine key metrics, covering plan participation, contribution rates, investment returns, and non-retirement-related withdrawals. Only by tracking measures such as these can sponsors be sure that they are (or aren't) delivering a competitive plan.

Finally, Chapter 21 considers the simple but useful steps a plan sponsor can take to help in the postretirement phase. In the decumulation phase, the sponsor has no legal obligation; a lump sum paid to the participant discharges all DC plan obligations. But the system actually needs sponsors to help in this phase, just as it needs them to play their role during the accumulation phase. What a waste for a plan sponsor to devote time, money, and energy to building a really strong program for the working years of their employees, only to see the benefit that might have been achieved squandered through neglecting the postretirement years.

A FINAL THOUGHT: FROM BIGGEST TO BEST

The United States is the world's biggest DC culture, in the sense of having the largest amount in DC assets. It is a more subjective judgment call to say what the best DC culture would look like. But the prescriptions that we set out would significantly improve the productivity of the DC system by reducing the waste currently inherent in it—and would do so to such an extent that, if the U.S. system were to do that, we think it would become the world's best.

The same prescriptions could equally make any other country's DC system the world's best, if other countries adopt them and the United States doesn't. But it's not a contest. The best scenario would be for every country to become the best, simultaneously!

CHAPTER 1

DC Version 2.0

The earliest versions of computer spreadsheet programs—from VisiCalc in the late 1970s on—were designed for experts: academics, accountants, and computer geeks.[1] Built by guys with beards and sandals for guys with beards and sandals. Functionality was very limited indeed by today's standards. Interest was low initially. Fast-forward 30 years and Microsoft Excel is everywhere. It is enormously superior to early spreadsheets. It can calculate the inverse matrix for a matrix stored in an array or the probability density function of a Weibull distribution, which is nice if that's what you want it to do. However, most of you don't want it to do that. While improved functionality in a spreadsheet program is important, what matters even more is that it is easy for a book club secretary to type a list of members' names and telephone numbers and distribute that list to the others. Yes, the software needs the power behind it to do an awesome range of complex things for the few, but that ability cannot be at the expense of how well the far simpler needs of the many are met.

DC plans (the most popular type in the United States are called 401(k) plans, because that's the section of the Internal Revenue Code under which their tax-favored status arises[2]) are almost as old as VisiCalc. They, too, have moved on. And the developments currently under way are so fundamental that we refer to the new breed of 401(k) plan as version 2.0.

The lesson of Microsoft Excel applies to version 2.0 of the 401(k) plan. Broad-ranging success will depend on how well the needs of the many are met, more than on the esoteric features that have been built for the most expert users of the system. The ability to trade daily, for example, provides enormous flexibility for the few who really want it. Daily trading was one of a number of developments built into version 1.0 (around version 1.5, perhaps, if we want to get very literal with our analogy) that were driven by the wishes of the most interested users. Other such developments were education and advice programs, brokerage windows, mutual funds, and specialist investments such as technology funds.

But underpinning version 2.0 is the realization that these features are not the main point and that it is far more important for individuals who do not hold strong investment views to be provided with a simple-to-use but robust vehicle for retirement saving. These—the many—are the ones who most need an effective 401(k) system. These are the ones for whom version 1.0 did not work well (and version 1.5 possibly even less well), and whose needs are now really driving change. We will see again and again that what makes the new breed of 401(k) plan different is how it addresses the needs of the many, not the bells and whistles designed for the few.

COMING OF AGE

In this chapter, we will argue that the 401(k) plan is undergoing a complete redesign in corporations across America. That's not necessarily how any individual corporation sees it; they may feel that they are simply responding to changes in their regulatory and competitive environments. But behind those changes and the corporate response to them lies a fundamental reassessment of what a 401(k) plan is for. If we go beyond the plan-by-plan situation and look at the retirement system itself, the picture that emerges is a transition, led by large employers, to a totally new type of 401(k) plan.

The seeds of change were sown when the 401(k) plan stopped being regarded as a supplement to a DB plan, and instead became seen as an alternative to it. Since their inception in the early 1980s, 401(k)s have grown to cover 47.5 million workers[3] and to total more than $3 trillion[4] in assets. In the process, they outgrew their old skin. Over time, they reached a tipping point at which they stopped being merely a convenient, tax-efficient way to save, and instead became the primary vehicle for providing financial security in retirement for Americans working in the private sector.

Because 401(k) plans now play a central role in the nation's retirement provision, they have become a matter of public policy. Their new role at the center of the system became official, in a sense, on August 17, 2006, when President Bush signed the Pension Protection Act of 2006 (PPA) into law. The PPA's origins lay in the DB system's challenges, but by the time it became law it had evolved to address the pressing issues of the DC system as well. Behind the provisions lay a message: official recognition that 401(k) plans represented the future. At a stroke, the bar was raised and a spotlight was turned on these plans' weaknesses. Michael Barry of Plan Advisory Services has pointed out that, "Policymakers will not accept going from an efficient system to an inefficient one."[5]

Since the PPA was enacted, 401(k) plans—and the DC system of which they are part—have got serious about coming to terms with their new role. They are being upgraded. Before our eyes, and at a quite remarkable pace, 401(k) version 2.0 is being designed, built, tested, and launched. The new version starts with a different objective, allocates important responsibilities to different players, and indeed does just about everything differently from how version 1.0 did it. But existing 401(k) plans may be falling short in their new role.

THE NEW RETIREMENT SUPERPOWER

Few would now disagree that the 401(k) plan, not the DB plan, is the new retirement superpower. Nancy Webman, editor of *Pensions and Investments*, wrote shortly after the passage of PPA that "the new law clearly signals Washington's acceptance of the growing dominance of defined contribution plans."[6]

With the role of retirement superpower comes a world of responsibility, and 401(k) plans are now firmly in the spotlight of regulators, the press, and the public. Expectations are correspondingly higher.

Serious questions have been raised about whether 401(k) plans are able to handle this new role. Alicia Munnell and Annika Sundén have noted that "... at every step along the way, a significant fraction of participants make serious mistakes. If 401(k) plans are to become a successful vehicle for providing retirement income, the system has to be changed."[7] This quote is taken from *Coming Up Short*, a book published in 2004. A great deal has happened in the short time since then, and these words seem prescient today. As the impact of changes such as the PPA play out, the system *is* being changed. And it is being changed at just about every step along the way.

As attention has turned to the weaknesses of the 401(k) system, some of the specific areas that are receiving most attention are:

- *Participation*. In 1988, 43 percent of workers eligible to participate in a 401(k) plan did not do so. This figure has trended downward, reaching 21 percent as of 2004; however, that is still a significant proportion of the workforce that plans were failing to provide for.[8]
- *Contribution levels*. Of course, it is not enough just to participate. Typical contributions into DC plans are lower than into DB plans and there is no mystery here: What does not go in will not come out.
- *Investment decisions*. The quality of decision making within 401(k) plans is frequently poor. For example, allocations to company stock

were often higher than sound investment principles would dictate, a problem for which Enron became the poster child.[9]

- *Fees.* There is concern among some policy makers that 401(k) fees may be unreasonably high, or that undisclosed fees may be leading to conflicts of interest. There is much regulatory and other activity on this front.

- *Early withdrawals.* Munnell and Sundén estimate that, in 2001, 14.1 percent of those who could borrow from their 401(k) plans had done so and that 15.9 percent of workers had received a lump-sum distribution at some point. That using 401(k) assets for other purposes (notwithstanding the tax consequences) is relatively easy and is sometimes seen as normal practice reduces their effectiveness as a retirement savings vehicle.

That is by no means a complete list of the criticisms that have been made. We will examine each of these as well as other, more subtle issues that are likely to be different in version 2.0 of the 401(k) plan. But, first, it is informative to note how, like any successful occupying power, DC is incorporating elements of the old regime. Indeed, version 2.0 of DC will look in some regards remarkably like DB.

COMING SOON TO A DICTIONARY NEAR YOU: DBization

To capture this trend, the term *DBization* has entered the retirement-planning vocabulary. It is not in any dictionary you can buy—yet. But the term has gained traction because it rings true: Many of the most obvious weaknesses of DC in its new role are weaknesses the DB model has been able to (more or less) successfully address.

After all, DB plans were built explicitly with the goal of income replacement from the very beginning; they allow wide participation, without burden, to participants; investment decisions are made by qualified experts; and so on.

It is hardly surprising that the new challenges being faced by 401(k) plans are being met with solutions largely borrowed from a system that faced the same challenges in the past. As we look at the features that will be built into version 2.0 of the 401(k) system, we have a chance to learn from what was effective in the DB system, as well to learn from the factors that led to its weakening and decline.

AT THE HEART OF VERSION 2.0:
A DIFFERENT OBJECTIVE

Let's begin with the basics: What is the purpose of a 401(k)?

Ted Benna, who was involved in one of the earliest applications of the 401(k) provisions, describes becoming interested in the potential for Section 401(k) of the Internal Revenue Code to enable higher-paid employees to save their bonuses in a flexible, tax-efficient way. The fact that the saving was for retirement was largely incidental—and perhaps even a drawback in that "most of the employees weren't thrilled to have the cash bonus replaced by a plan that tied up their money for retirement."[10]

But version 2.0 of the 401(k) can much more easily be understood if it is thought of as a pension plan, rather than as a savings plan. This is, for example, why participation is an issue: Wealth management is for the wealthy, but retirement planning should be for everyone. In Benna's world, broad participation was a hoop to be jumped through ("The one catch was that I had to get the lower-paid two thirds to put enough money into the plan.") Broad participation was necessary in order to gain the tax break needed for the executive suite, but was not a basic principle, as it is for a DB plan.

The language we use can be revealing; it is still common in the United States to use the term *pension* to refer specifically to a DB benefit, but not to 401(k)s or other DC plans. Benna talks of a 401(k) savings plan, not a 401(k) pension plan. Indeed, the comments President Bush made when he signed the PPA included the term *pension plan* to refer to defined benefit plans. But terminology is changing. Internet searches show that the term *401(k) pension plan* is gaining ground in government and corporate web sites. This subtle change in language is one sign of the changing role that underlies the move to version 2.0.[11]

INCOME REPLACEMENT

If a savings plan is about a pot of money, a pension plan is about providing income. In the case of a DB plan, the income replacement objective is obviously central to the whole design and operation. And many of the changes occurring today are driven by the growing realization that income replacement has become the name of the game for DC plans, too.

Reporting is going to be affected. An individual participant in a 401(k) plan has been accustomed to seeing a statement that might say something like: "You have saved $50,000." A DB plan participant, in contrast, might see a statement that says: "You have accrued an annual pension of $5,000." As the DC focus shifts to income replacement, the accrued value figure will need to be supplemented with more information—information that is relevant to what the plan is there for, perhaps something like: "This $50,000 is likely to provide you with about $X in monthly income, which should be enough to replace about 15 percent of your salary, if you retire at age 60."

Left to their own devices, most people do not make this connection between their savings and their retirement income needs. For example, the 2008 EBRI Retirement Confidence Survey (its 18th annual) reveals that 53 percent of respondents had not tried to figure out how much money they will need in order to live comfortably in retirement.[12]

This reframing from a savings perspective to a pension perspective applies to the plan sponsor, too. At present, plan sponsors have little real gauge of how effective their 401(k) plan is in terms of retirement income. They know how much money is going *into* the plan. They know the accumulated value of the assets. They know, usually, the return that has been earned on those accumulated assets. But they do not know how this all fits together—that is, how effective the overall program is in terms of its fundamental purpose. In version 2.0 of the 401(k) plan, plan sponsors will have a clearer view of this big picture.

Income replacement is a high bar to set. In our previous example, $50,000 may well sound like a lot of money to the typical plan participant, but the implied level of income replacement may be much less reassuring. Income seems especially puny when interest rates are low and when life expectancy is increasing.

Income replacement in retirement for the many is a much tougher task than tax-efficient accumulation of wealth for the few.

IS THIS THE FIRST NAIL IN THE COFFIN OF DEFINED CONTRIBUTION?

Version 2.0 is being asked to do a lot more than version 1.0 and is going to be judged to a higher standard. In many cases, 401(k) plans will not compare favorably to DB plans. While DC plans *can* provide DB-like levels of benefit, they will require DB-like levels of contribution to do so. And the growth of DC has been driven in part by a desire to cut costs, so those DB-like levels of contribution are the exception, rather than the rule.

As a result, clearer reporting may lead to some dissatisfaction. When the question of income-replacement reporting first came up several years ago, one colleague, John Gillies, posed the question: "Is this the first nail in the coffin for DC?" His point: Clear reporting reassures if projections are acceptable and provides advance warning if they are not. The arithmetic must be confronted and assumptions must be laid bare. If better income-replacement reporting throws light on low levels of contribution and other inadequacies in the system, it is better to do that today—unwelcome as that news may be—than to be confronted with the social strains it would produce in 15 or 20 years' time.

This is an important point. The twin realities that lie behind any retirement system are, first, that retirement provision is expensive and, second, that investment returns are uncertain. A key factor in the decline of the DB system was that these twin realities were for a long time not fully acknowledged, with neither the cost nor the uncertainty fully reflected on corporate balance sheets for many years. Reporting changes came after falls in equity markets and at a time when interest rates were low—so the system was less well placed to face what the reporting changes revealed than it would have been a few years earlier. There are lessons from DB about what *not* to do, and this is one of them.

Moving from DB to DC removes a significant source of uncertainty from corporate balance sheets but that uncertainty does not go away: It is moved onto the balance sheets of individuals. In the DC system, people do not know how much income their plans may provide. Similarly, retirement provision is expensive no matter which way you go about building it.

DC's eventual success may well depend on better reporting, even though in the short term that will draw attention to some inconvenient realities.

"HOLD ON A SECOND . . ."

Not everybody will agree with what we have just said. In particular, many plan sponsors will balk at the idea that 401(k) plans are now pension plans, designed for the provision of retirement income, rather than savings plans. Focusing on income replacement is more complex and demanding than focusing on savings. This new world would mean that plan sponsors can no longer just hire a record keeper, put in their company match, and call it good.

When confronted with the notion of 401(k)-as-pension-plan, plan sponsors vary in their responses. Some welcome the idea: They view a Version 2.0 DBized 401(k) plan as a superior benefit, and they want to be part of it. Others wonder what is in it for them: After all, many of them have just closed their DB plans in order to get out of the business of providing retirement income, and they have no wish to be back in it. In part, this just reflects different corporate cultures. Whatever the reason, there are many plan sponsors who would take the view that version 1.0 was fine, thank you very much.

But whether or not plan sponsors feel this way is, in a sense, irrelevant. There are wider societal forces that are driving the 401(k) system to reinvent itself. The changes in the PPA signal that the effectiveness of the system is now a matter of public policy. DC is new again; we have a chance to build it better this time.

One

The Dynamics of the Retirement Plan

In one sense, the way that a retirement plan works is not very complex: Money is set aside for a number of years and then, later, that money (along with any additional money that those savings have been able to generate through investment returns) is withdrawn to support an individual once they are no longer working. What makes it complex is that there are so many variables that can affect the operation of a plan like this. In the four chapters that follow we will explore the nature of the most important of those variables.

This section is intended to lay the groundwork for the rest of the book: For example, in order to understand why the design of the decumulation products available to retirees is important, it is first necessary to have a feeling for what the biggest financial risks faced by retirees are. It is background for all of our intended readers: plan sponsors and their advisers, individuals and their advisers, and opinion leaders.

The first of the four chapters is devoted to the question of life expectancy (or longevity). This is a subject that has been largely ignored in much of the retirement savings debate in the past. However, if the goal of a retirement system is to provide income throughout retirement, it is important to know how long that retirement is likely to be.

The second variable that we will explore is the level of saving that is put into the plan: How much is enough? And how confident can we be in our answer? The third variable is investment returns. These obviously matter, but it is easy to miss just *how much* they matter. Finally, we will explore the dynamics of the spending policy: how much money is taken out of the plan each year after retirement.

Together, these four variables (how long you will live, how much you save, how much your savings earn in the investment markets, and how much you spend) will determine whether a retirement plan is effective or not.

Armed with the principles set out in these four chapters, we will be ready to turn from the theoretical basis for a retirement plan to the world as it actually works. (Which is just our way of saying: If you find the going gets a bit heavy in places, feel free to skip ahead.)

CHAPTER 2

More than You Ever Wanted to Know about Life Expectancy

We're living much longer than we used to. In this chapter we look at that simple statement in more detail. The reason it's relevant is that the longer we live after our income from work stops, the more we need to save during our working years to last through our post-work lifetime. As mentioned in the Introduction, for the average American couple these days, it's pretty much a 50-50 proposition that at least one member of the couple will survive to age 90.

WHAT IS "LIFE EXPECTANCY"?

The life expectancy of a group of people is the average number of future years of life expected to be lived by that group. The group is typically defined by age and gender. For example, if you were to define a group as "male Americans aged 65" and look up the relevant National Vital Statistics Report published in 2002,[1] you would find that the average future expectancy for this group was 16.3 years. That means that, if you took, let's say, a group of 1,000 male Americans aged 65, randomly selected, they would have been expected (at the time—these estimates vary each year) to live for a total of 16,300 more years. How long would any one of them live? It's impossible to predict. Some would live a long time, perhaps more than 35 years. Some would die soon. Together, their individual life spans would be distributed over a wide range of time. But the average expectancy was then 16.3 years—and that's what people mean when they talk about the life expectancy of American males aged 65.[2]

Life expectancy is actually measured by recording two sets of things. First, how many people are alive at any given time, grouped by age (and gender and whatever other classification is of interest)? For the population as a whole, this is recorded at every ten-year census. And second, what proportion of people at each age die in the following year? For the population as a whole, this is averaged over the year of the census and the immediately preceding and following years. The average mortality rate for each age is then calculated. The proportion that survives can then be calculated. And by aggregating the survival rates, the average future expectancy results. Because death rates change from year to year, so too does the future life expectancy.

When the future life expectancy is calculated from birth, it is typically just called the population life expectancy. In the 2002 Report (which was based on the 2000 national census) that number was an average life expectancy of 76.9 years for the population as a whole. (Actually, it was an average of 74.1 years for males and an average of 79.5 years for women.)

How can males have an average life expectancy of 74.1 years at birth and 65-year-old males have an average expectancy of 16.3 years? Shouldn't the 65-year-olds expect, on average, to live to 74.1, so that their future average life expectancy should be just 9.1 years? No. The average life expectancy at birth is for all males. Some die before 65, some die after 65. Those who die before 65 bring the average down. Those who survive to 65 are longer-lived than the early-dying group. Those who survive to 65 die, on average, at age 81.3 (that's 65 plus 16.3). Those who die before 65 die, on average, much younger. Across both groups (those who die before 65 and those who die after 65), the average age at death is 74.1 years.

When we're just born, we don't care about our future life expectancy. It only really starts to matter when we reach our older years. At that point, it's the future expectancy we're interested in, measured from our current age.

HOW LIFE EXPECTANCY HAS CHANGED

Around 1900, average life expectancy at birth in the United States was just over 49 years. Because of healthier foods and lifestyles and medical advances, it has kept increasing. Measured every 10 years (based on the 10-year censuses that we have), it finally passed age 70 in 1970, hitting 70.8 years. Based on the 2000 census, it reached 76.9 years in 2000. The progression of life expectancy at birth throughout the twentieth century is illustrated in Figure 2.1.

Much of the improvement came about because deaths at younger ages started to decline. Thus, for the average survivor to age 65 (a relatively small group in 1900), the future life expectancy was then 11.9 years. That increased to 15.0 years by 1970. That means that, of the total increase in life expectancy at birth (from 49.2 years to 70.8 years, an increase of 21.6 years), only a small portion came from higher survival rates after reaching

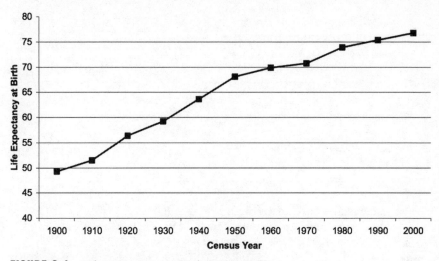

FIGURE 2.1 Life Expectancy at Birth, 1900–2000

age 65; the other 18.5 years of the improvement between 1900 and 1970 came from fewer people dying at ages below 65, because they didn't die in their infancy or their youth.

In 2000 the average life expectancy at age 65 reached 17.9 years. The increase since 1970 in the average expectancy at birth is 6.1 years (from 70.8 to 76.9), while the increase in expectancy after age 65 is 2.9 years (from 15.0 to 17.9), so the effect of survival rates after age 65 has been proportionately much bigger in recent years. This is because there is now much less scope for increasing longevity between birth and age 65; most of the improvement has already taken place. In the future, most of the improvement in life expectancy at birth is likely to take place after age 65, as medical science continues to improve our chances of survival when disease hits us in old age. Figure 2.2 illustrates the increase in life expectancy at age 65 over the past century.

Of all Americans born, the proportion reaching age 65 as of the 2000 census was just above 82 percent (about 78 percent for men and 86 percent for women). Figure 2.3 shows the percentage of Americans reaching age 65 from 1900 to 2000.

BUT AN INDIVIDUAL'S LIFE SPAN IS UNCERTAIN

The authors are in the investment business, and more mathematically oriented than the average person. And we're used to the idea that the future is uncertain. Telling us what the average outcome is expected to be in the future isn't enough for us. We want to know how uncertain that average

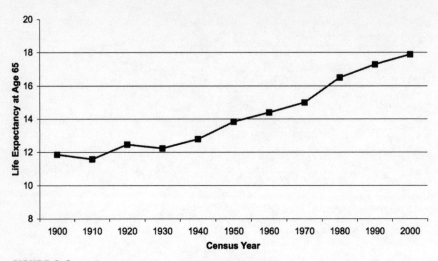

FIGURE 2.2   Life Expectancy at Age 65, 1900–2000

is. And we need to incorporate that uncertainty into our planning, because retirement lasts *exactly* 16.3 years for very few people. Is the distribution of possible outcomes tightly clenched around the average, or is it widely spread? That makes a difference. If it's tightly clenched, we can pretty much count on the average happening, or something close to the average. If it's a wide distribution, then the average doesn't tell us much.

So, when the oldest among the authors hit age 60, a natural question for him to ask was not just "What's my future life expectancy?" but to add "And

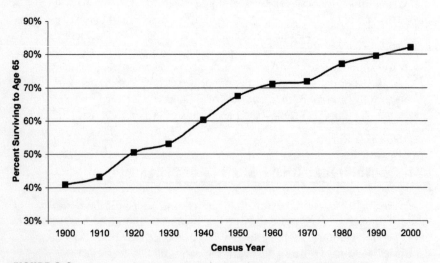

FIGURE 2.3   Percent of Americans Born Reaching Age 65, 1900–2000

what's its standard deviation?"—the standard deviation being a measure of how wide the distribution is. Strangely, nobody seemed to know. And for all the volumes of publications available, none that we found specified the standard deviation.

Friends didn't even understand the concept. "How can you have a standard deviation? You're either dead or alive. When you die, that's it. That will tell you what your longevity is. It's just one number."

Yes, of course. In just the same way, when one looks back, one has experienced only a single rate of return over one's lifetime of investing. But when one looks forward, there's uncertainty. In the same way, looking forward, 21 years might be the average number of years that a group of 60-year-old males will continue to live; but they'll all live for different lengths of time. Their ages at death will form a distribution. How wide is that distribution? That's what the standard deviation of life expectancy measures.

So that author did the calculation himself. He used the relevant table to project how many 60-year-old males would die after living one year, how many after living two years, and so on. That produced the distribution. And then the standard deviation followed.

He asked five mathematically oriented friends what they thought the standard deviation might be. One year? Five years? Ten? Longer? Three of the five people thought 5 years, one thought 10, one thought 15. It turned out to be a little more than 9 years. One colleague, an actuary, clearly had the right mind-set. He said: "A few will live to 100. Let's say that's a two-standard-deviation event. If the average age at death is 81, then 19 more years will be roughly two standard deviations. So, in round numbers, I'd say 10 years is the standard deviation."

Two surprising thoughts emerged through all of this. One is that the distribution is extremely wide. Plot the proportion of deaths at each age, and you get a distribution wider and less peaked than the typical investment return distributions we are used to. That suggests that longevity is a big risk, and we need to consider it seriously, particularly those of us who are risk averse. We'll consider this thoroughly in Part Five of the book, where we deal with issues faced by any individual planning to decumulate.

The other surprising thing is how wrong the admittedly small sample of friends turned out to be in their estimates of the standard deviation of longevity. One was right; three were 50 percent too low; one was 50 percent too high. Imagine the same range when considering the standard deviation of equity returns. Let's say it's roughly 16 percent per annum. Imagine that we think it's only 8 percent (too low by half). Or that it's 24 percent (too high by half). We would make completely inappropriate asset allocation decisions if our estimates of the standard deviation were 50 percent off the mark. Yet that may be the state of affairs with the uncertainty of longevity.[3]

If we don't have a rough, intuitive idea of how large the uncertainty is, we will make decisions that are totally inappropriate.

Clearly, financial planning for decumulation requires us to understand longevity risk just as deeply as we understand investment return risk. With that in mind, let's look at some statistics on life expectancy and its distribution.

LONGEVITY DISTRIBUTIONS: LET'S TAKE A LOOK

Let's start with a picture of a longevity distribution. In this case it is based on a life expectancy table called RP 2000, which is the one required by the Internal Revenue Service (IRS) for use in certain pension fund calculations.[4] This table has a number of components. The specific survival rates used here are those for "healthy annuitants."

Figure 2.4 shows, for a large group of males of various ages, the proportions that are projected to die after one year, two years, and so on, according to RP 2000.

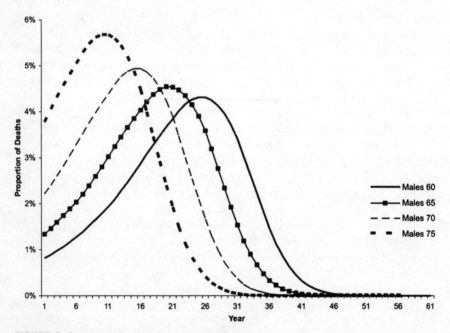

FIGURE 2.4   Longevity Distributions for Males

Several aspects of Figure 2.4 are worth noting. The curves look almost normally distributed, for those ages.

There is a right-hand tail, because a very few are expected to survive to extreme old age. But the distributions clearly don't have a left-hand tail, because at those starting ages a noticeable proportion of the group is expected to die within the first year. There would be a left-hand tail if the starting age were very young, because relatively few die young.

Although RP 2000 projects a few survivors to age 120, in actuality virtually no males aged 60 are expected to survive for more than about 45 more years, nor males aged 75 for about 30 more years—that is, beyond age 105.

These curves are flatter than the one-year distributions we're accustomed to seeing for equity returns. Assuming a standard deviation of 16 percent per annum, the equity return distribution peaks at about a 10 percent proportion on the vertical axis; that is, it's much steeper than these longevity curves, implying a tighter distribution. And, of course, a typical one-year bond return distribution would be even tighter and more peaked than an equity return distribution. Figure 2.5 shows the patterns for women.

The patterns in Figure 2.5 are all but identical to those in Figure 2.4, although of course the careful reader will notice that the numbers are different.

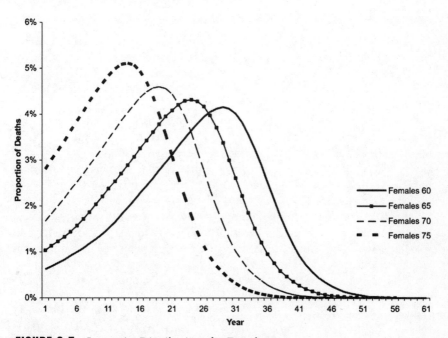

FIGURE 2.5 Longevity Distributions for Females

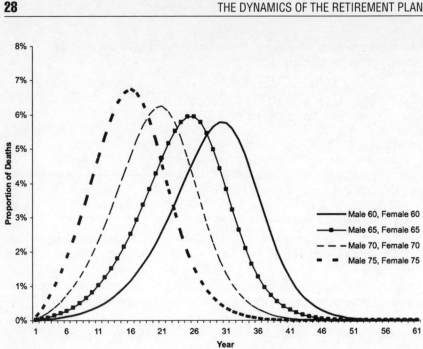

FIGURE 2.6   Longevity Distributions for Second Death, Males and Females

Typically, financial planning for decumulation involves a couple rather than a single person, and has as its goal that the income is required to last (although perhaps at a lower level) as long as the second-to-die of the couple survives. So it might be interesting to see the longevity curves for the second-to-die of a couple (Figure 2.6).

Once again, the general shape of the curves is unaltered; though this time the curves do seem to start very close to 0 percent on the left-hand side, because the chance that both partners will die early is small.

Notice that the curves do stretch a little further to the right, meaning that the second death takes place at a later age than if we were considering only a single individual.

Because of the lower starting point on the left, the curves appear to be a little bit more concentrated in the middle than are the curves for males and females separately. This is confirmed in Table 2.1, which shows numerical summary statistics.

The standard deviations for second-to-die combinations are typically smaller than for single lives because the curves are pushed closer to the right-hand end of the distributions, but the right-hand ends are all forced by the RP 2000 tables to stop by age 120. Hence the slight squashing effect, resulting in lower standard deviations.

TABLE 2.1 Average Life Expectancies and Standard Deviations in Years*

Male age	Expectancy	Std Dev
60	21.6	9.1
65	17.6	8.2
70	13.9	7.2
75	10.6	6.1

Female age	Expectancy	Std Dev
60	24.2	9.9
65	20.1	9.0
70	16.2	8.1
75	12.7	7.1

Second-to-die combinations

Male/female age	Expectancy	Std Dev
60/60	28.4	7.4
65/60	26.8	7.8
65/65	23.9	7.0
70/65	22.3	7.3
70/70	19.5	6.6
75/70	18.1	6.8
75/75	15.5	6.0

*Calculated from RP 2000 tables for healthy annuitants.

Because the distributions are not symmetrical, the standard deviations themselves are far from perfect representations of the width of the distributions—although their relative sizes do seem to capture the main characteristic of how wide the distributions are.

WHAT DOES THIS MEAN?

As promised in the title of this chapter, this is probably more than you ever wanted to know about longevity. But here is the point. Once we have reached age 60 or 65, the average ones among us are likely to live for a long time yet, probably much longer than you guessed. And the average among us are married. Let's look at the second-to-die combinations in Table 2.1.

For a man and a woman both aged 60, the second-to-die expectancy is 28.4 years. That's the average period until both have died. If you're making plans for the future, at least one half of the couple is likely to be alive until age 88.4. For a 65-year-old couple, it's until age 88.9. For a 70-year-old couple, it's age 89.5. All those numbers are close to 90. For the typical couple starting out on their retirement years, there's a good chance that at least one of them will live close to age 90 or beyond.[5]

And that is the average future life expectancy for the survivor of the couple. If you want to plan to have money for longer than the average expectancy, add another five years to your planning horizon to give yourself a 75 percent chance of having enough money, and a further four years to give yourself a 90 percent chance of having enough money. (And even then, 1 couple in 10 will have the survivor still alive at that age.)

That's what all of this means. An exciting prospect, if we can stay healthy. A scary prospect: saving enough to enjoy it.[6]

AND WILL LONGEVITY IMPROVE EVEN MORE?

Most experts think that longevity will continue to improve. While a full discussion would go far beyond the scope of this book, we encourage you to look at Bryan Appleyard's book *How to Live Forever or Die Trying* to learn more.[7]

CHAPTER 3

Retirement Is Expensive

Typical savings rates in a DC plan are around 10 percent of earnings, 7 percent coming from employees and 3 percent from employers.[1] Is this consistent with an aspiration for the plan to replace a significant portion of an individual's salary in retirement? How much does a retirement system require in terms of contributions if it is to satisfy the expectations of workers and, indeed, of society? Those are the questions addressed in this chapter. Based on a simple model of wealth accumulation over a working lifetime and wealth decumulation in retirement, we will explore the interaction of savings and investment growth and reach two main conclusions. The first conclusion is that income replacement in retirement is expensive. The second conclusion—one that is far less widely recognized—is that we cannot with any great degree of certainty be sure exactly what sort of savings rate will deliver a meaningful income replacement level in retirement.

Recall the fundamental pension equation that underlies any retirement system:

$$\text{Contributions} + \text{Investment returns} = \text{Benefits}$$

This applies to both defined benefit (DB) and defined contribution (DC). In both systems, investment returns are uncertain. The difference between the two lies in which of the other two components of the equation is held constant. In DB the benefits are defined, so contributions are uncertain and depend on variations in investment returns. In DC it's the other way around; the contributions are defined, so the benefits are uncertain and depend on investment returns.

THE GOAL IS A TARGETED LEVEL
OF INCOME REPLACEMENT

Since the whole point of the DC plan is to provide retirement income, it is sensible to have an idea of how much income we are aiming for. It is normal to think of this in terms of income replacement. That way of thinking has a couple of advantages. The first is that it is fairly easy for anyone—no matter what their income—to grasp roughly what the targeted income level would mean. The second is that it automatically adjusts for the effects of inflation. If you earn $50,000 today, then a savings program designed to provide $50,000 a year in 20 years' time might sound more than adequate ... but $50,000 in 20 years' time will not go as far as $50,000 today (remember how much candy cost when you were young?). If that same program was expressed as targeting 50 percent of final earnings, then it is easier to understand what that might mean in terms of standard of living.

Several people have done some good thinking about what the right level of targeted income replacement should be. Aon Consulting, in a joint study with Georgia State University,[2] concluded that someone earning $30,000 a year should aim for a total income in retirement of 90 percent of their working income (it is less than 100 percent because, for example, the retiree typically gets an income tax break at 65, does not face commuting costs, and is no longer saving for retirement). Further, they calculate that Social Security would provide 59 percent income replacement, leaving a shortfall of 31 percent to be met from other sources. For someone earning $60,000, they estimate a required replacement ratio of 78 percent of preretirement earnings, with 46 percent coming from Social Security and the shortfall of 32 percent to be met from other sources. For someone earning $90,000, the numbers are: 78 percent required replacement ratio, 36 percent from Social Security, and 42 percent from other sources.[3]

So it appears that a reasonable target for an average American worker might be to replace 80 percent of preretirement income, and for a DC plan and additional personal saving to replace 40 percent of the participant's income, although depending on circumstances, a higher or lower target for the DC plan may well make sense.

Let us add two notes of caution, both of which suggest higher targets. One is that, over the years, this series of studies has shown a trend to higher and higher targets. For example, at $30,000 the 2001 study suggested a target of 81 percent, which by 2008 had risen to 90 percent; at $90,000 the 2001 target of 75 percent had risen to 78 percent by 2008. The other cautionary note is that these replacement ratios are for workers with similar health care benefits provided by their employers before and after retirement. For workers with preretirement but not postretirement health care benefits, the study suggests a further $5,000 a year be added to the replacement target income.

Some experts have told us that we should use an overall target of at least 85 percent as our base case, with at least 45 percent coming from a DC plan and additional personal saving. We have used 80 percent and 40 percent in what follows, not from a conviction that it's right and 85 percent/45 percent is wrong, but simply because it's easy enough for readers to adjust our results to any targets that they think make sense, and in any case one of our messages is that there is no single right number for anything when future investment returns are involved.

THE FUNDAMENTAL PENSION EQUATION AND THE DEFINED BENEFIT SYSTEM

In the context of the DB system, the fundamental pension equation has meant that a great deal of talk and energy was devoted to finding appropriate rules for determining contributions. The latest development was the Pension Protection Act of 2006 (PPA), which was intended to reduce the risk of DB funding proving to be inadequate. It increased the pace at which shortfalls need to be made good, with the result that contributions may need to increase rapidly following periods of poor investment performance. Even before PPA, contributions were volatile and unpredictable. For example, according to its annual reports, oil giant Exxon-Mobil made no contribution at all to its U.S. DB pension plan in 2004 or 2005. In 2006, it contributed $2.383 billion. Many other corporations have faced similar volatile funding costs.[4]

This uncertainty that corporations face in the DB world is transferred—in a DC world—onto the individual. The same dynamic that leaves corporations like Exxon-Mobil flip-flopping in their view of what the contribution needs to be in the fundamental pension equation is still there in DC. But in DC its impact is on the benefit component of the equation.

All of this serves to underline just how important the investment returns are in a retirement system. So much so that it is impossible to say much that is meaningful about contributions or benefits without recognizing the interaction between them. To demonstrate this basic truth, we will introduce a simple model of retirement saving, which will reappear at various points throughout this book.

A SIMPLE MODEL OF RETIREMENT PLAN
ACCUMULATION AND DECUMULATION

The model that we will describe is basic in nature, but incorporates all of the main dynamics affecting retirement savings. Interested readers who would like to explore those dynamics further will be able to duplicate the model on their own computers, using their own spreadsheet programs, and test the impact of different assumptions. In this and subsequent chapters, we will spell out our own main conclusions.

In the base case of our model the participant joins the DC plan at age 25. His or her salary is taken to be $25,000 at that point in time (although we should note that this assumption is of little importance, because we will concentrate on percentage savings rates, and percentage income replacement ratios, so an individual earning $50,000 would accumulate double the savings, but those savings would produce exactly the same retirement income as a percentage of earnings). Our individual puts 4 percent of before-tax earnings into the DC plan. Our model awards them a 4.75 percent pay increase each year on their birthday. They are assumed to retire at age 65. Investment returns are assumed to be earned each year on the account at the rate of 7.5 percent a year. This return is applied in full to the account balance at the start of each year, and half of it is applied to contributions in the year that they are made. (This is approximately equivalent to assuming that contributions are made evenly throughout the year.)[5]

That first set of assumptions allows us to model the buildup of the retirement account over the 40 years of our individual's working lifetime, and to calculate the account balance at retirement. Our base case takes a very simple approach to modeling decumulation (in a later chapter, we will make some variations to this approach, in order to explore some of the questions facing those in that stage—but for current purposes, the simple approach is perfectly adequate). This approach is to assume that distributions will begin from the plan at retirement and will rise by 3 percent each subsequent year (reflecting an increasing cost of living) until death at age 90, which you will recall from Chapter 2 is roughly the median age at death of the second-to-die for a healthy American retired couple. The level of distribution that we assume is chosen so as to leave the account balance at exactly zero at the point of death.

BASE CASE RESULTS

Table 3.1 shows the year-by-year experience of our model participant under the base case assumptions. One observation we can make about this base

TABLE 3.1 Base Case Retirement Savings Model with 7.5 Percent Investment Rate of Return Both Pre- and Postretirement

Participant's Age	Accumulated Savings at Start of Year	Contribution Made to Plan	Distribution Made from Plan	Rate of Investment Return	Investment Gain	Accumulated Savings at End of Year
25	0	1,000	0	7.5%	38	1,038
26	1,038	1,048	0	7.5%	117	2,202
27	2,202	1,097	0	7.5%	206	3,506
28	3,506	1,149	0	7.5%	306	4,961
29	4,961	1,204	0	7.5%	417	6,582
30	6,582	1,261	0	7.5%	541	8,384
31	8,384	1,321	0	7.5%	678	10,384
32	10,384	1,384	0	7.5%	831	12,598
33	12,598	1,450	0	7.5%	999	15,047
34	15,047	1,518	0	7.5%	1,185	17,751
35	17,751	1,591	0	7.5%	1,391	20,732
36	20,732	1,666	0	7.5%	1,617	24,016
37	24,016	1,745	0	7.5%	1,867	27,628
38	27,628	1,828	0	7.5%	2,141	31,597
39	31,597	1,915	0	7.5%	2,442	35,953
40	35,953	2,006	0	7.5%	2,772	40,731
41	40,731	2101	0	7.5%	3,134	45,965
42	45,965	2,201	0	7.5%	3,530	51,696
43	51,696	2,306	0	7.5%	3,964	57,966
44	57,966	2,415	0	7.5%	4,438	64,819
45	64,819	2,530	0	7.5%	4,956	72,305
46	72,305	2,650	0	7.5%	5,522	80,477
47	80,477	2,776	0	7.5%	6,140	89,392
48	89,392	2,908	0	7.5%	6,813	99,114
49	99,114	3,046	0	7.5%	7,548	109,707
50	109,707	3,190	0	7.5%	8,348	121,245
51	121,245	3,342	0	7.5%	9,219	133,806
52	133,806	3,501	0	7.5%	10,167	147,473
53	147,473	3,667	0	7.5%	11,198	162,338
54	162,338	3,841	0	7.5%	12,319	178,499
55	178,499	4,024	0	7.5%	13,538	196,061
56	196,061	4,215	0	7.5%	14,863	215,138
57	215,138	4,415	0	7.5%	16,301	235,854
58	235,854	4,625	0	7.5%	17,862	258,341
59	258,341	4,844	0	7.5%	19,557	282,743
60	282,743	5,074	0	7.5%	21,396	309,214
61	309,214	5,316	0	7.5%	23,390	337,919
62	337,919	5,568	0	7.5%	25,553	369,040
63	369,040	5,832	0	7.5%	27,897	402,769
64	402,769	6,110	0	7.5%	30,437	439,316
65	439,316	0	29,017	7.5%	31,861	442,159
66	442,159	0	29,888	7.5%	32,041	444,312
67	444,312	0	30,785	7.5%	32,169	445,697

(*Continued*)

TABLE 3.1 (*Continued*)

Participant's Age	Accumulated Savings at Start of Year	Contribution Made to Plan	Distribution Made from Plan	Rate of Investment Return	Investment Gain	Accumulated Savings at End of Year
68	445,697	0	31,708	7.5%	32,238	446,227
69	446,227	0	32,659	7.5%	32,242	445,810
70	445,810	0	33,639	7.5%	32,174	444,345
71	444,345	0	34,648	7.5%	32,027	441,723
72	441,723	0	35,688	7.5%	31,791	437827
73	437,827	0	36,758	7.5%	31,459	432,527
74	432,527	0	37,861	7.5%	31,020	425,686
75	425,686	0	38,997	7.5%	30,464	417,153
76	417,153	0	40,167	7.5%	29,780	406,766
77	406,766	0	41,372	7.5%	28,956	394,350
78	394,350	0	42,613	7.5%	27,978	379,716
79	379,716	0	43,891	7.5%	26,833	362,657
80	362,657	0	45,208	7.5%	25,504	342,953
81	342,953	0	46,564	7.5%	23,975	320,364
82	320,364	0	47,961	7.5%	22,229	294,631
83	294,631	0	49,400	7.5%	20,245	265,476
84	265,476	0	50,882	7.5%	18,003	232,597
85	232,597	0	52,409	7.5%	15,479	195,667
86	195,667	0	53,981	7.5%	12,651	154,337
87	154,337	0	55,600	7.5%	9,490	108,227
88	108,227	0	57,268	7.5%	5,969	56,929
89	56,929	0	58,986	7.5%	2,058	0

case is that our plan participant receives payouts totaling $1.06 million, while having contributed less than $114,000. So 90 percent of the distributions represent not the return of the original contributions, but rather the investment returns earned. We will come back to this observation in the next chapter.

At this point, we want to concentrate on another relationship within the numbers: the ratio of the contribution (4 percent of earnings) to the distribution (which is a retirement income of 19 percent of final salary). This income replacement of just 19 percent is well below what most people are looking for from their 401(k), and it is fair to conclude that the main reason for this is that a 4 percent savings rate is too low. But our model appears to quantify exactly how much is required for a chosen level of income replacement. Based on this result, you could easily conclude that anyone could set any retirement income target they choose and back out the required savings rate: So if the target for the DC plan is 40 percent income replacement, then a savings rate of 8.4 percent of earnings would be needed.

That doesn't actually sound particularly expensive. Unfortunately, things are not quite that simple for two reasons.

One reason is that this result ignores the contribution made to the Social Security system. Employers and employees together contribute 12.4 percent of wages covered by Social Security.[6] Add an 8.4 percent DC plan contribution, and a U.S. worker requires contributions of roughly 20 percent of pay for an adequate replacement ratio.[7] Now that's expensive.

In a country without this sort of Social Security system, the 80 percent target replacement ratio would, in this base case, require a contribution rate of 16.8 percent of annual pay. That too is expensive.

But there is a second reason we can't just cite the base case result as a precise quantification of how much we need to save. As we are about to see, the results can vary if the key assumptions vary. We will look at two of the most important of these assumptions: the age at which saving begins and the investment returns earned. And we will look at only the DC plan, ignoring its integration with Social Security.

WHEN TO START SAVING

Our base case looked at a 40-year savings program. Our worker joined the plan at age 25 and saved 4 percent of his salary every year until retirement at age 65. That's a good model, but not necessarily what happens in practice. So we need to test how much the results change for different ages of joining the plan. Rerunning the base case with a start date of our worker's thirtieth birthday (5 years later) sees the income replacement rate fall to 15.4 percent of final earnings. Now a 40 percent replacement target would no longer call for a 8.4 percent savings rate, but 10.4 percent. If the start date is pushed back to age 35 then that same 40 percent replacement target requires a savings rate of 12.2 percent, and if saving does not begin until age 40 (giving the worker just 25 years to save for a retirement that may well last just as long) then the required savings rate jumps to 16.8 percent of earnings—double what was needed in our 25-year-old base case.

From this we conclude that, while it is better to start saving sooner rather than later—and a high retirement income replacement ratio becomes less attainable (or more expensive) the longer one waits—all is not lost if a worker is not signed up and locked into a savings plan by age 25. If they are, that is a terrific start to a good program. But if they are not, it is still worthwhile to join later when they can.

THE BASE CASE MAY NOT BE A RELIABLE GUIDE

Now, the base case is fine as far as it goes, but it does not replicate the actual experience that any individual will have. Not only will the date at which saving starts vary, but savings rates may fluctuate, salary progression may fluctuate, or retirement may occur earlier or later than age 65. And, most importantly of all, investment returns will not be exactly 7.5 percent each year, year in, year out, steadily and surely growing our plan participant's savings in a reliable, predictable progression toward a reliable, predictable retirement.

Instead, the rate of return will move dramatically from year to year (anyone with even a passing interest in the stock market knows that much), and the consequence of those fluctuations is to make even the long-term averages far less predictable than is widely assumed.

To illustrate this, consider the return that you would expect the U.S. equity market to deliver on average over the next 20 years. We do not, however, want a single estimate. We want you to think about a good case outcome and a bad case outcome, and to produce a range of possible average returns that you are 90 percent confident will encompass the actual outcome. Take a moment to decide what your range is—remember that we want you to be highly confident (90 percent) that the actual outcome will fall within it.

Before we tell you whether you did a good job of picking your range or not, let us mention that we chose a period of 20 years because our model is based on a working lifetime of 40 years, with saving occurring throughout that working lifetime. So some dollars will have 40 years to grow before retirement and some will have hardly any time to grow—and, on average, each dollar will have about 20 years of preretirement investment return.

Maybe you said 4 percent to 12 percent. So what happens if we plug a 4 percent preretirement return into our base case model? Now the retirement income replacement of our individual is no longer 19 percent, but 9.4 percent. That's less than half of the result we obtained a moment ago with a 7.5 percent investment return. A 40 percent targeted replacement ratio now calls for a savings rate of 17 percent of salary—a far cry from the 8.4 percent we found earlier.

Maybe things will turn out well (after all, most people tend to be quite optimistic that things will work out in the end). What happens if we plug a 12 percent preretirement return into the model? The 19 percent retirement income replacement jumps up to a very nice 55 percent—the higher assumed investment return has turned $114,000 of contribution into more than $3 million of retirement income. If investment returns are good enough, maybe there's not such a great need to panic over our 401(k) contributions after all.

Sadly, we don't know—and cannot control—whether investment returns will average 4 percent a year for the next 20 years or 12 percent. And that realization should start to throw some light on a very important fact about the question of how much saving really needs to be done if DC plans are going to meet the retirement expectations of current workers: *We simply don't know* just how much saving is really going to be needed. Investment markets are too unpredictable. And we have actually been understating our case; as an appendix to this chapter, we will explore what the uncertainty associated with investment returns really is—and the impact will turn out to be even greater than this comparison of the impact of a 4 percent annualized return and a 12 percent annualized return.

HOW TO ACT IN THE FACE OF UNCERTAINTY

Having pointed all of this out, it would be quite reasonable for the reader to ask: Just what action is our individual supposed to take in response? If we kept the story simple ("you need to save at least X percent of your salary over your working lifetime if your 401(k) is to provide a decent level of retirement income") then that at least would be easy to understand and would encourage better savings rates than we see today, even if we know that in reality the claim is quite likely to prove either wildly optimistic or wildly pessimistic. But since the story is not that simple and it is difficult to be sure exactly how much saving is enough, we must explore the implications; it is certainly not our intent to make anyone simply give up in despair.

In fact, there are a number of steps that can be taken to deal with this uncertainty.[8] These take advantage of the fact that a savings plan that runs for a working lifetime gives plenty of opportunity for adjustment in response to experience.

Choice 1: Be Prepared to Vary the Savings Rate

Higher savings rates produce higher retirement income. That much, at least, is certain. So following a period of poor returns, higher contributions probably make sense, if the retirement savings plan is to stay on track. Few individuals or DC plan sponsors would want to see their contributions fluctuating as much as DB plan contributions do (one reason that many corporations closed their DB plans in the early years of the new millennium is that they wanted to prevent a recurrence of the extreme jumps in contributions that resulted from the bear market of 2000–2002). But if an individual is saving with an eye on a particular level of income replacement in retirement, then they should be prepared to make some adjustments to their level of saving as experience unfolds.

Unfortunately, what we observe is that in bad times employers sometimes reduce their matching contributions, which in turn can prompt lower contributions from employees—doubly disturbing behavior.

Choice 2: Be Prepared to Vary the Retirement Date

Another variable with a big effect on the end result is the assumed age of retirement. An earlier retirement would mean a shorter period during which contributions are being made to the plan. It also means a shorter period for those contributions to grow with investment returns. And it means a longer period during which distributions are being made by the plan. These three factors all lead to lower income-replacement rates. Retire later, and the same three factors each lead to higher income-replacement rates.

Not everyone is in a position to keep working for longer than planned, in the event that their retirement savings do not build up as fast as they had hoped. But for those who are, this can be a valuable (if, perhaps, unwelcome) safety valve. Gradual retirement is a variation on this theme—shifting to part-time status rather than exiting the workforce completely.

We also believe that it is helpful to think of the retirement date as something that can be brought forward in the event of strong investment returns. We do not want our demonstration that phenomenally good income replacement is possible with a relatively low savings rate (in the event of a rampant stock market) to discourage prudent saving. Rather, we'd prefer people to think, "If things turn out really well, I'll be able to bring my retirement date forward—more time to travel or relax on the boat."

Choice 3: Be Prepared to Adjust Your Expectations

If savings rates and the retirement date cannot be changed, then the impact of investment experience will be felt in the level of benefit provided by the plan. That follows from the fundamental pension equation with which we started this chapter. Indeed, when much of corporate America—and other nations around the world—moved from DB to DC, the message to workers was "we are no longer going to promise you a certain level of retirement income." With employers no longer underwriting the level of benefit, workers have to accept that their retirement security is now tied—for good or ill—to the experience of their 401(k) investment portfolios.

Choice 4: Manage the Investment Program

In this chapter, we have looked at the impact of investment returns on a retirement savings plan. We have not looked at the ways in which investment experience can be managed. This can be done to some extent through investment strategy (the way in which the investments are balanced between riskier assets such as equities, or less risky assets such as bonds or cash). There is a basic principle that lies behind much of this: The higher the return aspiration, the more the investor needs to be prepared to take risk in its pursuit.[9] This is the subject to which we will turn our attention next.

APPENDIX: FURTHER ANALYSIS OF THE UNCERTAINTY ASSOCIATED WITH INVESTMENT RETURNS

This appendix sits between the chapter on required contribution rates and the discussion of investment returns to which we will turn next. It serves as further analysis of the results in the former and as an introduction to the challenges of the latter.

You will recall that we asked you to think of a 90 percent confidence range for the average annual investment return on the broad U.S. stock market over the next 20 years. What was your range? We asked a number of colleagues this exact question—all of them involved in the investment business and all highly aware of the short-term volatility of stock markets, since that is something that they live through every day in one form or another. Even so, many of them produced ranges that spanned only a 2 percent or 3 percent range: 7 percent to 10 percent was a popular choice.

We will explain later why this range is far too narrow as a 90 percent confidence range. As we shall explain in Chapter 10, there is a human tendency to produce ranges that are too narrow when confronted with a question such as this. So if your range was a similarly narrow one, then you are in good company. But our exercise shows that a significant number of well-informed individuals working in the investment business do not intuitively sense how uncertain stock market returns are over the long term (even though well aware of it in the short term). And, as we have already seen, uncertainty in investment returns translates into uncertainty in how much contribution will be needed to achieve a targeted level of benefit. So the impact of investment uncertainty on retirement outcomes is something that is not intuitively grasped by plan participants.

What sort of a range would really be reasonable, to be 90 percent sure that the actual outcome will lie within it? One way to answer this question is to look to a really good 20-year period that has actually happened. We don't have to look far back in history for that: From 1980 to 1999 the broad-based Russell 3000 index returned 17.1 percent a year on average. The widely followed S&P 500 index returned 17.9 percent a year over the same period (slightly higher because the S&P 500 is a large-cap index, and large-cap stocks did especially well in those years). So we don't think it's asking too much to say that the top of the range ought to be stretched up to 17 percent or even more.

At the bottom of the range, we will look a little further back in history, to the crash of 1929 and its aftermath. Data histories become patchier the further back one goes, but back-history of the S&P 500 shows a total average return of 3.1 percent over that period. However, that may offer false reassurance. Prolonged periods of negative returns have occurred in recent history in the Japanese market, for example. And we cannot count on every bear market's being quickly followed by a subsequent bounce back, even though that has frequently been the case in the past. It is possible that pattern will continue, but that cannot be taken for granted. A 20-year stock market return of around zero should not be ruled out.

So bearing in mind that the future is less certain than the past, we see that it's quite possible to get to a range more like 0 to 17 percent. Indeed, a number of colleagues did come up with ranges on that scale. Those who did so tended to arrive at their ranges by thinking more about what *could* happen than by relying on their intuition about what they *expected* to happen, which is not how most people naturally think.

Such a range can be confirmed using a more quantitative approach, derived from the strategic planning models that investment consultants use for helping institutional investors set their asset mix policies. We will not labor our point by getting into the details of those models, but if you have the opportunity to see the long-term output that they generate, you will probably find that it is closer to our distinctly unintuitive range than it is to the one you thought of.

Plug those numbers into the preretirement period of our base case model and the range of retirement income replacement rates based on a 4 percent rate of saving becomes 5 percent to 202 percent. And that's just a 90 percent confidence range. The other 10 percent of possible outcomes are even more extreme. So while we can say that providing for retirement is an expensive proposition, be wary of anyone who claims to know exactly how expensive. The stock market is no less uncertain in the long run than it is in the short run.

CHAPTER 4

Investment Returns Are All-Important

The magnitude of the role played by investment returns in retirement provision has long been understood within the defined benefit (DB) system. As long ago as 1989, one of the authors modeled DB plan growth and found that "80¢ or more comes from investment returns; contributions account for the remaining 20¢ of each benefit dollar."[1] The same paper found that "for any one plan member, the largest part of the investment return ... accrues during the payout stage." DB investment programs are accordingly built around the realization that return generation is a key element in the cost-effective provision of pension benefits.

Exactly the same is true in a defined contribution (DC) or 401(k) plan. The dynamics are similar but not identical; instead of a series of cohorts of different ages with new entrants replenishing the system as older participants retire and eventually die, there is only a single life to consider in a DC plan. Neither investment risk nor longevity risk is pooled in DC as they are in DB plans that do not make lump-sum distributions. And, unlike in DC, contributions in DB tend to be back-loaded (there is a significantly higher cost attached to the accrual of a DB pension at advanced ages than at younger ages).

The result is that the 80-20 split of DB looks more like 90-10 in DC. The finding that the bulk of the investment return is earned during the payout stage remains true in a DC world but takes on added significance because of the absence of intergenerational pooling of investments. Growing realization of these dynamics is one reason for the greater focus on investment considerations within DC plan design—it is becoming less common to see investments play second fiddle to record keeping, participant communication, or other considerations.

THE 10/30/60 RULE

In Chapter 3 we introduced a simple model of retirement plan accumulation and decumulation. The example we used there was of a 25-year-old participant who starts to save a level percentage of an increasing payroll stream and earns a uniform annual return until retirement at age 65. The participant starts to draw down an inflation-indexed annual amount from 65, so calculated as to exactly exhaust the savings at death at age 90. Continuing with the simple construction of the model, we assumed, in the baseline scenario, annual inflation at 3 percent, pay increases at 4.75 percent, and investment returns at 7.5 percent.

We will discuss in a moment the impact of varying the input assumptions. But, first, let us look at a result that startles every group we have shown it to.

In the baseline scenario, there are total distributions of $1,057,951, accounted for as shown in Table 4.1.

In other words, of each dollar drawn down in retirement, a little more than 10 cents came from the original contributions, a little more than 30 cents came from investment earnings in the accumulation phase, and a little less than 60 cents came from the investment earnings in the decumulation phase. We call this the "10/30/60" rule of thumb for the sources of DC retirement income.

This is such an unexpected result that we encourage readers to play with the numbers in a spreadsheet tool such as Microsoft Excel. It's the only way to make the power of the investment return intuitive. We show the results of some of the variations we've explored.

TABLE 4.1 Total Savings, Investment Returns, and Distributions in the Baseline Scenario

	Total ($)	Percent of Total Distributions
Savings	113,678	10.7%
Preretirement Investment Earnings	325,637	30.8%
Postretirement Investment Earnings	618,636	58.5%
Total Distributions	1,057,951	100%

The 10/30/60 Rule Is Fairly Robust under Different Input Assumptions

- If investment returns are uncompetitive, then the 10/30/60 rule can cease to apply. For example, replacing the 7.5 percent return assumption with 5 percent each year changes the result to 23 percent/30 percent/46 percent.[2] But it is the preretirement return assumption that matters most: If only the postretirement return assumption is reduced to 5 percent the result becomes 14 percent/40 percent/46 percent.[3]
- Other changes have far less impact on the result than changing the investment return assumption. For example, using a starting age of 35 (rather than 25) produces a result of 15 percent/27 percent/58 percent.
- A retirement age of 60 changes the pre- and postretirement contributions, but does not significantly increase the proportion represented by contributions (11 percent/25 percent/64 percent).
- If death is assumed to occur at age 85 rather than 90, the result becomes 13 percent/37 percent/51 percent.
- If contributions are assumed to escalate at 7.5 percent (which may reflect auto-escalation of contributions, or an increasing rate of saving over a working lifetime), the result becomes 14 percent/28 percent/58 percent.
- If postretirement drawdowns are level in nominal dollars rather than increasing with inflation, then the result becomes 12 percent/34 percent/54 percent.

So we can see that the basic 10/30/60 pattern is fairly stable even in the light of changing the input assumptions from our baseline scenario, with the exception of the preretirement investment return assumption, which is critical.

What the 10/30/60 Rule Does Not Mean— And What It Does Mean

It would be wrong to conclude that the 10/30/60 rule means that the contribution level is not important in a DC plan. Indeed, without contributions, there can be no investment return—an adequate rate of saving is an indispensable starting point for successful retirement planning.

However, as the DC system continues to grow and a greater number of Americans become increasingly dependent on it, it is important that plan design is based on a clear understanding of the economic dynamics that underpin a DC vehicle. In particular, with roughly 90 percent of distributions being generated by investment earnings (not by contributions saved), and the majority of that 90 percent being earned after retirement, sound investment programs are critical if DC plans are to be effective in meeting their goals.

The investment earnings themselves result from a combination of the market returns available from different asset classes and how much of the participant's account is invested in each asset class (i.e., the asset allocation). So we now turn to the investment principles that themselves underlie the choice of an asset allocation policy. We have found that participants crave an understanding of how capital markets work: not the day-to-day mechanics, but the principles that help them understand why there's no easy money to be found, why some asset classes are more volatile than others, and so on. We have also found that a casino analogy both engages participants and helps give them that understanding.

GAMES AT A VIRTUAL CASINO

Come with us, friends, on a virtual trip to a virtual casino tonight. We're taking over the casino. It's our own private function. And the good news is that the odds at this virtual casino, unlike a real one, are stacked in your favor. Does this sound like easy money? Well, we'll see about that. Anyway, let's enter. What, no slot machines? No, all we see are three doors, cheerfully decorated, with the labels Game 1, Game 2, and Game 3. Okay, then, let's enter into the spirit of the evening and head for Game 1.

Here's the casino official. He tells us it's a simple game. He'll toss a coin. If it comes down heads, every player will win $1,000. If it comes down tails, every player will win $500. Yes, please, you'd all like to play! One of you says: "This really is easy money!" But wait, the casino official hasn't finished speaking. He says, "Before you play, I have three questions for you. The first question: Would you pay $400 for the right to play this game?" You're all still cheerful. "Of course," you all agree.

"The second question: Would you pay more than $400?" A moment's hesitation; then, realizing you haven't been asked what's your limit, you all agree: "Yes." And so to the third question: "What's the most you would pay?" Oh, that's more difficult. The shouts start: "$401." "$450." One wit calls out, "$800!" Everyone laughs: He can't be serious (or he has such a lust for gambling that he'll pay anything just to experience the thrill). The bidding (yes, that's what it has become) settles down at $749: Just enough to keep the game in your favor. Some have backed out. It's hardly worthwhile at $749. They want a better margin in their favor. One in particular says: "That's too much. The game is still in my favor at $749, but I can get a better return with complete certainty buying a Treasury bill." Oh, he's a spoilsport: He's making this an investment question rather than fun.

Actually, the game is over at that point. The game was not really to toss a coin; it was to see how much you'd bid and how the bidding developed. Oh, this is a learning game, not a gambling game. How disappointing! Well, we're here, we might as well continue.

Let's go to Game 2. Another casino official. He's going to toss a coin. If it's heads, every player wins $1 million. If it's tails, every player wins $500,000. Might as well get to the point quickly: What's the most you would pay for the right to play this game? One of you shouts out: "$740,000." He preempts the bidding. Nobody challenges him with a higher bid. Nobody goes to $749,999, even though the game is still in your favor at that level. You've evidently taken the spoilsport's T-bill comment to heart; there are easier ways to make money, with much less risk.

The casino official has one more question: "Why do people typically offer to pay less than 1,000 times as much to play Game 2 as to play Game 1?" One of you says: "Well, Game 2 is like playing Game 1 1,000 times, so I'd be willing to pay 1,000 times as much, as long as the margin was a bit more in my favor, like $650 for Game 1 and $650,000 for Game 2." Yes, but you were willing to pay more than $650 for Game 1, weren't you? "Yes." So, then, if your limit for Game 2 is $650,000, your bid is less than 1,000 times your bid for Game 1. "Right." "Okay," says the casino official, "I accept your offer of $650,000. Let's play Game 2! Put up the money." Our friend says, "It's virtual money!" No, it needs to be real money. "What d'you think I am, crazy? I'd never risk $650,000 at a time." And there endeth the second game.

And We've Already Learned Two Important Lessons

- *In a free market, there's no easy money.* As long as people have enough information to understand the game and anybody can play, the price gets bid up to the point where there's no easy money, just a risk/reward calculation.
- *The higher the potential loss, the higher the upside potential that people demand in order to be willing to play the game.* People don't like losing, but their aversion to losing increases as the potential loss increases, so the bigger the risk, the more they want the payoff tilted in their favor.

Remember, there's still Game 3 to be played. Another casino official: "I'm going to draw a card from a standard deck of 52 cards. If it's an ace, every player loses $100. If it's any card but an ace, every player wins $100." This might be starting to sound familiar, but no, this time the question is different: "What's your reaction if you win?" Several cries: "It was bound to happen." "This is too easy!" "Let's play again!" And one final question:

"What's your reaction if you lose?" A quick shout: "It's a fix!" Laughter, then silence. Then several of you say: "Let's play again!"

Two More Lessons

- *Even good strategies can have bad outcomes.* Playing Game 3 for no entry fee is clearly a good strategy, because it's tilted so strongly in your favor, and even if you lose, the loss is bearable. But there's still a chance you'll lose; that's just bad luck, but bad luck does happen sometimes.
- *With a good strategy, the more often you can play the game, the more likely you are to win over the long term.* That's why you said, "Let's play again!" even if you lost Game 3 the first time it was played. The chances are so much in your favor that you're highly likely to come out ahead if you play, let's say, 10 times, and even more likely if you play 100 times.

INVESTMENT ANALOGS

The lessons of our casino games apply to investing for retirement. To show how, we are now going to look at how various types of investments have behaved in the past, and the characteristics that should be assumed for their future behavior.

Here's a way to think about investing. Think of stocks (often called equities), bonds (often called fixed income), and cash (often called Treasury bills) as being three different investment games, with three different pay-off patterns. But there are a couple of significant differences between our casino games and these investment games. Unlike our casino games, these investment games don't just have two "either/or" outcomes: They have a continuous range of intermediate outcomes. And unlike our casino games, these investment games don't come with precise odds and payoffs known in advance. History is all we know. That's an obvious starting point, but there's no guarantee that the future will be like the past.

But, as we'll see, all four lessons that we learned in our virtual casino still apply when we play the investment game. There's no easy money. As the potential loss increases, you want a disproportionate increase in the potential reward before you're willing to play the game. Even good strategies can have bad outcomes. And with a good strategy, the more often you play, the more likely you are to eventually win. What does that mean, to play the game often? Think of it this way: The younger you are, the more often you can play, because it's the passage of time that constitutes a play.

```
                                     2006
                                     2004
                     2000 2007 1988 2003 1997
                     1990 2005 1986 1999 1995
                     1981 1994 1979 1998 1991
                     1977 1993 1972 1996 1989
                     1969 1992 1971 1983 1985
                     1962 1987 1968 1982 1980
                     1953 1984 1965 1976 1975
                     1946 1978 1964 1967 1955
                2001 1940 1970 1959 1963 1950
                1973 1939 1960 1952 1961 1945
           2002 1966 1934 1956 1949 1951 1938 1958
           1974 1957 1932 1948 1944 1943 1936 1935 1954
      1931 1937 1930 1947 1929 1947 1926 1942 1927 1928 1933
-80  -70  -60  -50  -40  -30  -20  -10   0   10   20   30   40   50   60   70   80
                              Annual Return Percents
```

FIGURE 4.1   Calendar Year Returns, U.S. Large Cap Stocks, 1926–2007
Source: Morningstar, 2008 Ibbotson® SBBI® Classic Yearbook.

HISTORICAL RETURN PATTERNS

Let's consider a calendar year as constituting a play of each game; not because there's any magic to calendar years, but just because it's convenient. Figure 4.1 shows returns from 1926 through 2007 for U.S. stocks.[4] Each year's return is placed in the appropriate 10-percentage-point range.

Notice that the middle portion of the range occurs with greater frequency, while the frequency fades away as the returns become more extreme on the left and on the right. What's the best year? And the worst? And the mean (the average) and the standard deviation (which we were introduced to in Chapter 2)? How about if we look not at individual years, but at chunks of 10 consecutive years? All of that appears in Table 4.2.

Notice that the best year was more than two standard deviations better than the mean, and the worst was almost three standard deviations worse than the mean. With 10-year chunks, the best and worst aren't nearly so extreme. The best 10-year chunk shows a very healthy average

TABLE 4.2   Summary Statistics, U.S. Large Cap Stocks, 1926–2007

Best Year	54.0%	(1933)
Worst Year	−43.3%	(1931)
Arithmetic Mean (Annualized)	12.3%	
Standard Deviation (Annualized)	19.8%	
Best 10 Consecutive Years (Annualized)	20.1%	(1949–1958)
Worst 10 Consecutive Years (Annualized)	−0.9%	(1929–1938)

Source: Morningstar, 2008 Ibbotson® SBBI® Classic Yearbook.

annual return. The worst is slightly worse than breakeven. Now let's look at the corresponding numbers for U.S. bonds over the same time period.

Figure 4.2 and Table 4.3 are the bond analogs of Figure 4.1 and Table 4.2. Notice how much more clustered the bond return distribution

```
                                    2007
                                    2006
                                    2005
                                    2004
                                    2003
                                    1996
                                    1992
                                    1990
                                    1983
                                    1977
                                    1973
                                    1972
                                    1968
                                    1966
                                    1964
                                    1963
                                    1962
                                    1961
                                    1960
                                    1957
                                    1955
                                    1954
                                    1953
                                    1952
                                    1950
                                    1949
                                    1948 2002
                               1999 1946 2001
                               1994 1945 2000
                               1987 1944 1998
                               1981 1943 1997
                               1980 1942 1993
                               1979 1941 1991
                               1978 1940 1989
                               1974 1939 1988
                               1969 1938 1986
                               1967 1937 1984
                               1965 1936 1976
                               1959 1935 1975
                               1958 1930 1971
                               1956 1929 1970
                               1951 1928 1934
                               1947 1927 1933
                               1931 1926 1932 1995 1985 1982
 -80  -70  -60  -50  -40  -30  -20  -10   0   10   20   30   40   50   60   70   80
                                  Annual Return Percents
```

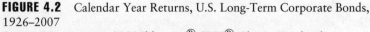

FIGURE 4.2 Calendar Year Returns, U.S. Long-Term Corporate Bonds, 1926–2007
Source: Morningstar, 2008 Ibbotson® SBBI® Classic Yearbook.

TABLE 4.3 Summary Statistics, U.S. Long-Term Corporate Bonds, 1926–2007

Best Year	42.6%	(1982)
Worst Year	−8.1%	(1969)
Arithmetic Mean (Annualized)	6.2%	
Standard Deviation (Annualized)	8.4%	
Best 10 Consecutive Years (Annualized)	16.3%	(1982–1991)
Worst 10 Consecutive Years (Annualized)	1.0%	(1947–1956)

Source: Morningstar, 2008 Ibbotson® SBBI® Classic Yearbook.

is, compared to the stock return distribution. This is a game with less extreme outcomes.

The numbers in Table 4.3 confirm that the worst bond year wasn't nearly as bad as the worst stock year. And even the worst 10-year period showed a positive average annual return. But in exchange for the downside protection, bonds didn't give as high an average return as stocks, nor was the upside as big.

By now we can anticipate what we see in Figure 4.3 and Table 4.4, which are the cash analogs of the stock and bond numbers.

Figure 4.3 is almost completely concentrated in the 0- to 10-percent range. Only in a highly inflationary period 30 years ago did cash return more than 10 percent in one year. And yes, that's not a misprint: Treasury bills really have shown a negative return.[5]

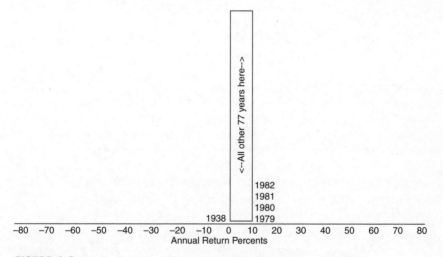

FIGURE 4.3 Calendar Year Returns, U.S. Treasury Bills, 1926–2007
Source: Morningstar, 2008 Ibbotson® SBBI® Classic Yearbook.

TABLE 4.4 Summary Statistics, U.S. Treasury Bills, 1926–2007

Best Year	14.7%	(1981)
Worst Year	−0.02%	(1938)
Arithmetic Mean (Annualized)	3.8%	
Standard Deviation (Annualized)	3.1%	
Best 10 Consecutive Years (Annualized)	9.2%	(1978–1987)
Worst 10 Consecutive Years (Annualized)	0.1%	(1933–1942)

Source: Morningstar, 2008 Ibbotson® SBBI® Classic Yearbook.

Given the almost complete downside protection from loss,[6] this cash return distribution has a very small average return and very little upside potential.

WHAT ARE THE LESSONS?

Let's check the four lessons from our casino games. First, there's no easy money. That's certainly true. The closest to being risk free (in the sense of not experiencing a negative return—though that's far from the only, or even the most sensible, definition of risk) is cash; and the return certainly doesn't scream "Easy money!" Stocks give the best potential, but that comes at a big risk, so again it's hardly easy money.

Second, you need a tempting reward to be induced to take a risk. That's true. Stocks have the biggest risk. But they don't just have to offer the best upside potential to tempt you in; they also have to offer the best long-term average return. The stock return distribution isn't just more extreme on both sides than bonds and cash; it also has a central point (a long-term average) that's higher than both bonds and cash.

Third, even good strategies have bad outcomes. Investing in any of these asset classes is a paying strategy, over the long term, in the sense that they all tend to add some positive return to your investment. But every one has had a bad outcome at some stage. There are no guarantees.

Fourth, with a good strategy, the longer you play, the greater your chance of ending up a winner. Look at the 10-year outcomes. Even with stocks, there was only one 10-year period that had an overall negative outcome.

A word of caution that our colleagues (and any expert) would want to be thrown in here: We're grossly oversimplifying. Of course. Our purpose is not to suggest that anybody who grasps these four lessons is now an expert (heaven knows, we argue against that conclusion throughout the book).

Rather, we are aiming to illustrate the basic dynamics of investment markets and the inevitable uncertainty that is attached to them, so that nobody reading this book is under the illusion that there is a simple answer to the challenges of retirement saving if only you can crack the code of the markets.

There's a fifth lesson that we should see in the numbers: The past has not always been a reliable guide to the future. Here's something you can try yourself. In Figure 4.1 (where it's easiest to do because the distribution is the most spread out), find the year of your birth. See which column it appears in. Then check the following year, and the one after, and so on for 20 years. You won't find a pattern appearing, of good years routinely following bad years (or the reverse), or of two good years followed by two bad ones (or the reverse), or anything that offers a formula for predictability. Too bad. It's almost as if the pattern is random.

And that leads to our final observation, which comes in response to the objection that often arises after this presentation. What about all the experts who predict whether the economy will pick up or slow down, whether investment markets will do well or badly, whether specific securities will do well or badly? Don't they know? Can't we use them to predict? Surely it can't all be random.

The answer is: You're right, it isn't all random. But, in some ways, it might as well be.

Start with the economy. Most years it shows growth. That's not random. It even has cycles that are moderately predictable, although experts disagree as to exactly what the growth will be. But even if we can get that right, it doesn't take us very far because there's no security that we can invest in that's tied exactly to the level of economic growth. So we have to predict what effect economic growth will have on different kinds of investments, like stocks, bonds, and cash. That's much more difficult. And on that score, experts disagree much more. The other thing is that their average forecast is already built into security market prices; in that sense, when you buy, you're buying the average. So, to make more money than the average investor, you have to guess whether a particular expert predictor is more likely to be right than the other expert predictors, all of whom have pretty much the same access to the same information. That's very tough. And when it comes to specific sectors of the market or to specific securities (where again the average forecast is already built into the buying price), it becomes even tougher.

So, although it's not random, the fact that forecasts are widely distributed and the average forecast is built into the buying price makes it very difficult to predict a precise outcome, or even what asset classes or securities will be the winners over the short term, like a year. Yes, it is possible to skew the odds a little in your favor if you have above average skill. But only a little. (And fewer people really do have above average skill than think that they do.) That's why those outcomes may appear to be random. (Think of it like betting on American football games. We may all agree that Team A is highly likely to beat Team B. But spread betting builds the expected margin into the bet. If the spread is, say, $6^1/_2$ points, we need Team A to win by at least 7 points, or Team B to be no more than 6 points behind at the end of the game, to win the bet. That's a much more difficult bet to win consistently.) In contrast, broad comparisons over the very long term (like stocks versus bonds versus cash) are more likely to be predictable. But who can wait for the long term? That takes discipline, which is one reason that the most successful long-term investors tend to be those who are the most disciplined.

WHAT FOLLOWS?

All of this has been just an introduction to some broad investment concepts. We've said nothing about correlation (the extent to which investments move with or in opposite directions to each other), diversification (what happens when you mix different kinds of investments), efficiency in constructing portfolios (getting the most expected return bang for your risk buck), your risk tolerance, and so on—all of which are necessary parts of any decision as to how to invest your assets.

In fact, that's part of our purpose: to whet your appetite but show you how much is involved in really becoming sufficiently expert to call your own shots. Most participants aren't expert (as we'll see in Chapter 10) and never will be. For them, expertise needs to be built into default options, so that they can tap into expertise without ever having to acquire it themselves. How this can be made to happen is the theme of Part Two of this book.

In this chapter on investment principles, we conclude with an overview of the fundamental question of how much investment risk you can handle.

HOW MUCH INVESTMENT RISK
CAN YOU TOLERATE?

We have said nothing, to this point, about risk tolerance and what goes into the assessment of how much risk a participant can take. Yet it is fundamental. Suppose a group of experts all agreed on the prospects for the various asset classes: What is the central rate of return most likely for each asset class over some agreed investment horizon, how uncertain that return is likely to be, and so on. They would still not all select the same asset allocations for their own investment accounts. Why? Because some will prefer to play the investment game characterized by a high potential reward for taking a large risk, while others will prefer to eschew risk and live with the prospect of a relatively low return.

Who is right? Potentially, they're all right. The point is that there's no right or wrong tolerance for risk. It's just a question of what you're comfortable with.

In fact, we often explain it to participants by saying that your essential choice is to decide where you place yourself between two extreme goals: to eat well and to sleep well. This typically draws a round of nervous laughter. Surely that has nothing to do with investing. Surely it's too simple a characterization. No, it's accurate and not oversimplified.

Typically, those who are at the "eat well" end of the spectrum are long-term investors. They want to accumulate enough wealth to be able, as the goal states, to eat well in retirement, to live their desired lifestyle to the fullest extent. They know, because they understand the principles in this chapter, that most of that wealth will come from the investment return, and that, in seeking a high return over the long term, they must endure a high degree of short-term uncertainty and volatility. To take the analogy of eating a step further, they know they might have to endure a gut-wrenching ride on the way to their meals. But they are willing to do so, even though they also know that, at the end of the ride, there is no guarantee that they will have succeeded.

Those at the "sleep well" end of the spectrum are also long-term investors, but can't live with that sort of uncertainty. They can't sleep at night if their future is profoundly uncertain and seems to vary in its prospects from day to day, with every gyration of the markets. So, even though they realize (because they too understand the principles in this chapter) that cutting back on risk also means cutting back on opportunity, they choose to live with low risk.

Both groups understand that opportunity comes with risk. The two investment features are inseparable. Sure, we'd all like the opportunity to make a large riskless return. But the first principle we learned is that there's no easy money.

Which end of the spectrum is more sensible? The answer is: They are both sensible. Being sensible isn't a matter of seeing who ends up with the most money. It's a matter of making a choice you can live with. People are different. Being sensible means knowing what sort of person you are, in this context. Whenever we explain it to an audience this way, we are invariably approached by people afterwards telling us privately of their own family situations, in which the family members clearly have different degrees of tolerance for risk, but all have to live with the decision made by one of them. Our explanation finally confirms to them that they are different, and they often resolve (though, sadly, few harbor high hopes of success) to raise the subject at the next family meeting to see if they can get a discussion going about risk tolerance.

Most of us are probably somewhere in between the ends of the spectrum. We're not entirely risk averse. Equally, we're not willing to take enormous risks. What determines a sensible place in the spectrum?

Essentially, there are two sets of inputs. One is financial and one is psychological.

The financial aspect has to do with a comparison of your goals and your current situation. We explore this in more detail in Part Five, where we look at the financial issues facing any individual. For now, we summarize it by saying that you can explore how much of a difference it makes if you vary the amount of risk that you take in pursuing your goals, and that can give you some idea of how much risk you *need* to take. Whatever the outcome of your exploration, it's always helpful to look at this aspect long before you retire, when you really have a chance to do something different for a substantial length of accumulation time, rather than leaving it until you've arrived at decumulation time and find that you wish you had started earlier.

The psychological aspect is more subjective. Essentially, it is about determining in advance how bumpy a ride you will be able to live with. It is relatively easy for an investor to be relaxed about the prospect of bearing risk (in pursuit of higher returns) as long as the conversation is conceptual. But the reality of risk is normally a sharp drop in portfolio value, quite possibly during a worrying period of economic or political uncertainty. That reality tends to create a different set of emotions than some story about a series of coin flips that may turn out to be tails once in a while. And if the investor decides at that point that his risk tolerance is not so high after all, then he may well bail out of the market. This is a strategy that pretty much guarantees you will be in the market for the bad times but not the good ones. It is far better to be realistic in advance about how much risk you can take, and to steel yourself in the sure knowledge that this tolerance will be tested.

CHAPTER 5

Sustainable Spending

The four basic dynamics that lie behind a retirement plan are how long you live, how much you save, how large an investment return you earn, and how much you spend in retirement. We have dealt with the principles of longevity, saving, and investment in the preceding chapters. In this chapter we discuss spending.

We will see, when we discuss individual issues in decumulation, that the relationship between the amount of money saved and the amount of spending it will support is badly misunderstood by most people, and that many are overconfident as they approach retirement. Later, though, they realize that their challenge has changed from how to accumulate enough wealth to making their wealth last as long as they can. Many people fear running out of money in old age. This is an understandable fear. We need to be attentive to the risks but not overly cautious. Doing so can create another problem: living at an unnecessarily low standard of living. As a colleague put it, "the basic challenge for a new retiree is to spend enough today so as not to starve, but not so much today that they will starve tomorrow."

It is common for people planning for retirement to ask, "How much of my retirement money can I safely spend each year?" There are two ways to provide an answer. One is to look at purchase rates for an immediate annuity. The other is to make some assumptions as to how long they will need to sustain a proposed rate of spending and what their future investment returns will be. With a distribution of possible answers to these two questions, we can run a series of scenarios through what is known as a Monte Carlo process. The result of a Monte Carlo simulation is a probability of success for a given set of circumstances.

LIFETIME ANNUITIES

Annuities are a way in which individuals can turn their wealth into an income. We'll have more to say on them later. For now, what matters is that the cost of an annuity provides us with an external reference point for how much spending a particular level of wealth might sustain.

Lifetime annuities can be purchased to provide fixed-dollar payments or payments that increase with inflation. So it is possible to see how many fixed dollars can be guaranteed for a given amount of savings, or how many initial dollars that will gradually increase with inflation—or perhaps a bit of both. It is also possible to base the annuity on the life of one person, or for as long as at least one of two people survives, or a variety of other arrangements.

Because rates vary all the time as interest rates change, we haven't quoted numbers here, but it's easy to check by going to a web site like www.incomesolutions.com.

As a quick guide, we include as an appendix to this chapter a table of annuity multiples over a range of interest rates and life expectancies.

SIMULATIONS

Some individuals will feel that they have enough wealth to last for a long time, and would rather invest their money and draw it down gradually, at least for a number of years. Then, if later they feel they are at risk of outliving their wealth, they might contemplate buying a lifetime annuity at an advanced age. We illustrate simulations for a couple that feels this way.

Figure 5.1 shows the results of such a simulation. This chart shows the probability of success for different spending rates in retirement. Success is defined as the ability of a couple to spend a certain amount of money each year for 20 years, and after 20 years have enough money left to buy an immediate annuity with a joint and 100 percent survivor option. The amount of money is related to the initial amount of their wealth and starts at the percentage shown; for example, it might start at 5 percent of their wealth. From that point, the withdrawals from their invested portfolio are increased each year with inflation. We also assume that both members of the couple are aged 65 at the start of their withdrawal plan, and that their retirement portfolio is invested 60 percent in equities (stocks) and 40 percent in fixed income (bonds).[1]

Consider a withdrawal rate that is 5 percent of the initial wealth; for example, if the wealth amounts to $300,000, the withdrawals amount to 5 percent of this number, or $15,000, each year. In this example, Figure 5.1 shows that there is approximately a 59 percent probability of this level of withdrawal being sustainable for 20 years with enough left to purchase an annuity at that time for the couple, guaranteed to pay the inflation-adjusted equivalent of $15,000 a year for as long as at least one of them is alive.

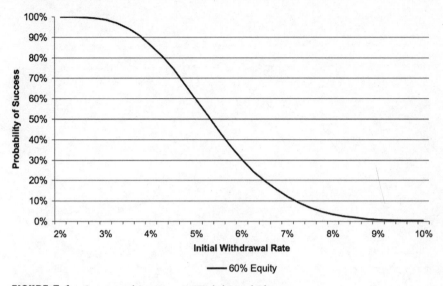

FIGURE 5.1   Success of Systematic Withdrawal Plans

Looking at all of Figure 5.1, we can see that this couple has approximately an 86 percent chance of being able to spend an amount that starts at 4 percent of their initial retirement assets at age 65 each year for 20 years, and have enough left over at age 85 to buy an immediate life annuity equaling the inflation adjusted, value of that same spending amount. And then the immediate life annuity they purchase at age 85 will continue paying this amount until the last of the two members of the couple dies. Figure 5.1 also shows that this same couple has less than a 10 percent chance of success if their spending rate is greater than 7.25 percent of their retirement assets at age 65.

This illustration is meant to give directional rather than specific guidance as to how much you can spend in retirement. Based on this set of assumptions, an inflation-adjusted 3.5 percent to 4.5 percent spending rate seems sensible; spending rates higher than these quickly seem to be unreasonably risky. These types of simulations can be run with an endless number of different assumptions. For instance, the ages of the couple can be changed; the spending amount can be in nominal dollars rather than inflation adjusted; and the assets can be assumed to be invested in a different mix of investments. Every unique combination will yield different results, but the results in Figure 5.1 stay directionally unchanged.

To make this point, we also show this same scenario run with a range of asset allocation assumptions rather than just using a static 60 percent equities, 40 percent fixed-income portfolio. Figure 5.2 shows the range of

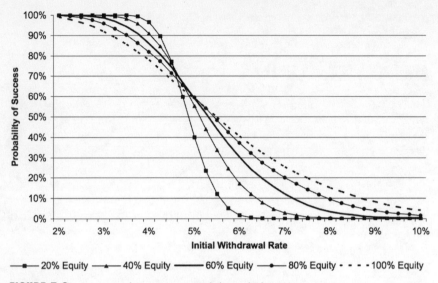

FIGURE 5.2   Success of Systematic Withdrawal Plans

success probabilities for a series of simulations where the assets were invested in different portfolios, ranging from conservative (20 percent equities and 80 percent fixed income) to aggressive (100 percent equities).[2]

To interpret Figure 5.2, look at a withdrawal rate of 4 percent of the initial portfolio value. The probability of success ranges from about 78 percent for an aggressive (100 percent equity) portfolio to about 96 percent for a conservative (20 percent equity/80 percent fixed-income) portfolio. Similarly for other rates of withdrawal, there is a range of probabilities of success.

What is significant about the results in Figure 5.2 is that the pattern of success probabilities retains the same general shape, even though we have a wide range of investment portfolios. The asset allocation does have a meaningful impact; however, it is the spending rate that has a greater influence on the success pattern. All of this is meant to make a single point—spending rates in retirement have a meaningful impact on people's ability to sustain their spending throughout their remaining life.

This analysis looks at the initial spending rate that a new retiree might choose, based on the assumption that the amount of spending will not vary over time (except that the withdrawals are increased each year for inflation). In practice, of course, retirees will periodically review whether their level of spending continues to make sense. But in this chapter, we simply wanted to establish the place of spending policy within the context of the dynamics of a retirement plan.

As a rule of thumb, an initial spending rate of 3.5 percent to 4.5 percent (in inflation adjusted dollars) carries a high probability of success. The higher the spending rate, the greater the chance you have of running out of money during your lifetime.

APPENDIX: THE MULTIPLE

The multiples in this table relate your annual spending to the amount of assets needed to support that spending. Multiply your annual spending by the multiple to calculate the required assets. These multiples have been calculated based on the spending amounts remaining constant each year; in other words, the spending amount is not increased each year with inflation.

Specifically, Table 5.1 shows the "fair value" multiples for a given life expectancy and a given interest rate. For example, the multiple if you have a life expectancy of 20 years and are considering an interest rate of 6 percent is 11.81. So, for annual spending of $100,000, you'll need assets of $1,181,000.

The relevant life expectancy could be, for example, your own life expectancy or the second-to-die expectancy of you and your spouse. You have to get these expectancies from somewhere else; an expert planner is a possible source, or Table 2.1 might give you a rough approximation.

The interest rate is the one that's relevant for buying a lifetime annuity. As a first approximation, you could use the current yield on long-dated Treasury bonds. That's because insurance companies typically invest your annuity purchase price in bonds. The yield on long corporate bonds is typically a little bit higher. You could use that, too. For conservatism, use Treasuries.

That's the relevant interest rate for traditional lifetime annuities, the ones that pay you the same dollar amount every month. That amount is set when you buy the annuity. It is not subsequently adjusted for inflation. Inflation-proofed annuities are rare.[3] But at least some of the expenditures

TABLE 5.1 Fair Value Multiples

Future Life Expectancy in Years	Interest Rate			
	2%	4%	6%	8%
4	3.85	3.70	3.57	3.44
8	7.40	6.87	6.40	5.98
12	10.68	9.57	8.64	7.84
16	13.71	11.89	10.41	9.21
20	16.51	13.86	11.81	10.21
24	19.10	15.55	12.93	10.95
28	21.49	17.00	13.81	11.49
32	23.70	18.23	14.51	11.89

in your spending plan will need inflation-proofing, and for these the interest rate that you use should be the current bond yield minus the inflation that you expect. For example, if bond yields are 6 percent and you're hoping to be able to support inflation of 2 percent each year, use 6 percent − 2 percent = 4 percent. The multiple for this purpose, for a life expectancy of 20 years, is 13.86.[4] That same $100,000 annual spending that we considered earlier now needs assets of $1,386,000 to support it, if the spending is to increase by 2 percent each year.

You may want to separate your spending into portions that are fixed and portions that are inflation-dependent. Whatever you choose to do for planning purposes, Table 5.1 enables you to make a first approximation as to how much money you need to support that spending.

The spending, assuming you are using after-tax spending estimates, needs to be grossed up to the pretax amount you'll need every year.

Finally, note that these are called "fair value" multiples. Why? What's an "unfair" value? A fair value is one that allows for life expectancy and the relevant interest rate—as the table does. But you can't expect an insurance company to sell you a lifetime annuity on that basis. They'll charge you more, for several reasons. First, they need a margin, in case their estimates of life expectancies prove too short. (And these days, with longevity rising, they need a substantial margin.) In addition, they have expenses: selling to you, maintaining the appropriate records, setting up reserves that comply with insurance laws, and so on. And they're in business, so their shareholders will want some profit margin. For all these reasons, they'll charge you a higher multiple than Table 5.1 shows.

The gap between what they charge and what the table shows is called, in the literature, "actuarial unfairness."[5] In what they call "money's worth" calculations, academics estimate of the size of this aggregate margin as being anywhere from 2 percent to 20 percent, when they use annuitant mortality tables. (When they use population mortality tables, the margin is much larger, because population mortality projects people dying earlier than self-selected purchasers of lifetime annuities.) Therefore, once you have used the table to estimate the assets you need to support your lifestyle, you ought to add a further margin to allow for the loadings that you will encounter if you have to buy a lifetime annuity. But the margin varies from time to time, and it is also generally bigger the older the age of the purchaser. We don't have a rule of thumb as to what you should add—you should check out annuity purchase rates at the time you're evaluating your situation. The numbers in Table 5.1 therefore provide a floor to the amount you'll need.

Opportunities in the Accumulation Phase

In Chapter 1 we explained that defined contribution (DC) version 2.0 has taken over as the main vehicle for employment-based retirement saving. We identified some of the hurdles it needs to rise above if it is to succeed in creating adequate retirement incomes. Because of the increased importance of DC, addressing these issues is now a matter of broad public interest.

In the four chapters that follow, we will look more closely at ways in which the current system—which has catered up until now more to the needs of the informed few rather than to the needs of the broader population—falls short in this new role. These chapters will look at the preretirement period: the accumulation phase of DC. We will return to the postretirement decumulation phase in Part Five. So we address this part to readers who are interested in making the current DC system more effective: plan sponsors, consultants, and opinion leaders.

As anyone who has ever read a self-help book knows, shortcomings are really opportunities. And in the case of the DC system, the issues that we will address in these four chapters are indeed opportunities for change. The issues, by and large, are well known. So, too, are the routes to solutions—solutions that are needed if version 2.0 of the DC system is to become fully formed. Some of the routes have been embarked upon, others not yet.

We have divided this analysis of opportunities during the accumulation phase into four sets:

- Inadequate access to or use of DC plans
- Leakage of assets
- Inefficiencies in investment management
- Fees

Anyone without access to a DC plan can have an individual retirement account (IRA), and many DC plan participants can have an IRA. In this book, we have framed our analysis in terms of DC plans rather than IRAs, but virtually everything that we recommend would serve to improve the efficiency of IRAs as well.

Indeed, most commentators assert that IRAs are typically less efficient than DC plans. For example, unlike DC plans, IRAs do not have the benefit of expert screening of investment choices to narrow down the choices to those that best suit the participants, nor do they benefit from institutional fee pricing.

CHAPTER 6

Save More

Not every worker participates in a defined contribution (DC) plan. And of those who do, some start late, some make inadequate contributions, and some who change jobs lose the opportunity to make their participation in the system continuous. In this chapter we discuss each of those four aspects of the DC system. In each case, we will describe the issue and quantify as best we can how big an impact it has. We will explain why it occurs. Lastly, we will describe the solutions that might be possible.

EMPLOYERS WITH NO PLAN

If society is looking to the DC system as the private sector's primary vehicle for retirement provision, then it is pretty obvious that there is a problem if employers do not offer a plan. But many do not.

In 2008 the Government Accountability Office of the U.S. Congress published a study on savings in DC plans, based on the 2004 Survey of Consumer Finances.[1] It reported that:

- Sixty-two percent of workers were offered a retirement plan (either defined benefit [DB] or DC) by their employer. Of those offered a plan, 84 percent participated. Since DB participation is essentially 100 percent, the DC participation rate is clearly below 84 percent.
- Looking at DC alone, 36 percent of workers were enrolled in a DC plan with their current employer. But among the young, only 24 percent of workers aged 18 to 29 were enrolled in a DC plan with their current employer.
- Only 25 percent of workers in the lowest-income quartile were offered a DC plan, and only 8 percent were actually enrolled in a DC plan with their current employer.

So almost 40 percent of workers are not offered any type of DB or DC plan by their employers, and this figure is higher among the low paid. Individuals who work without an employment-based retirement savings vehicle are left to their own devices—their own motivations, their own skills—to save for retirement. In a world of day-to-day pressures, individuals evidently find it extremely difficult to meet that challenge. That is not good for them or for the retirement saving system.

Why Does This Happen?

Why don't all employers sponsor a plan? There's no secret about the answer. For all employers, but particularly for small ones, sponsoring a plan requires a commitment of time and money and a search for expertise. And so there have been many approaches suggested, all aimed at providing a default solution that reduces the time and money involved and builds expertise into the default, so that the employer doesn't need to embark on an independent search for that expertise.

It is important to acknowledge another perspective on this topic. In September 2008, the Investment Company Institute® released a report entitled *Who Gets Retirement Plans and Why*. One of their key findings was: "Younger and lower-income households are more likely to report that they save primarily for reasons other than retirement, such as to fund education, to purchase a house, to fund other purchases, or to have cash on hand in case of unexpected need." The report goes on to suggest that it is possible that employers who have a large percentage of these types of workers (often small employers) do not offer DC plans simply because workers do not value them.

Possible Solutions

The solution is conceptually obvious: Make it easier for employers to install a plan. The GAO report outlines three kinds of proposals to increase coverage.[2]

The first is the "State-K" proposal. State governments would design and administer a 401(k) plan that any employer in the state could offer to its employees. By pooling resources and sharing costs across many employers, and offering very simple features, both administrative and investment costs would be much lower than for a single employer, particularly a small employer. In our discussions with states that might sponsor such schemes, there has been a general reluctance to take on fiduciary responsibility for any but their own employees. This means that the State-K proposal, if implemented, would probably leave fiduciary responsibility with the employer. This seems to us to make it less likely to be widely adopted.

A second proposal is the "automatic IRA," which overcomes the fiduciary issue by providing access to individual savings plans rather than a central DC plan.[3] This, too, envisages pooling as the source of administrative and investment cost reduction. Employers would not be permitted to make direct contributions to an individual's account. A new entity would take on responsibility for creating simple investment default and other options, and that is where investment fiduciary responsibility would lie.

The third proposal is "universal accounts." Its differentiating feature is that the federal government would administer it, with possibly a partial contribution match provided by the government in the form of a tax credit. Again, pooling reduces costs.

All of these plans have the same intent: to make it simple for the employer. All the employer has to do is to make employees aware of the plan; to remit employee contributions to the vehicle; and to make and remit employer contributions if the employer chooses to design its own contribution formula. As we will see in Chapter 12 on the way in which Australia runs DC plans, this relief of employer responsibility is an important feature in enabling widespread coverage.[4]

EMPLOYEES WHO DO NOT ENROLL

Even where a plan is offered, not every eligible employee participates. As noted before, the DC participation rate is well below 84 percent.[5] You do not need to replicate the base case analysis we provided in Chapter 3 to be able to calculate that if a worker does not participate in a plan the retirement income it provides drops from 19 percent (in our original base case) to exactly zero.

Why Does This Happen?

This question of participation has been one of the most studied and commented-on aspects of DC plans, and has almost universally been ascribed to inertia on the part of workers. They intend to join, but never quite get around to it.

We should acknowledge a second reason. As we said earlier, perhaps saving for retirement simply isn't worthwhile for really low-paid employees. They already contribute to Social Security, which will replace a substantial proportion of their preretirement income. Some may also receive supplemental benefits in retirement, if their postretirement income is low. Direct taxation and affluence testing of state-provided benefits together could constitute a very high effective marginal tax rate on these benefits, if low-paid participants save additionally and generate postretirement income that reduces state-provided benefits. So it is not just the problem of finding money to save when they are working and have other more immediate priorities for their work income, it is the very design of state-provided benefits that takes away the incentive to save. Some commentators assert that some of the loans and hardship withdrawals we see (and which we discuss in the next chapter) are simply a reflection of low-income DC participants taking advantage of the liquidity of the DC system to get an employer contribution match.

Possible Solutions

Once it had been decided that the problem was due to inertia, an obvious solution presented itself: auto-enrollment. This case was well argued by a number of experts, including a paper by four academics from Harvard, Chicago, and Penn called "Saving for Retirement on the Path of Least Resistance."[6]

Auto-enrollment means that an employee is automatically enrolled in the plan unless he or she explicitly elects not to participate. In one sense, the question of participation or nonparticipation still rests entirely with the worker. In reality, however, the outcome of their inertia has been changed: Inertia pushes people toward the plan, rather than away from it. It makes a big difference.

This is the solution that the Pension Protection Act of 2006 (PPA) endorsed. This endorsement came in the form of an exemption from a nondiscrimination testing requirement for plans that auto-enrolled eligible workers. Perhaps of even greater importance was the signal that this sent, that this was seen as a desirable feature of the DC plan of the future. And, as we think of what we really mean by version 2.0 of the DC plan, auto-enrollment is an obvious and fundamental feature.

Some employers, indeed, are going further, and taking PPA as the opportunity to automatically reenroll employees who have passed the eligibility date and never elected to participate; those employees are being told that they will participate unless they now consciously elect not to.

A 2005 joint study by the Employee Benefit Research Institute and the Investment Company Institute[7] concluded that if all employers with plans adopted auto-enrollment, the median replacement rate for the lowest-income-quartile employees would increase from a modeled baseline of 23 percent to 37 percent, even under the conservative assumptions of a 3 percent contribution rate and a money market default investment. When the default contribution rate was raised to 6 percent and the default investment was changed to a target date fund, the median replacement rate for this group increased further to 52 percent. Auto-enrollment is a powerful mechanism.

EMPLOYEES WHO START SAVING TOO LATE

Individuals who start their saving program late are at a disadvantage, as we showed in Chapter 3. We found, for example, that if our base case model is changed so that saving begins at age 30 rather than 25, the savings rate required for a 40 percent income replacement rate increases from 8.4 percent of salary to 10.4 percent. Start saving at age 40 and the required savings rate jumps to 16.8 percent.

Why Does This Happen?

People have many reasons for starting late: early-in-life expenses such as repaying education loans, buying and furnishing a home, starting a family, and so on. In addition to these pressures, there are some behavioral factors that we will explain in Chapter 10, which include a tendency to pay too little attention to the future, causing people to undervalue the benefit of saving; and being put off by having too many choices to make.

Perhaps the most important factor is that beginning income levels tend to be low, and typically unable to support even the modest lifestyles that young people often have, let alone leaving room for retirement saving. Indeed, this simple observation led economists, including subsequent Nobel Prize winners, to postulate the life-cycle model of consumption. This hypothesizes that individuals have a consumption path that is much smoother than their income path. This means that they are, in effect, borrowing against future income in their early years, and then subsequently repaying their borrowings and starting to save for their retirement years, when their earned income ceases and they draw down their savings to finance consumption.[8]

Yet another reason for delayed participation is that employers may impose a waiting period, perhaps 6 to 12 months, during which new employees are not eligible to participate in a DC plan, to save the administrative expense that goes with short-service employees, particularly in high-turnover industries.

Finally, many employees in companies that do not pay for health insurance would rather buy health care coverage first, and find that they don't have enough to save for retirement, too.

In short, many of the reasons are financially understandable, but many are also behavioral. It is these behavioral ones, in particular, that are the focus of strategies to enroll employees early.

Possible Solutions

Auto-enrollment, described earlier, not only gets more workers into the plan, it gets them in earlier.

A more long-term solution, which is desirable in its own right and would reinforce auto-enrollment, is to increase financial literacy among the young, so that they understand budgeting, saving, making financial choices, and compound interest as it relates both to the cost of borrowing and the growth of savings.

EMPLOYEES WITH LOW SAVINGS RATES

We saw in Chapter 3 that retirement is expensive. Most people do not realize just how expensive it is. A survey published in 2008 by the MetLife Mature Market Institute helps to quantify the extent to which misunderstanding exists.[9] They report that, in the sample of more than 1,200 representative individuals aged 56 to 65:

- "There remain many widespread ... misconceptions around retirement income that could put many at risk for outliving their assets in retirement."
- Most underestimate postretirement longevity. Indeed, they do not even understand the concept of life expectancy. Told that an individual who reaches age 65 has a life expectancy of 85, 60 percent of the sample believed that implied much less than a 50-50 chance of living beyond 85.
- Many do not understand that they will probably need 80 to 90 percent of their preretirement income—counting all sources, including Social Security and so on—in order to maintain the same standard of living after retirement. "Half (49 percent) indicated that they would need 40 to 50 percent or even just 20 to 30 percent ..."
- "[A]lmost seven in ten (68 percent) respondents overestimate how much they can draw down from their retirement savings—with 43 percent saying they believe they can withdraw 10 percent or more each year while preserving their principal—even though most retirement experts suggest a withdrawal rate of no more than 4 percent annually."

To quantify the extent to which current savings rates fall short for many people, we could cite studies of how little has been accumulated in DC plans so far, but that would be an unfair, distorted set of statistics because the current generation of employees has not yet passed through a lifetime of dependency on DC plans. Most are only partway through their careers; and of those DC participants approaching retirement, most have spent part of their careers covered by DB. Nevertheless, we do not need studies of savings to make our point; the MetLife survey alone is enough to explain why participants save inadequate amounts. Indeed, many participants do not contribute enough even to attract the maximum employer match, thus forsaking free money.

Why Does This Happen?

The behavioral explanations are a by-now-familiar list: inertia, a dramatically greater focus on the present than on the future, and being put off by having to make decisions.

Possible Solutions

One element that helps to solve this problem is the auto-escalation of contributions, now explicitly recognized in the Pension Protection Act and starting to be used by many employers. Once again, it's a simple idea: Increase contribution rates over time in a predefined way until some maximum contribution rate is reached. Again, the direction of inertia is reversed and contribution rates automatically increase unless the participant consciously elects not to implement the increase.

However, the power of auto-escalation is not as strong as the power of auto-enrollment, because the default savings rates (even the escalating savings rate) tend to be set on the low end of what employees would choose to contribute on their own. And those contribution rates themselves tend to be somewhat below what most projections (including our base case) would imply are robust rates for retirement income provision on a par with what DB would have provided.

This leads in turn to quite a basic question about the DC system: Who should be paying for it? It was, by and large, the employer who paid for a DB plan.[10] Version 1.0 of the 401(k) plan was seen as being funded by the employee (admittedly with an employer match in many cases).[11] If version 2.0 is going to meet its retirement income goals, both employee and employer are going to have to pitch in—employees alone may be unable to bridge the gap. With increased expectations around the employer match, funding of version 2.0 probably needs to be seen as a shared responsibility, somewhere between the old 401(k) model and the DB model.

In the meantime, if it is employees to whom we are looking to put more into their DC plans, auto-escalation alone cannot do it. Indeed, once there is a default basic contribution level, plan participants may become anchored on that contribution and fail to put more money in when they should be doing so.

So, despite the hoped-for power of default paths, there is still a role for financial education in the DC system. Not so much the old-style education about the nature of different asset classes, about diversification, and so on. But, rather, education about how much saving is likely to be needed to reach certain financial goals, about what can (and what cannot) reasonably be expected from the financial markets. We will see in Chapter 12 on the Australian DC experience that education about targeted incentives to contribute is successful there.

Education needs to be complemented by better reporting than is available today. That's another subject we will return to. But general financial education will not do much to change behavior. It is only if somebody sees the track that they are on, and the likely outcome—in terms of their postretirement standard of living—of different rates of saving, that they will be able to make informed decisions on this question.

Yet another suggestion that has been made is to use a higher ceiling for the maximum contribution rate (currently 10 percent). Clearly, this would be more effective at increasing the overall savings rate (by allowing those who save a lot to save more) than it would at helping those who save the least.

One more point: We add here a reminder of something we mentioned in Chapter 3. Saving for retirement is a long, difficult, and long-term-focused endeavor. Because a temporary downturn in the market is discouraging, employees sometimes tend to reduce their contribution rate then, whereas holding steady (or even increasing it) is a more sensible reaction. Similarly for employers after a temporary downturn in the economy: Holding steady is much to be recommended rather than decreasing the match.

EMPLOYEES WITH GAPS IN CONTINUOUS PARTICIPATION

Auto-escalation is not enough. Even with auto-escalation in force, events conspire to keep contribution rates low.

Why Does This Happen?

When a worker moves from one job to another, he or she becomes a new employee with the new employer, and thus routinely drops (even with auto-enrollment and auto-escalation) to the lowest level of contribution with the new employer. That's because there is no continuity of record keeping from the old to the new employer, and you cannot rely on employees to remember what was the contribution rate with the former employer, to be able to start again at that rate and escalate from there. Indeed, in an auto-enroll world, it may be difficult to find out.

We can compare the experience of the base case projection described earlier in this book (which assumed a constant 4 percent contribution rate) to another individual with an identical pay scale and investment policy, but who starts contributing at the rate of 1 percent, increasing 1 percent each year to 4 percent, then switching jobs and restarting the 1 percent-to-4 percent pattern, 10 times in all. The second worker accumulates roughly 62 percent of the assets by age 65 and generates roughly 62 percent of the retirement income that the first worker does. While this is an oversimplified case, it does show that a sawtoothed savings pattern causes a gap that it is very beneficial to fill.

Possible Solutions

When it comes to dealing with issues such as gaps in continuous coverage, we find that the auto-solutions reach the limit of their effectiveness. An employer can institute a sound savings program for its own workers, but have no practical way to dovetail that with the programs of previous employers (or those to come).

To some extent, plan design can recognize this challenge. For example, if an employer decides to wait six months before allowing a new employee to join the plan (in order to avoid the administration burden if that employee leaves quickly), then perhaps a catch-up period could be set in place thereafter to make up the contribution shortfall that was missed.

But, when all is said and done, no employer-based savings program can completely solve the retirement savings challenges of workers who change jobs frequently. *That* would demand another level of system redesign altogether—one as fundamental as the Australian redesign or a federal program that could rival the Social Security system. For now, however, we will continue to concentrate on how to improve the system we have.

CHAPTER 7

Limit Leakage

Continuing with our theme of the shortcomings/opportunities in the defined contribution (DC) system as it currently operates, in this chapter we will address some of the ways in which assets can leak out of the system. This happens because when workers participate in DC plans, they sometimes tap into their accumulated savings prior to retirement. Some cash out a lump-sum distribution for nonretirement purposes. Some use them as security for a loan that the participant receives from the plan. Some take what are known as "hardship distributions" from their accounts. We will follow a similar structure to the previous chapter and consider for each of these forms of leakage the extent of the issue and the reasons. Because the possible solutions are essentially the same in all cases, we will address them together.

As we mentioned in Chapter 6, it may be that some participants, particularly the low-paid ones, use these leakage features as a way to make contributions to DC plans, get an employer contribution match, and then effectively take back their own contributions because they really can't afford to save. To that extent, they are less likely to respond to the solutions we discuss.

CASHING OUT

When workers change employers, they sometimes choose to withdraw—or "cash out"—their retirement savings account. Since taking money out before retirement is not really the point of a retirement savings vehicle, the tax system is designed to discourage this: Preretirement withdrawals typically incur a 10 percent tax penalty in addition to being taxed as earned income in the year received. So if you cash out before age $59^{1}/_{2}$, you might have been better off saving in some other way than through the DC system.

Nevertheless, lots of people do cash out. The 2008 Government Accountability Office (GAO) study cited in the previous chapter states that "of the 21 percent of households reporting that they had received lump sum distributions from previous jobs' retirement plans, about 47 percent cashed out all the funds, 4 percent cashed out some of the funds, and 50 percent rolled over all the funds into another retirement account."[1] In other words, about half the people changing jobs and receiving a lump sum cashed out wholly or partially. There is a link between account size and cashing out: Larger amounts tend to be rolled over, while smaller amounts are more likely to be cashed out. The GAO reports that the median amount rolled over was $24,200 and the median amount cashed out was $6,800. Unsurprisingly, it is the short tenured and the lower paid who seem to be most prone to this form of leakage.

There is evidence that the lump-sum distribution issue is declining over time. Another study compares what happened in 1993 and 2003.[2] In 1993, 19 percent of preretirement distributions were completely rolled over into other retirement accounts; this increased to 43 percent in 2003. In 1993, 23 percent used the entire distribution for consumption; in 2003 this declined to 15 percent.

Why Does This Happen?

One likely reason that many people cash out upon changing jobs is that cash in hand is helpful at a time of financial strain. Another reason may well simply be that they do it because they can: Psychologically, many people may be unwilling to leave assets in the care of an employer with whom they are severing their ties. 401(k) accounts can accumulate like old comic books and become difficult to keep track of: Each one is just another organization that needs to be notified every time you change your address. And once you've made the decision not to leave the assets in the old employer's plan, well, it's just so tempting to take the windfall rather than to be responsible and roll it over into another retirement account. Finally, some take the distribution with the intent of rollover and forget to do it.

LOANS

Most 401(k) plans allow participants to borrow against their accounts, and this can have the same effect as withdrawing money. A loan from one's own 401(k) account usually represents a more cost-effective proposition than a loan from a commercial source: Interest is normally lower and, even better, the interest is paid to the account, not to an external lender. (Strictly speaking, the rate of interest on the loan is economically irrelevant, since the plan participant is both the borrower and the lender. The real cost comes from the fact that the assets borrowed are no longer in the retirement account earning investment returns.) A loan can adversely affect retirement prospects in another way, too. If not repaid in full, it is treated as a withdrawal, reducing the account balance at retirement and possibly subject to a tax penalty.

The GAO study cites the statistic that roughly 85 percent of employers offer a loan option, and that at the end of 2006, loan balances amounted to 12 percent of the accounts of participants who had loans.[3]

Why Does This Happen?

Why do participants take out loans from their DC plans? Because these loans require no approval outside the plan administrator and incur dramatically lower transaction costs. And up to a point, loans are a helpful feature of a 401(k) plan: If there are unexpected hospital bills to pay and the choice is between borrowing from the 401(k) plan or running up credit card debts, participants are probably better off borrowing from the 401(k). But to the extent that 401(k) accounts are *too* easy to dip into—so that they become used to increase consumption, rather than in cases of necessity only—they do not fit with their new role. Version 2.0, you will recall, is meant to be a retirement savings account, not a supplementary savings vehicle. It is possible that use of these features will become less common as a result of a change in attitudes and general discouragement of their use, which may flow from the other changes we have already covered—the reliance of more participants on auto-enroll and default options, and so on.

HARDSHIP WITHDRAWALS

There is also a third form of leakage: hardship withdrawals. Plans are permitted to make provisions for these distributions, if the criteria are explicitly defined and are limited to the amount of an immediate and heavy financial need of the participant (or his or her spouse or dependent). The distribution is taxable and may be subject to a tax penalty. It does not need to be repaid. After taking a distribution, the participant is (by law) not permitted to make elective contributions to the plan for a further six months. Thus, a hardship distribution has more of a long-term impact on an account balance than a loan of the same amount.

Why Does This Happen?

Apart from the obvious comment that hardship withdrawals allow participants access to their money if they turn out to genuinely need it prior to retirement, there is a subtler reason why loans and hardship features are common features of 401(k) plans. They help the account balance to feel more like the participant's own money. The monthly deduction from salary feels less like a tax going to some distant entity that only vaguely and indirectly benefits them. The account balance is available—if it is really needed—at any point, not just at a distant retirement age decades away. And that, many employers argue, has been a factor in persuading workers to sign up for the plans in the first place.

Does all of this—the cashing out, the loans, and the hardship withdrawals—make a serious dent in the system? The GAO performed simulations of what might happen if various changes take place in participant behavior. The study states: "Assuming that workers do not withdraw money from their accounts while they are working—that is, no leakage occurs—raises overall average annuity income from DC plans by 11 percent and reduces the percentage of those with no DC savings at retirement by over 25 percent." The impacts are particularly high among low-income workers. In short, this is still a significant issue.

During the economic downturn of 2008, lawmakers were alarmed at the apparent increase in hardship withdrawals and borrowing from 401(k) plans—so much so that the Senate Special Committee on Aging called for hearings on the matter in July 2008. We mentioned in Chapter 3 that the combination of low or negative market returns and reduced contribution rates was especially harmful to a successful accumulation strategy. Here we see a similar problem, the combination of low or negative market returns and increased hardship withdrawals from accounts.

Possible Solutions

Are there obvious approaches to improve the end result? Of course. If employers were to limit or eliminate loan, hardship, and early withdrawal provisions and make rollovers the default option for job changers, the amount of money staying in the retirement savings system would undoubtedly increase, particularly for low-income workers. In fact, employers are currently required, in the absence of participant direction, to automatically roll DC account distributions between $1,000 and $5,000 into an individual retirement account (IRA) or leave the money in the plan.

Psychological aspects may also be helpful. For example, although workers would be upset by restrictive changes to their plans, they accept that under Social Security there are no loans and no hardship provisions, so there is no automatic notion that saving for retirement is unbearable without leakage provisions.

It may also be that general financial education has a role to play. Given the tax penalties associated with early distributions, hardship withdrawals, and loans that are not fully repaid, any arrangement under which a participant's finances outside the plan could be rearranged to accommodate the hardship or help the loan to be repaid in full would be of great benefit. Preventative education and access to financial advice at the time of the hardship or the loan initiation may be constructive.

CHAPTER 8

Invest Better

Of the many parts that go into a retirement savings program, investment is where many large opportunities for improvement lie. We have already looked at the 10/30/60 rule, which tells us that only around 10 percent of the distributions in our base case savings model came from contributions: The remainder were earned in the investment markets. And we'll see in Chapter 9, which covers the question of fees, even a small drop in the annual investment return results in a meaningful pay cut for our base case saver. So the impact of a good or bad investment program is enormous. But investment is a complex subject. It's easy to get it wrong. And it's hard to balance the risk of investment, which we want to reduce, with the returns, which we want to increase.

That's why a good defined contribution (DC) system needs to find a way to get investment right. If there are ways to increase returns with no adverse consequences, they should be considered seriously. If at the same time there are ways to reduce the market risk to which those savings are exposed, that would be even better. In this chapter we show how both of those goals—higher returns and lower risk—can be achieved.

EVIDENCE OF WASTE

Throughout our analysis of the opportunities in the DC system, we have started by identifying the issue and its impact. When it comes to investment, the root of the problems lies in the fact that, for the most part, workers are not investment experts.

Here's a simple but powerful piece of evidence. Even though as late as 2005 the most popular default in American DC plans was a money market or stable value fund,[1] one industry survey found that 40 percent of DC plan participants believed that money market funds included stocks and only 8 percent knew that they contained only short-term exposures.[2] That's as basic a lack of knowledge as is possible.

Another piece of evidence relates to diversification. The average American defined benefit (DB) plan has 44 percent of its assets in U.S. equities and 16 percent in non-U.S. equities (in addition to illiquid asset classes such as private equity and real estate), thus diversifying its equity exposure to some extent around the world. Now, even this 44-to-16 ratio displays too strong a home-country bias. But the average American DC plan's equity exposure is even less diversified: 56 percent in U.S. equities and 6 percent in non-U.S. equities.[3] This is not the choice of a sophisticated group.

Until recently, the DC system was based around the premise that individuals had to make their own investment decisions. Compare this to DB investing, which is typically carried out by a small group of experts.[4] Given the inexpertise of DC participants, it is no surprise that, in the aggregate, DB returns tend to be higher than DC returns. There are several studies that point in this direction. We will cite three.

The Center for Retirement Research at Boston College reports that, over the period 1988 through 2004, DB plans outperformed 401(k) plans by an average of 1 percentage point a year.[5] As we've already seen, 1 percent a year is a very big deal indeed.

A long series of studies by Watson Wyatt Worldwide points in the same direction.[6] In the latest comparison, they find "that between 1995 and 2006, DB plans outperformed DC plans by an average of 1 percent per year," adding that "earlier studies also found that, over time, DB plans attained higher returns than did 401(k) plans."

In fact, an annualized 1 percent is at the low end of what studies report. A study by Burgess and associates[7] looked at more than 162,000 participants in John Hancock's record-keeping database. Participants who made their own choices were each compared to one of Hancock's "lifestyle" funds based on the lifestyle fund that most closely matched the risk level of the participant's own asset allocation. The comparison showed that 89 percent of participants would have done much better than they actually did if they had chosen "lifestyle" funds corresponding to their risk profiles. How much better? An average of 2.96 percent per year better.

That study shows that participants waste returns. They did not need to take higher risk in order to get higher returns. It was their own poor investing behavior that caused the opportunity for higher returns to be wasted.

We will return in Chapter 10 to some of the reasons why individuals frequently make poor choices. Often, it comes down to the way we are as human beings and the way human beings make decisions: We are overconfident, chase returns, have a herd mentality, and don't like facing up to mistakes. For now, let's look at the solution. It comes in two parts. The first part is to design a good default option and nudge participants toward it. The second part is to allow knowledgeable participants to customize their choices.

THE IMPORTANCE OF A GOOD DEFAULT OPTION

Traditionally, the default option was an afterthought in a DC program. Because the expectation was that each individual would take care of his or her own investment allocation, the default (which is where the investments would end up if the participant didn't make any active choices) was chosen by the sponsor for convenience.

The old system was able to duck many investment questions by passing them to the individual. Version 2.0 cannot do that. In part, this is because so many participants are now auto-enrolled. In part, it's because, as we have seen, the old way of doing things didn't work particularly well. The old model tried to raise the quality of the decisions being made by millions of nonexperts to the standard set by full-time professionals. Version 2.0 abandons that effort.

Behind this change of approach lies a rethinking of what it means to be a fiduciary in a DC plan. For a long time, it was easy to see DC as the soft fiduciary option. But it is actually *more* difficult to be a good investment fiduciary in a DC plan than in a DB plan. That's because the fiduciary is ultimately responsible for everything that is done in the plan—yes, even for the choices that individual DC participants make. That doesn't mean that the fiduciaries are responsible for the outcomes; no, they can't control the outcomes. But they are responsible for the thought process that made the outcome possible. That means they are responsible for thinking about the chance that an option could lead to a bad outcome. And while they are not supposed to shut down everything that could lead to a bad outcome (that's impossible), they do have to think along the lines of: "Knowing about the inexpertise of participants, how likely is a bad outcome?"

It becomes clear, then, that one of the things fiduciaries ought to do, as part of participant education, is to tell them about the dangers of inexpertise. (Ironically, this is 180 degrees away from the traditional direction of education, which is based on the implicit assumption that any participant can become an informed, successful investor. We will explore this aspect more thoroughly in Part Three of the book.)

Another thing that fiduciaries ought to do is to build their own investment expertise into the default option and nudge participants into the default. In that way, the essential difference between the fiduciary structures of DB and DC investment decision making—the cause of wasted returns in DC—is minimized, because if expertise is built into the default and a participant accepts the default, the participant's own inexpertise is side-stepped. We know that inertia plays a big part in participant behavior: Make it the fiduciary's ally rather than a hindrance to success. And in the United States, the PPA permits this. That's why a well-designed default option is so very important in DC plans.

THE "TARGET DATE" SOLUTION

Participants are individuals. No default option will ever fit all of their different circumstances, goals and attitudes, though it can fit the average participant reasonably well. That means the fiduciaries need to define the characteristics that they believe represent the average participant, design the default accordingly, and publicize the characteristics so that those participants who want to do something different are able to adjust their exposure to the default to better reflect their own circumstances.

No matter what the characteristics, there is one particular approach that has suddenly become overwhelmingly popular in the United States in designing the asset allocation policy contained in the default.[8] We applaud this approach wholeheartedly. It is the "target date" approach (also called target retirement, life cycle, and a confusing variety of other names). Its main feature is that the asset allocation has what has become known as a "glide path," with its equity exposure declining in a predetermined way as the participant approaches the target date for retirement.

There are differences in the exact glide paths chosen in practice by different plans and different fund companies. We will shortly discuss what affects them. But they all have that common glide path feature of a declining equity exposure. Why? There are two ways to explain why: an academic way and a practical way. They lead to the same conclusion—that a glide path of some sort is sensible.

Glide Path: The Academic Explanation

This goes back to the notion we mentioned in the previous chapter, developed by Nobel Prize–winning economists: the life-cycle model of consumption. The point is that an individual's total wealth is not just their financial assets, but also their future earning potential, which the economists call their human capital. It's illiquid and it's not an asset that the person can cash in, of course, but it has a value to the person so it's a sort of asset. And it's an asset that for most people acts more like a bond than an equity.

In fact, at any given point in time, an individual can think of their total wealth as a combination of their human capital (future earnings) and their financial capital (invested assets).[9] This is illustrated in Figure 8.1.

It's easier to understand what this means for a retirement savings plan if you equate the human capital to the future contributions that have not yet been made to the plan. They are part of what will provide for the final benefits, but they're not available for investment yet.

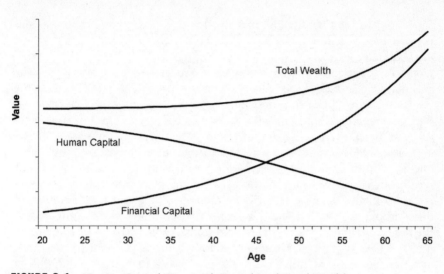

FIGURE 8.1 Human Capital, Financial Capital, and Total Wealth

So at the very start of the participant's investment life, there are no financial assets, only human capital, which is bondlike. Too bad! There's no way to give the total assets some equity exposure.[10] Then, as financial assets are created, it makes sense to invest them in equities, since there's so little exposure to equities so far. It's 100 percent of the plan account, but only a small amount of the sum of human capital and financial assets.

In time, the financial assets become big enough that the equity exposure—as a percent of those financial assets—can start to be reduced. And as the human capital declines relatively quickly in the last few years before retirement, its bondlike exposure needs to be replaced with an accelerated exposure to fixed income in the financial assets. By retirement, there is no more saving to be done, no future contributions yet to be made. At that point, the assets are entirely financial assets.

The equity exposure in the financial assets alone, then, will start off at 100 percent, stay there for some time, and eventually start to decline, doing so more quickly as the target date for retirement approaches. That's the glide path.[11]

Sequential Risk: The Practical Explanation

Although it was this academic concept that led to the notion of a glide path, in practice most people find it easier to set aside notions like human capital and think of the question a little differently, using the idea of sequential risk.

Sequential risk can be thought of as the risk of experiencing bad investment performance at the wrong time, when poor returns do the most damage. For example, a year of poor returns during the first year of DC saving would be unwelcome but have very little impact on the retirement income eventually generated. If the same poor returns were to be experienced in the year immediately prior to retirement, they would do a lot more harm.

It is possible to quantify this difference by varying the investment returns in our base case. Recall that in our base case, the accumulated assets at retirement (assuming a 7.5 percent return each year) were $439,000, producing total distributions of $1.06 million. If we substitute an investment return of −20 percent into the first year of the plan (when the participant is 25 years old), then the assets at retirement still amount to $437,000 and distributions to $1.05 million, a drop of barely 0.5 percent compared to the base case. In contrast, if the same negative return were to be substituted into the base case in the year immediately prior to retirement, the assets at retirement would be just $328,000 and total distributions $789,000—a drop of more than 25 percent.

So the risk associated with poor investment returns is different at different points in time. The interaction between timing, risk, reward, and asset allocation is far from simple. However, the upshot of sequential risk is that for any constant asset allocation applied to contributions, we can always find a different asset allocation path—in particular, a path with a higher equity exposure in the early years and a lower equity exposure in the later years—that will give us the same best estimate of accumulated wealth at retirement but with lower risk.

Here's a simple way to see why the glide path method is superior. With the glide path, as the dollars exposed increase, the equity exposure decreases, so that the potential dollar decline doesn't increase. The downside risk exposure from a high-equity allocation can be frightening at the end of a career. That's why taking more risk when the dollars are small and less risk when the dollars are large is a more desirable allocation of risk exposure over a contributing lifetime.

When you use this sort of glide path, the best estimate of the accumulated wealth at retirement is the same as for a constant equity exposure, but the distribution of possible outcomes has a much more controlled downside exposure. No wonder this has become the most popular form of default asset allocation policy.

What Goes into a Glide Path?

To design an appropriate glide path, assumptions are needed about the characteristics of the average investor: starting age for contributions, target retirement age, the projected level and shape of the salary path, the projected level and shape of the participant's and the employer's contribution percentage, the desired wealth or retirement income goal, and the assumed risk tolerance. All these factors are relevant. The equity exposure at any point in the glide path is not an isolated number; it is a number in a continuous and logical sequence that constitutes an investment plan that goes with the contribution plan.

Change any of the characteristics, and the glide path should change.

Consider, for example, a low-paid group. Much of their retirement income will inevitably come from Social Security. In other words, their assets already include a chunk of preannuitized wealth. Their 401(k) will add a slice of nonannuitized wealth. Whatever their ending equity exposure in the 401(k), it will place less of their aggregate retirement income at risk than will be the case for a high-paid group, for whom more of their wealth will be in 401(k) form. So an optimized glide path based on the lower-paid group ends up with more equity at the end of the glide path than it would for a higher-paid group. It also means a shallower decline over their career to get to that end point.

Another way in which a glide path will vary with circumstances is that some groups may traditionally retire before their Social Security commences. For example, this used to be compulsory for commercial airline pilots. For that sort of group, the objective will probably include a high bridging income for the first few retirement years, followed by a lower income once Social Security kicks in. Since pilots often start their commercial flying careers relatively late (if, for example, they have served in the military), their glide path of equity exposure will typically be higher than for the average participant in other jobs, because they have less time in which to accumulate their retirement wealth.

Now, given the assumptions that need to be made, and the fact that the optimal path is only strictly optimal for someone who exactly fits the assumed characteristics, one should not get carried away with the notion that an optimized glide path is vastly superior to every possible alternative. For every optimal solution, there are usually many others that produce expected outcomes that, for all practical purposes, are equally good. But not every solution produces close-to-optimal results. By optimizing, we can be assured that a robust solution has been found that serves well the needs of a very large group whose broad characteristics are roughly those on which the optimization is based.

The point here is that intelligently designed glide paths are not arbitrary sequences of numbers. They have a rationale. They are meant to be solutions to specifically defined problems. They should be arrived at using a sound process. Any supplier of a target date solution should be able to explain clearly exactly what is the problem for which the glide path is the optimal solution. Without that sort of clear (and clearly explained) rationale, what will the supplier do when the problem changes? For example, consider the group of commercial airline pilots. When legislation changed and permitted them to retire from their jobs later, this clearly changed the problem to be solved and should have resulted in a change in the optimal glide path.

What to Do If You're Not the Average Employee

A glide path fits a specific definition of the average employee. Some employees know they are not average. They may not fit the demographic characteristics: They may have started saving later, their expected salary curve may be steeper, they may be more willing to increase the rate at which their contributions increase—whatever. They may also not fit the risk tolerance profile. They may, for example, consider themselves to be more risk tolerant than average; perhaps they have a defined benefit from a prior employer, or non-employment-related wealth. Or they may be less tolerant of risk; many simply can't live with the thought of a high-equity exposure, no matter how necessary it is to their retirement aspirations.

Publishing the assumed characteristics of the average participant allows these other participants to decide whether they want to turn the investment risk dial up or down, relative to the default glide path. They can, of course, attempt to find expertise and customize an asset allocation for themselves. Most won't. Also, there is a great convenience in the automatic feature of a target date plan that changes the allocation at predetermined times and rebalances back to the glide path when investment markets take the allocation away from the path.

There are at least two obvious ways to turn the risk dial up or down. One is to mix the target date fund with a chunk of something riskier (for example, 80 percent glide path and 20 percent equities, to turn the risk dial up) or something less risky (for example, 70 percent glide path and 30 percent fixed income, to turn the risk dial down). But then the participant needs to rebalance back to the 80/20 or 70/30 mix from time to time, since the allocation inevitably drifts away from the targeted balance if left alone. The other way is for the participant to choose a target date allocation that corresponds to a date earlier than his or her own prospective retirement date, to turn the risk dial down, or a later date, to turn the risk dial up. For example, if a participant plans to retire in 2030 but wants to turn the risk dial up, he or she can sign on for the target date 2035 or 2040 fund, so that his or her glide path stays on a higher-equity exposure. Similarly, electing a 2025 target date fund forces the experienced glide path to turn down earlier.

Purists will argue that selecting an artificial-year glide path results in a suboptimal path. Quite true. But as we mentioned before, the optimal path is only strictly optimal for those who exactly fit the assumed characteristics. The real beauty of target date glide paths is that they are close to optimal for just about everyone else. This is why they work so well as multipurpose vehicles, including for turning the risk dial up and down.

Implementing the Glide Path

We have concentrated on the asset allocation glide path because it is the single most important feature of the investment program in a DC plan. It is only the beginning of a sound investment program, however. There are other ways in which the standard of DC investment falls short of the bar set by DB. In particular, as long as responsibility for investment of the assets was seen as lying mainly with the participant, there was little scope for applying the finer details of institutional best practices. But increased engagement by the plan fiduciary leads to the application of institutional standards—where success and failure are measured not in percentage points, but in basis points (one-hundredths of a percentage point)—and to a greater emphasis on investment efficiency.

Sophisticated practices, such as securities lending, transition management, overlay programs, and the like, will become increasingly common in DC plans run by engaged fiduciaries.[12] In addition, fiduciaries have the opportunity to free themselves from the fetters of participant behavior (like performance chasing and daily liquidity needs) and broaden the opportunity set of investments used in target date options to include DB-type asset classes such as real estate, emerging markets, and so on.

The greater emphasis of version 2.0 on default options works directly toward this end, because it encourages the plan sponsor to focus attention on the highly effective management of a small number of core options.

AND FOR THE INVESTMENT EXPERTS?

We have said that there are two parts to the investment solution for DC. Part one, the default, is the most important part because it deals with the greatest number of people, and it deals with the people who most need help. But there will always be those who have, or feel they have, enough expertise to plot their own path. What should the fiduciaries offer them? Essentially, there are two levels. For those who know enough to match their risk tolerance to an asset allocation, a choice from target risk funds (in which the allocation is maintained constant at a predetermined risk exposure—also called "lifestyle" funds or "balanced funds" or any of a variety of other names), or asset class funds that can be self-assembled by the participants into their desired allocation. Target risk funds are like target date funds, except there is no glide path; they have a constant overall risk profile. The point is that these choices should be assembled with all the fiduciaries' expertise built in, and (assuming the desired asset allocation fits the participant's risk tolerance) the chance of a bad outcome in any of the funds is low—as low as is the case in a DB plan.

Remember the evidence that, after adjusting for asset allocation risk, do-it-yourself participants' returns are dramatically lower than the returns from identical-risk fund choices assembled by knowledgeable fiduciaries. That is the form of waste that can be avoided by funds that contain the built-in expertise of the fiduciaries: No more return chasing, trading too much, and so on.

This would be a big change. But there is evidence that participants in fact have weak preferences as investors. Professors Shlomo Benartzi and Richard Thaler have shown that when participants create their own asset-allocated portfolios, they assemble portfolios that do not match their risk preferences. They also give much higher satisfaction ratings to portfolios that are assembled by professionals (or even to the median allocation in their plan), when they are presented with the range of retirement income each participant can expect.[13]

What about those who still want to make their own decisions in all regards? There is no need for the fiduciaries to offer a selection of narrowly defined funds, such as industry funds. Instead, for those who want to make bets on industries or factor exposures or countries or currencies or specific securities (or whatever), permit them a mutual fund or brokerage window in which they essentially proclaim that they are rejecting the fiduciaries' expertise and want to be responsible for their own investment fate.

CHAPTER 9

Reduce Fees

As we search the defined contribution (DC) landscape for leakage and inefficiency, one topic stands out as especially contentious, and we will award it its own special chapter. That topic is fees. In DC, unlike in defined benefit (DB), fees have a direct impact on the benefit received by the plan participant. This creates a different set of dynamics. One danger is that those in a position to monitor and manage fees (the plan fiduciaries, most notably the plan sponsor) have less direct incentive to do so.[1] The result can be that fees are inadequately managed. Another danger arises when awareness of this first danger grows: Controlling fees becomes a goal in itself. This produces the opposite—but potentially just as damaging—outcome: The cheapest route is chosen even where this acts against the interests of participants.

THE IMPACT OF FEES

In Chapter 4 we showed how very important investment returns are. Anything that reduces those returns unnecessarily is a waste, and potentially very damaging. Because fees are paid year after year, their impact can add to a lot over the course of a lifetime. In our base case example, for instance, an 8.4 percent savings rate produced a 40 percent income-replacement ratio. That was based on an annual investment return (after the impact of fees) of 7.5 percent. Suppose a further $1/2$ percent a year were to be lost to fees, reducing the effective return to 7 percent. Now, the same 8.4 percent savings rate produces just 34 percent income replacement: a 15 percent pay cut for the plan participant. Alternatively, a 9.8 percent savings rate would now be required to produce the same 40 percent income-replacement rate. So, other things being equal, an apparently small reduction in fees adds up to a big gain in plan effectiveness. Are other things equal? To answer that, we need to look at what the fees are paying for.

FEES FOR WHAT?

DC plans don't run themselves. There is a lot of administration and investment activity required and all of that costs money. Plan fees and expenses generally fall into three categories: administration fees, investment fees, and individual service fees.

Administration fees cover record keeping, accounting, legal, and trustee services, required on a day-to-day basis. Investment fees are those fees and expenses associated with managing plan investments. Individual service fees are those associated with optional features of plans, typically charged to the accounts of the individuals who elect to use those features.

Individual service fees tend to account for the smallest slice of the pie. And, because they tend to be clearly linked to specific services received by specific individuals, they tend to be relatively easy to assess and manage. We will not worry about them here.

The lion's share of total fees is typically made up of investment and record keeping, a fact that has been highlighted by the U.S. Government Accountability Office (GAO):[2]

> For example, a 2005 industry survey estimated that investment fees made up about 80 to 99 percent of plan fees, depending on the number of participants in the plan. Plan record-keeping fees ... are the second-largest portion of plan fees. ... Investment fees, which are usually charged as a fixed percentage of assets and deducted from plan returns, are typically borne by participants. Plan record-keeping fees are charged as a percentage of a participant's assets, a flat fee, or a combination of both. Although plan sponsors pay these fees in a considerable number of plans, they are increasingly being paid by participants.

LOOKING FOR FEE LEAKAGE

One might suppose that the simplest way to measure the extent of the fee leakage would be to compare actual fees to some bare minimum level. That, however, would miss the point. Cheapest is not always best. What we need to do, therefore, is to look for whether fees are legitimate—does the service that is being paid for justify the expense or not? This is a necessary exercise, not only because fees can make such a big impact on the end result, but also because there is evidence that the DC system as a whole suffers from some degree of fee leakage. The problem may not be as simple as some would like to paint it, but it is a real problem.

We will now look at three reasons why fees may be higher than a bare minimum. The first is fee-sharing arrangements. The second is the different levels of fees paid by large institutions compared to individual, or "retail," investors. The third is active management of investments. Before we begin, we have two simple and general comments to make about investment management fees.

First, whatever level they are at, the participant should be looking at the investment returns earned net of fees. In some cases the employer pays the investment management fees. This is not usual, but it is permissible and constitutes potentially a very important benefit to participants, because it is not considered an employee benefit for income tax purposes. In these cases, participants can think in terms of the investment return gross of fees because gross and net amount to the same thing for the participants. In other cases (most of the time, in fact), participants can only eat their net-of-fee returns, so net returns become the only relevant consideration in making investment choices.

Second, whatever the fees are, they need to be defensible. This is actually a more subtle statement than it appears at first sight to be. Why that is so should become clear as we look at the details.

FEE-SHARING ARRANGEMENTS

Some fees may be partly a form of compensation for other services provided by a supplier, with the total fees subject to a fee-sharing agreement of some kind. For example, a record keeper receives fees from mutual funds on its platform, and these fees offset the record keeper's costs for its administrative services. This kind of deal has triggered the ire of legislators in the United States in recent times, and there is a cry for complete disclosure of hidden fee-sharing arrangements.

It's not that revenue sharing is itself an ignoble practice. But a hidden fee-sharing arrangement lacks transparency. And that prevents pricing efficiency.

We've stated that fees should be defensible. A hidden fee-sharing arrangement prevents a fee from being defensible. In the example in the previous paragraph, nondisclosure means that the sponsor may think the record keeper's explicit fee charged is a very competitive one rather than an indirectly subsidized one; and the sponsor does not know if the undisclosed revenue constitutes a big incentive for the record keeper to include that family of mutual funds on its platform. Nondisclosure is not conducive to sound management: Where the incentives on the various parties making decisions are complex, it is essential that a transparent structure is in place to allow everyone to see what is being paid, by whom, and for what. Only then can we start to be confident that fees are not fatter than they need be, and that competitive pressures have a chance to come into play.

As for the revenue that is the subject of the fee-sharing arrangement, perhaps that is in itself defensible and perhaps it is not. Bringing the arrangement into daylight requires the party receiving the fee as well as the plan sponsor to explain why the fee is defensible. The explanation can then be considered on its own merits. Once full disclosure is made, the stand-alone fee can be evaluated.

INSTITUTIONAL VERSUS RETAIL FEES

The second reason that fees may be more than a bare minimum is that the investment management fee may be what is called in industry jargon an institutional fee or it may be a retail fee. An institutional fee is one that is charged to a large pool of assets, such as a DB pension plan or a large DC plan or an endowment or foundation. It is typically much lower than a retail fee, which is charged by mutual funds to individual investors and may include not only investment management fees but possibly also fees used to pay commissions to brokers and other salespersons, advertising costs, and so on.

When DC plans were a small supplement to a DB plan, convenience often dictated that retail mutual funds constituted the range of DC choices. It was also partly because of their size: DC plans started out small and took some time to get bigger (many are still small in institutional terms). When you're small, retail fees are all that are available. Which made sense when DC plans were supplemental savings vehicles, but less sense for version 2.0—because version 2.0 of the DC system is largely replacing a DB system. And it can't do that effectively if it's paying significantly higher fees for investment management. So when DC becomes the sole, or the main, form of retirement saving, convenience becomes less important, and the search for ways to find economies of scale in investment management becomes more important.

One approach, for example, may be to combine the assets of two or more pension funds for investment purposes, unitizing the combined pool or pools so that the portion owned by each fund can be easily tracked and valued. For example, a sponsor with both a DB and a DC plan could create a pool from the assets in each of several asset classes in its DB fund. This would enable the pools to be used in the creation of default choices or asset-allocated fund choices or even as the list, or a portion of the list, of single asset class funds for sponsors who want to provide that level of choice. Unitizing each of the pools enables the asset classes to be bought and sold in the DC plan, retaining the institutional pricing of those assets and transferring the institutional pricing to the DC plan.

Indeed sponsors can go further. They can aggregate their assets with those of other sponsors for even greater economies of scale, via so-called collective trusts or commingled funds.

ACTIVE MANAGEMENT

Finally, whatever the fee arrangement, fees paid for active management are higher than fees paid for passively tracking a specified market index. If active management is chosen then fees are higher.

A bare-bones fee would therefore be a stand-alone institutional fee for passive management with no revenue sharing.

Now, because it is net-of-fees returns that matter to the investor, the question of whether active management is worth paying for is crucial here. When one considers all investors in any market, the aggregate of all their activity is what defines the passive return for the market.[3] Thus, it is inevitable that the average of all their active returns will be the same as the passive return—before paying for investment management fees. And so, because passive fees are lower than active fees, the average active return net of fees will be below the average passive return net of fees. Active management is worthwhile, net of fees, only for those who are more skilled than the average investor—essentially, therefore, a minority of investors.

Consider what investment markets do. They are, in effect, a price discovery mechanism. We can go into a market and discover what price others are willing to pay for a particular asset, or at what price they are willing to sell one that they hold. Prices change until the balance of prospective buyers and sellers becomes equal. If we believe that we have a better insight into what a particular price ought to be than those who are trading in the marketplace, then we can make money from our insight, buying or selling (as appropriate)—and when other market participants eventually come around to our view of the price (after thinking about things in the different ways that they do), then the price moves to what we thought it ought to be, and we are better off.

But it's not just *when* they come around to our price; it's also *if* they do. And if they don't, then we don't do as well as others in the marketplace. So it's only those with superior insights (which could come from better information or better analysis, both of which cost money to generate) who should bet actively on prices. The rest should be content to take whatever is the average opinion of all the market participants. And that means accepting prices passively, whether they turn out to be right or wrong.

But that's not the end of the story. Most American DB funds are managed actively, at least in part. Most DB sponsors feel they can select an above-average consultant who in turn can select above-average managers. Of course, this represents aggregate overconfidence. Nevertheless, the belief system persists among sponsors that they can find skill, and that this skill will benefit the DB fund. This has interesting implications for the construction of DC default options.

As we saw in Chapter 8, the default option is designed by fiduciaries who are deemed to be expert or to have sought expertise, and who build that expertise into the default option, so that inexpert participants can overcome their inexpertise by accepting the default. But we observe that many American sponsors who use active management in their DB funds then turn around and use passive management in their DC default option.

Under the Employee Retirement Income Security Act of 1974 (ERISA), this must surely be difficult to justify. DB shows what economists would call the revealed preferences of the sponsors. In other words, active management is the choice they make when they are paying the fees out of their own pocket and they are the ones directly impacted by the success or failure of that decision (because the investment returns affect not the benefits but the contributions, and it is the plan sponsor who must pay the contributions). However, when they must make the decision about whether to pay active management fees out of someone else's pocket—when that someone else is the one directly impacted by the success or failure of the decisions—they make a different decision. We are pretty confident that one consideration in these decisions is that active management has periods of ups and downs—there are inevitably some periods during which it will underperform the passive alternative. Trustees want to avoid the necessary explaining—not to mention the fear of lawsuits—when the inevitable happens.

Of course, ERISA is quite clear that fiduciaries can't put their own interests ("don't want to be sued") ahead of the interests of their participants ("higher returns"). Remember, this is the default option we're talking about, reflecting solely the expertise of the DC fiduciaries (who, we assume in this argument, are the same as the DB fiduciaries). Not a comfortable position.

The irony here is that a side effect of the different incentives created by the DB and DC structures may be that some DC participants are not paying too much in fees, but (in one area at least) too little.

The question of active versus passive management is a far bigger subject than we can cover here. Despite our earlier comments, we do not mean to take sides: We believe that there is a role—indeed, a need—for both forms of management in properly functioning markets and in a properly functioning DC system. But passive management should not be regarded as a panacea for all of DC's ills; this is a more subtle subject than that.

RECORD-KEEPING FEES

The cited GAO study itself cites an industry study reporting that plan record-keeping fees constituted 12 percent of total plan fees for plans with fewer than 25 participants, declining as a proportion of total plan fees to under 2 percent for plans with 1,000 participants.

Problems start to arise when fees are not charged on a stand-alone basis. For example, if record-keeping fees are charged partly as a percentage of fund assets and partly on a per-participant basis, then investment management fees subsidize record keeping and high-asset participants subsidize low-asset participants. A cynic might say that participants are little enough aware of the fees they pay anyway, so what difference does it make? Our point is simply that anything that moves the situation in the direction of greater clarity is a movement in the right direction. And that is what the initiatives on fee disclosure are all about.

Even though participants tend to pay record-keeping fees, they are in fact negotiated for the plan as a whole by the sponsor, who therefore bears a fiduciary responsibility to the participants to negotiate an arrangement that is defensible. At the time of writing, we see the forces between plan sponsors and record keepers shifting.[4] The supply of record-keeping services still lags behind the demand for them, giving record keepers the upper hand. Indeed, in many cases record keeping drives investment, with record keepers dictating which funds are available on their platform, because there is zero tolerance for record-keeping errors. But a simple analogy shows that this cause-and-effect relationship cannot last. There is also zero tolerance for errors in a sponsor's payroll function; but the supplier of payroll services does not dictate which forms of employee compensation can be considered. Record keeping must become the servant of investment choices, not the master.

As we will see in Chapter 12 on the Australian DC system, employer associations and unions in that country have come together to form buying pools of investment and record-keeping services, bringing down the cost of these services. This is not a major feature of the U.S. scene, though it is happening with professional associations and multiemployer plans.

One final closing thought concerns disclosure. We've argued for better disclosure in this chapter, and we are hardly a voice crying out in the wilderness in doing so. Regulators appear to have hung their hats on better disclosure as a vehicle for identifying and reducing fee leakage in the DC system. But the threat of more substantive legislation is never far behind, should disclosure still leave fees perceived as too high.

Three

We Need the Right Sort of Education

In the first two parts of this book, we established the basic dynamics of a retirement plan, and looked at the main areas of leakage during the savings phase. In Part Three, we will take a look at how the individuals within the defined contribution (DC) system act and what sort of help they need. We will look at some of the lessons of behavioral finance—a relatively new field of economics that looks at how the actual behavior of real people differs from that assumed by traditional economics. This is an important consideration as we look at the design of the DC system, since an effective system must be built around an understanding of the choices that participants actually make in various circumstances, not around the choices that they ought in theory to make.

Following from that is a discussion of what sort of education would do the greatest good. Since the decisions of individual participants are central to the DC system, the success of the system depends in part on their making appropriate choices. The challenge of improving financial literacy may appear overwhelming, but there is evidence that a surprising amount of progress appears to be possible, if education efforts are focused in the right areas.

We think all our readers will be interested in these two chapters. Individuals (and their advisers) will understand their personal decision making better. Sponsors (and their advisers) will understand why their educational efforts have borne relatively little fruit. And opinion leaders will see that financial education and investment education are two different things.

CHAPTER 10

Why the Waste? Because We're Only Human

Are you an above-average driver? Research indicates that 80 percent of people in general will rate themselves as above-average drivers.[1] Of course, it is not possible for most people really to be above-average drivers. By definition, only half the population can be above average at this or any task. But it seems to be part of human nature to be overconfident in one's own abilities.

This tendency to be overconfident has been studied extensively. Many studies have focused on overconfidence as it relates to financial decisions. One study involving individuals' level of confidence when it comes to selecting investments found that participants were *more* confident when their investment decisions were *less* accurate.[2] The same study also concluded that as task complexity increases, overconfidence increases as well.

Another widely quoted demonstration of overconfidence asks people to provide estimates of 10 quantities (such as the diameter of the moon, or the number of members of OPEC), with the instruction that for each of these, a range should be provided that the respondent is 90 percent confident contains the true value. (You will recall that we used this form of question in Chapter 3 when considering what future stock market returns might turn out to be.) Because you are free to make the ranges as wide as they need to be to get to the 90 percent confidence level, most people should (in theory) find just one of the 10 true values to surprise them and lie outside their range. In practice, it's rare to find someone whose estimates are even 70 percent accurate—40 to 50 percent is most common.[3]

OVERCONFIDENCE IN RETIREMENT PLANNING

There is good evidence that overconfidence shows up in planning for retirement. The Employee Benefit Research Institute (EBRI) has conducted a retirement confidence survey each year for nearly two decades.[4] In their 2008 survey they asked the question: "Have you or your spouse tried to figure out how much money you will need to have saved by the time you retire so that you can live comfortably in retirement?" Of the 1,057 workers who were surveyed, only 47 percent responded that they had. This statistic may not be surprising by itself but there was another question that was asked of these same workers. They were asked how confident they were that they would have enough money to live comfortably in retirement. Sixty-one percent said they were somewhat or very confident. How could it be that 61 percent were somewhat or very confident they would have enough money to live comfortably in retirement yet only 47 percent had even tried to figure out how much they would need? The answer lies in our human nature to be overconfident. We'll note for the record that the percentage of workers who said they were *very* confident in the 2008 survey was down significantly from the previous surveys. We have to go back to 1993 to find a year in which the "very confident" response was as low as 2008. So an economic downturn can have some impact—but the basic pattern remains intact through thick and thin.

The result of overconfidence can be to encourage low or no saving. People may figure that: "Something will come up—it always has up to now. I can worry about old age later." No less an authority than Dr. Seuss has told generations of children: "And will you succeed? Yes! You will indeed! (98 and $3/4$ percent guaranteed.)"[5] Confidence is good but can lead to problems when it shows up in the wrong places. And retirement saving is one of the wrong places. When even Dr. Seuss's advice turns out to be part of the problem, we know we're in trouble!

BEHAVIORAL FINANCE

Overconfidence is just one of many psychological factors that influence financial decisions. There is abundant evidence that individuals don't always act rationally when making financial decisions. This makes managing the financial aspects of retirement more difficult.

This field of study is known as behavioral finance. It's become a hot topic in recent years among professional investors, because it yields insights into why markets behave as they do. Daniel Kahneman, a pioneer in the field of behavioral finance, was one of two winners of the Nobel Prize for Economics in 2002 for "having integrated insights from psychological research into economic science, especially concerning human judgment and decision-making under uncertainty."[6] More recently still, the field has been extended even further by researchers seeking to tie emotions and decision making to activities in specific regions of the brain: hence the name neuroeconomics for this new science.

One of the foundations of behavioral finance is the concept of the "heuristic." Researchers such as Kahneman have shown that individuals often use heuristics to simplify their financial decision making. A heuristic is a mental shortcut or common method for solving a problem. Heuristics are helpful (who wants to spend 20 minutes optimizing what drink to order before dinner at a restaurant?) but can lead to biases in our decision making, which in turn can be harmful.

For example, a heuristic that most people apply (consciously or subconsciously) is "when in doubt, don't change things." After all, we all feel much worse if something bad comes about because of our own actions, rather than just as the effect of fate. This leads to what is known as the status quo bias.

When it comes to making changes to one's investment portfolio, the status quo bias might be beneficial: It may prevent you from selling low and buying high. However, when it comes to starting a savings routine, the status quo bias can lead to procrastination, causing you to delay your savings. Here the same heuristic can be harmful.

In the early 1980s, defined contribution (DC) plans in America began to involve individuals in their funding and investment decisions with the advent of 401(k) and 403(b) provisions. Regulations incented plan sponsors to take a number of steps to avoid liability for participants' decisions, including the provision of educational materials. In response, plan sponsors increased the amount of educational materials provided to plan participants. A lot of money has been spent on trying to educate plan participants toward more rational investment decision making in hopes of better outcomes. Some hope! People continued to make their decisions based on simple heuristics, as they always had—it's hard to fight against human nature. So, despite the good intentions, this education effort has not yielded meaningfully better results.

As a result of all this work, today we have a greater understanding of how individuals make financial decisions. The task now is to evolve our DC system to avoid these behavioral traps, and to do so by working with human nature, rather than against it. In Part Two, we saw the results of suboptimal behavior by participants. In this chapter, we will explore some of the psychological reasons for this behavior. The aspects that we will focus on are low participation and savings rates, and poor investment returns.

LOW PARTICIPATION AND SAVINGS RATES

One explanation for why people do not save for retirement or, when they do, they don't save enough is that many simply don't know how much money they will need for retirement. They don't know either because they have not tried to determine the amount or because they have tried and found the task too complex to complete (which is quite understandable, given what we saw in Chapter 3 about the uncertainty attached to the answer). Beyond complexity or lack of effort, there are psychological factors influencing participation and savings rates. Two factors of significant importance are the tendency to pay too little attention to events in the future and the impact of choice overload.

Hyperbolic Discounting

We humans value immediate costs and rewards much more than future costs and rewards.[7] We discount the value of something in the future at a rate that is so high that researchers call it *hyperbolic discounting*. Think of the advertisement that promises that you can have an entire bedroom set delivered today, yet don't have to start making payments until (you fill in the year). Why does this sales tactic work? Because the reward, the bedroom set, is fully valued: It is being delivered today. However, the *cost* has been pushed out far enough into the future that it is deeply discounted in the buyer's mind.

The same thing works in reverse. If there's a cost today for a reward in the future, we feel the cost much more than we anticipate the reward. Indeed, it seems that we actually use different parts of our brain when making decisions that involve immediate versus delayed rewards.[8] So our brains are (almost literally) hardwired to think differently about immediate and delayed rewards.

Hyperbolic discounting plays havoc with our motivation to save for retirement. Because of hyperbolic discounting, the mental math of saving for the future is difficult to justify. I experience the cost today, yet experience the reward sometime far into the future. The reward is deeply discounted in my mind, yet the cost is fully valued. I'd rather spend the cash today. This is why for many people it takes an employer matching contribution to get them to contribute to a 401(k). Because an employer match feels like an instant reward ("free money from my employer"), the mental math changes, making saving more attractive.

Now think about auto-escalation of contributions. Inertia alone is sufficient to explain why, once we have selected a contribution rate, we'll tend to leave it there. How can a participant be persuaded to increase contributions in the future, as pay increases and as the time horizon for earning an investment return decreases? Answer: use hyperbolic discounting. The cost of future increases in contributions is discounted, because it occurs in the future. Once made, the commitment tends to stick because of inertia.

Is it wrong to do this? The morality of using (some would say exploiting) human nature to achieve goals that people consider socially desirable has been debated. The prevailing view, implicitly incorporated into the Pension Protection Act of 2006 (PPA), is that it is acceptable. The argument is that human responses are always influenced by the way in which a question is framed, and that there is no neutral way to choose a default position on questions like participation and escalating contributions: You're in or you're out, you escalate or you don't. Whichever you choose as the default position, the other choice is automatically disadvantaged. In these circumstances, one ought then to frame the question in a way that leads the responder to the desired outcome (a form of paternalism), while still giving the responder a chance to opt out (a form of libertarianism).[9]

Choice Overload

In the early days of 401(k), many plans did not allow their plan participants to choose where their accounts were invested. The participant contributed to the plan and the employer invested the money. Before long, however, plan participants began asking for the ability to direct the investment of their accounts. In response, plan sponsors offered participants a choice of investments. Once down that road, it became very difficult to turn back. Over the years, the number of investment options in 401(k) plans has increased steadily. By 2005, the average number of investment choices in 401(k) plans had grown to 17.4.[10]

You might think that the number of investment choices would not have an impact on participation rates or, if there were an impact, that it would be positive. As it turns out, the opposite is true. And again, the reasons reflect human tendencies, rather than rational investment considerations.

The classic investigation into choice overload had nothing to do with investing. It involved a supermarket display of an extensive choice of jams. On some days 24 varieties were displayed in a booth; on other days, 6. When 6 were displayed, 40 percent of shoppers visited the booth, and 30 percent bought something there. When 24 varieties were displayed, far more shoppers (60 percent) visited the booth, but almost nobody bought (3 percent). It was as if they were saying, "They're all good. I don't know which one I like best."

In a follow-up experiment, people who said they liked chocolates made a selection from 6 or from 30, and tasted their selection. They were asked for a satisfaction rating. Those who chose from 30 were less sure that they really liked what they chose.[11]

One of the researchers from the supermarket study, Sheena Iyengar, wondered whether these findings could tell us something about the behavior of participants in DC plans. So she, along with several colleagues, conducted their own statistical study of a database of 650 plans with 800,000 employees. After controlling for all sorts of differences (to ensure that their results were not biased by incidental differences between plans), they came to the conclusion that a multiplicity of choices doesn't just make choosing difficult and doesn't just reduce satisfaction with your choices—it actually reduces participation itself. They found that the probability of participation declined 2 percent for every 10 additional investment options.[12] It was as if the employees were saying, "I'm sorry, it's too complicated, I want no part of this." The moral of the story is to keep choices simple and few.

POOR INVESTMENT RESULTS

Low participation rates and low savings rates are not the only challenges faced by the DC system. DC plans, in aggregate, appear to earn lower investment returns than their DB counterparts, as we mentioned in Chapter 8. We believe that, to a large extent, this is related to the way in which individuals go about their decision making.[13]

Hyperbolic discounting and choice overload may help explain low participation and savings rates, but what explains poor investment returns? We suggest that a lack of sophistication, combined with overconfidence and return-chasing behavior, are among the prime (although probably not the only) reasons.

Lack of Sophistication

The vast majority of individuals are inexpert when it comes to investing, just as most people are inexpert at any profession that is technical in nature, such as dentistry or mechanical engineering. Again, we cited evidence in Chapter 8 of participants not understanding what a money market fund holds and of poor diversification.

Overconfidence

Selecting investments is a difficult and complex task even for the experts. Unfortunately, as we mentioned before, as task complexity increases so does the tendency to be overconfident. DC participants given a wide choice of investments are susceptible to the same behavioral tendencies as any individual investor.

In a paper written about individual investor behavior published in 1999, Terry Odean describes his and fellow researcher Brad Barber's analysis of

158,000 investment accounts from a discount brokerage firm.[14] The sample of accounts showed a wide range of investment trading frequency. They found that the accounts that traded the most actively earned the lowest average returns. They also found that, on the whole, the stocks within these accounts that individual investors bought underperformed the stocks they sold. Barber and Odean concluded that overconfidence played a role in the underperformance, stating: "Greater overconfidence leads to greater trading and to lower expected utility."[15]

Confidence itself is a helpful trait when survival is at stake. In a dangerous situation, who wants to follow someone who is consumed with self-doubt? Overconfidence, however, is not a helpful trait. It appears to be another contributor to individual investors' poor returns.

Chasing Returns

There is ample evidence that investors tend to chase returns[16]—that they jump in after an investment has been successful, and in so doing they tend to buy high. Then, when the investment (as it often does) fails to perform as they hope, they hang on too long and eventually sell low. Buying high and selling low is, of course, exactly the opposite of what successful investors do. The easy question is: Why do we persist in these tendencies? Authors Steven Beach and Clarence Rose have identified three causes of this behavior.[17]

The first reason that we tend to chase returns is a herd mentality. When we see what others are doing, we tend to follow them. (This is built deeply into our psyche. In the early days of humanity, it was an obvious way to enhance our ability to survive.) In investing, it means that we wait to see what has already done well—and then, when the evidence is clear, we buy, too. The trouble is that, too often, we buy too late to benefit much from the investment.

The second reason is regret aversion. We don't want to feel the pain of admitting a mistake. So we hold on—too long.

What is it that makes us hold on to losers? Typically, it's our mental accounting. That's the third reason. We know the price at which we bought. That's our benchmark for judging success or failure. If the price falls, we can avoid regret if we hold on until we break even again—and so we do hold on, giving up other opportunities.

Beach and Rose go on to do a long study, using data on large company stocks, long-term bonds, and Treasury bills, from 1926 through 2002, comparing the outcomes of return-chasing behavior and disciplined rebalancing of a portfolio to a predetermined asset allocation. The results won't surprise you at all. If you search for a static asset allocation (a portfolio rebalanced to some constant allocation each year) that had the same overall return as the chase portfolio (which invested everything in the previous year's best asset class), the rebalanced portfolio had a lower volatility. If you search for a rebalanced portfolio that showed the same volatility as the chase portfolio, the rebalanced portfolio had a higher overall return.

Experience tells us that if we subdivide the choices further, meaning that we have not just three broad asset class choices but dozens or hundreds of choices (as, for example, with mutual funds), our scope for making the wrong choice expands tremendously, and the superiority of disciplined re-balancing shows up even more strongly. The results in Chapter 8 are simply a reflection of this fact.

WHAT TO DO?

We have described in this chapter the impact on retirement saving of normal human behavior, behavior that is natural and understandable, but damaging within the DC system as it currently operates. It is possible to make the system more effective through some design changes that work with human nature, rather than against it. That is what we described in Part Two: ways to reduce the waste and so make DC plans more successful.

CHAPTER 11

Financial Education

Financial education is not the same thing as investment education. Financial education is like basic food, necessary for economic survival; investment education is like icing on top of the cake. There's little point in giving employees investment education until they have first received financial education. In this chapter we explain why we think so.

FACTS THAT SURPRISED US

See if you can answer either or both of the following questions.

- *Question 1:* If five people all have the winning numbers in the lottery and the prize is $2 million, how much will each of them get?
- *Question 2:* Let's say you have $200 in a savings account. The account earns 10 percent interest per year. How much would you have in the account at the end of two years?

If you got them both right, you are in a minority of the adult U.S. population. That startling insight comes from three authors[1] who took those questions from a longer list used in the 2004 Health and Retirement Study (HRS), a survey conducted with a nationally representative sample of almost 1,000 participants. They tell us:

"We label these questions 'Lottery Split' and 'Interest' ... Less than half were able to correctly answer the Lottery Split question. 60 percent of respondents answered the Interest question correctly."
In a footnote they add: "Note that we give the respondent credit for the Interest question if they provide either the correct simple interest response or the correct compound interest response."[2]

What's more, they point out that other authors have found that "[t]hese controls for financial literacy have some predictive power in explaining wealth differentials among the HRS Early Baby Boomers cohort."

Here's another surprise. United States Treasurer Anna Escobedo Cabral, whose signature is on U.S. banknotes, had a revealing statistic to share with the audience at a recent seminar:[3] 10.5 million people insist on a monthly Social Security check rather than a direct deposit into a bank account, because they are not familiar with the banking system or don't trust direct deposit—even though it's much safer than a physical check. Her point was that too many people don't have an understanding of the most basic aspects of everyday financial transactions.

And a third observation. David John, a respected researcher and commentator on national financial issues, and possibly the only person in Washington, D.C., with an e-mail address at the Heritage Foundation and the Brookings Institution (two think tanks that traditionally lean in opposite directions), says that when his daughter graduated from one of the finest local schools, she had taken two photography courses and two cooking courses, but there was nothing offered on personal finance.

These vignettes suggest that it would be helpful to large segments of the population to provide them with something that is all too rare: elementary education on personal finance.

In the context of this book, the vignettes lead to two simple but powerful conclusions. The first is that a population with these characteristics has no chance of being educated to the point of investment expertise, at least until they have a much more basic financial education. The evidence we cited in Chapter 8 now comes as no surprise. Indeed, the explanation in Chapter 10 of human foibles hardwired into our minds is no longer necessary as a general cause. Chapter 10 explains why even financially literate participants make obvious investment mistakes. Participants without basic financial knowledge are even further behind the starting line.

The second conclusion is that the entire retirement savings system needs to be designed to work for financially illiterate participants. Of course, the financially aware should be given opportunities to use their expertise. But the base needs to cater to the many rather than to the few.

ENTHUSIASTIC INITIATIVES

There is no shortage of initiatives. A few examples will make the point.

In the United States, the President's Advisory Council on Financial Literacy was formed in January 2008. Among its goals are:

- Improving financial education efforts for youth in school and for adults in the workplace.
- Promoting effective access to financial services, especially for those without access to these services.
- Strengthening and coordinating public- and private-sector financial education programs.

Its members have demonstrated a serious commitment to these goals. For example:

- It is chaired by Charles Schwab, whose eponymous firm is well known. Less well known is the Schwab Foundation for Social Entrepreneurship and its efforts, both in the United States and around the world, to address social problems in an entrepreneurial way.
- The vice-chair is John Bryant, founder of Operation HOPE, started in 1992 after the Los Angeles riots to eradicate poverty in our lifetime, now with a global scope.

Financial literacy is only one of the means these organizations use, but they have much experience with them. So, too, does another Council member, Laura Levine, executive director of the Jump$tart Coalition for Personal Financial Literacy—a name that needs no further explanation of its mission.

Around the world, there are numerous other initiatives.

An Australian colleague of the authors, Linda Elkins, is a member of the Advisory Board of Australia's Financial Literacy Foundation, a government body established to promote financial literacy. In 2006, it created the web site www.understandingmoney.gov.au. In 2007, it published "Financial Literacy: Australians Understanding Money," a generally upbeat report on Australians' self-assessment of their financial abilities. But it added that "the survey reveals a range of money attitudes and beliefs that are inimical to people investing the time and effort required in taking the steps to improve their money skills and behavior. As the survey indicated, stress and discomfort, boredom and disinterest, and personal relevance and procrastination are commonly held attitudes when it comes to money."[4]

In the United Kingdom, the *ifs* School of Finance (formerly the Institute of Financial Services), an educational organization with charity status, has as its prime objective "to advance knowledge of, and education in, financial services for the benefit of the public at large." Stating that "the state of financial capability in the UK is absolutely dire," it offers courses for teenagers, and in September 2006 succeeded in making its Foundation Certificate in Personal Finance available nationally for credit toward the

United Kingdom's national high school graduation General Certificate in Secondary Education (GCSE).

In March 2008, Amsterdam saw the global launch of Aflatoun, the brainchild of Jeroo Billimoria of Mumbai, India. In Arabic, *aflatoun* means explorer, and the name was used for a Bollywood cartoon character. As with many other organizations, it goes beyond financial literacy, using it as a tool for social education, too. It teaches children aged 6 to 14 about rights and responsibilities and personal values, in addition to financial ethics and the importance of balancing financial skills with the judgment to use them responsibly. Its vision is a balance of social and financial empowerment of children, enabling them to break the cycle of poverty.

A pipe dream? No, it was developed over 17 years in India before it was transplanted to 10 other countries, with even more ambitious goals for the future. What did it actually achieve in India?[5] Its children "imbibed" (to use their graphic term) the habit of saving, developed a sense of responsibility, an ability to handle money and bank transactions. In turn, this gave them confidence that they could change their lives and explore new horizons. Oh, and it got their parents to start saving.

Along the way they had to overcome numerous criticisms: Children are too young to understand concepts like money. They are too poor to save. Banks aren't interested in this. Schools won't welcome the concept. This will stimulate child labor and reduce school attendance. Parents will force their children to withdraw money saved. And so on. None of them turned out to be valid.

What got her to start this? Ms. Billimoria had earlier worked with street children in India and found that many of the children she helped were entrepreneurial; and she became convinced that, given better education, they could have done well in life. So relates *The Economist*, in a feature on financial literacy.[6]

The courses can be adapted for all sorts of environments. It has been adapted for Zimbabwe, for example, with changes incorporated that take into account the existence of astronomical inflation. What about rich countries? *The Economist* quotes Ms. Billimoria: "My mistake. I never thought it would be needed in developed countries." And it adds its editorial comment: "If only."

WHAT EXACTLY CAN BE TAUGHT?

What financial concepts can one teach a child in preschool?[7] Here are some.

Income is earned by working. If a part of the income is not spent today, it can be used for future purposes: That's called saving.

A goal is something a person plans to achieve sometime in the future. If you don't have enough money to buy everything on your "wish list," you have to make choices. The most valuable thing that you give up, or postpone, is called your opportunity cost. Every choice involves an opportunity cost.

Can't you just see a good teacher getting these concepts across? Some exercises would involve the whole class or groups of students; others would involve individual students. "Have you ever worked and been paid for it?" "What's on your wish list? How much do those things cost?" (That gets the kids to find out about prices.) "Divide the total cost of everything in your wish list by two. If that's how much money you have, which items will you choose to buy now and which ones will you keep for a future wish list? Why did you select those items?" And so on.

Really imaginative teachers will no doubt find a way to entertain the kids at the same time, because engaging them is crucial.

The daughter of one of the authors teaches English as a second language to young students in Harlem. She believes that these concepts can be absorbed by her students, even in a foreign language, which English is to them.

Later, the concept of budgeting becomes important, particularly once kids get part-time jobs or pocket money. Most adults—let alone kids—don't budget. So they don't know how much they spend in total, or how much in each of several categories. They don't know whether most of their expenditures are planned or unplanned. They don't know (other than vaguely) whether they spend more than they save. They don't know whether they have more fixed or variable expenses. But once they get into this kind of exercise, they can start making evaluations, such as whether some of their unplanned expenditures were bad decisions. And that leads to better planning, to saving, and so on.

And to the concept of borrowing, and to the cost of borrowing, which (again) most adults don't understand. Very few can tell you what interest rate they pay on their credit cards (let alone on less common sources of credit). And from there to compound interest. The power of compound interest is awesome. Not until you play with numbers yourself can you appreciate it.

One way to get kids to appreciate it is via the first lesson in a four-part course called MoneyMath: Lessons for Life.[8] The first part (talk about getting kids engaged!) is called "the secret to becoming a millionaire." In the teaching guide, the teacher is instructed to read the following scenario to the class:

Last week, Mrs. Addle told her students that they could become millionaires if they followed the rules she provided them. As a matter of fact, she guaranteed that if they followed her rules exactly, they would be millionaires in 47 years! Misha and the rest of her classmates thought that Mrs. Addle was crazy. If she had rules that would guarantee that someone could be a millionaire, why was she teaching seventh-grade math? Why wasn't she rich and retired? Why didn't she follow her own rules? Mrs. Addle told the students to go home and talk to their families about what she had said.

Misha went home and told her family what Mrs. Addle had said. Misha's mother knew a lot about money and financial matters. She just smiled at Misha and said that Mrs. Addle was correct.

Well, you can probably anticipate the secrets that the teacher shared with the class the next day: Save early and often. Save as much as possible. Earn compound interest. Leave deposits and interest in the account as long as possible. And so on. And, of course, there will be lots of side issues and lots of other learning (including math skills) and other stories to use as teaching tools. But it's not until the kids play with the numbers themselves that the lessons start to stick in their minds, because self-discovery is always the best way to learn.

That leads to the next notion. Perhaps financial literacy isn't enough. Perhaps what the goal should really be is financial capability.[9] What's the difference? Financial capability results when individuals develop financial knowledge and skills, but also gain access to financial policies, instruments, and services. According to one definition, financial capability incorporates skills, behavior, and knowledge in five areas: making ends meet, keeping track, planning ahead, choosing products, and staying informed. For example, many youths lack savings accounts and savings. As we've seen, too many adults don't have or don't trust bank accounts. These gaps are disproportionately high among some groups in society, typically low-income workers and minorities. That's why so many organizations that teach financial literacy have as their goal something broader than literacy: the use of literacy to climb out of poverty.

There is some limited evidence that linking people to financial instruments along with financial education makes a difference.[10] For example, people who had an allowance, bank account, or investment when they were children saved more of their income as adults. Low-income participants of a financial management training program scored higher if they had a bank account or filed a tax return. The use of mainstream banking services contributes to positive financial behavior.

It is far beyond our scope to get into further detail. But as we assembled the material for this chapter, we were reminded of how basic these life lessons are, how rarely they are taught, and how (unreasonably) ambitious it is to attempt to teach subtle investment skills on a base that lacks this foundation. That's the point we hope we have made.

WHY HASN'T THIS ALREADY BEEN TAUGHT?

Even though all the initiatives we cited at the beginning of this chapter have a recent date, the call for early financial literacy is an old one. So why hasn't the call been heard? Why are courses in financial literacy so rare? In the *Economist* article that we quoted earlier, Laura Levine of Jump$tart is quoted as saying: "Personal-finance education is not a hard sell conceptually, but only when it comes to getting it prioritized." School principals will usually agree that financial literacy is worth teaching, but they are reluctant to give it time and resources.

At present, only three American states require that students take a course in personal finance. Another 15 insist that it be incorporated in other courses. In the United Kingdom, schools must teach citizenship, but they do not have to include courses on essential financial life skills.

Why is it not compulsory? Again, it is beyond our scope and our ability to comment authoritatively on this question. In the literature, we have come across two sets of arguments that interested us.

One set of arguments begins by acknowledging that it is easy, in theory, to see why there would be social benefits.[11] But the practical reality might not be as straightforward or unequivocal. For example, if the compulsory course were an addition to the curriculum, students would have to devote more time to academic learning: What would be sacrificed? Or if the course were a substitute for another course, how large would be the net benefit when the benefit from the substitute course is subtracted? After all, the benefit would be a function of many inputs: the learning resources made available to the student, the capacity of the student to learn the subject, the effort that the student would make, and the time devoted to the learning, both inside and outside the classroom.

The other argument is that there is another path that may be more practical. Richard Thaler, a behavioral economist at the University of Chicago, says: "The depressing truth is that financial literacy is impossible, at least for many of the big financial decisions all of us have to make." Even he finds it hard to know the right thing to do. "If these things are perplexing to people with Ph.D.'s in economics, financial literacy is not the right road to go down." Instead, "focus on making the world easier": Build sensible default options into the design of financial products, so that the do-nothing option is itself financially literate.[12]

A LITERATE DEFAULT SYSTEM

We agree with the conclusion reached by Thaler, but not with the first quote cited in the previous paragraph. We draw a distinction between basic financial literacy, which we consider to be an essential life skill and within the capability of most people to acquire (if taught), and investment expertise, which is a much more advanced skill and unlikely ever to be mastered by the majority of people. In the quote, the "big financial decisions" that Thaler refers to are indeed probably beyond most of us to be sure of getting right—but they are also far beyond our definition of basic financial skills. So we believe that basic financial literacy, as defined by the things this chapter has focused on, is very valuable. But when we go beyond that to much more difficult decisions, then yes, it makes sense to build that advanced level of financial literacy into the default options in the system.

The rest of this book is entirely consistent with that theme. That is why we emphasize that the system needs to be designed for the many, not for the few who are lucky enough to have acquired investment expertise.

A FINAL ANECDOTE

Behind education lies the attitude of those at whom it is aimed. Just how ingrained these attitudes can be was illustrated on a recent visit made by two families to Disneyland. As the children played and explored, two of them, one from each family, ran to a particular ride. Their parents called out to them not to stray too far: "We may never see you again." To which one parent added: "In that case, bye-bye. Study hard!" That moment was a revelation to the other parent. It stunned him that his friend would say, as his final piece of advice to his child, "Study hard." Even though they were joking, the importance of education in the friend's family and his culture asserted itself instinctively. We have no idea what our one final piece of wisdom to a child would be; but we do admire the friend's instincts.

Four

Other Ways of Running Defined Contribution Plans

We have, up to this point, looked at the defined contribution (DC) system from a mainly American perspective. But while the principles behind DC do not change with geography, the specific circumstances and attitudes that have shaped the system in each country have differed. As a result, different approaches have been tried in different places. We can learn from these experiences.

Part Four therefore begins with a look at the Australian system. This moved from DB to DC in little over a decade, thanks to legislation passed in the early 1990s, to become in many senses the world's most advanced DC society. As a result, it is a natural place to look for lessons in system design, a veritable Petri dish of DC activity. We will also explore the collective DC approaches used by some plans in the Netherlands and Canada. Sandwiched in the middle of this world tour is a description of a bank savings approach to DC, of a fund supermarket approach, and of a retirement income approach. These three models of DC systems differ in what they set out to achieve and hence in how they go about achieving it. Our vision of DC version 2.0 is really a vision of moving from the second of these three models to the third.

So this part is addressed to plan sponsors, consultants, and opinion leaders.

CHAPTER 12

Case Study—Australia

In 1992, Australia was the first country with developed capital markets to commit its retirement system to a funded market-based defined contribution (DC) system.

It wasn't the first to use DC. Chile changed its equivalent of the American Social Security system to funded DC in 1981. But it didn't have developed capital markets. In fact, the change to DC was part of a linked set of other changes, one being to create investment opportunities by privatizing majority chunks of government-owned enterprises, and another being to register a number of investment managers who could then compete for the privilege of being chosen by the individuals to manage their retirement investments. The resulting launch was quite different from Australia's and from the American DC system.

Nor was Chile the first to use DC for all its workers. The Singapore Central Provident Fund, for example, was established in 1955. But it wasn't then a market-based system. The government used the contributions as it thought fit, and declared a rate of interest each year to add to each participant's account balance.

That's one reason we use Australia as a case study—we can look at it from its origins without having to say, "Yes, but this aspect was totally different from the United States." Of course, there are many aspects that are still maturing. Not until an entire generation passes through the system, from starting work through retirement to death, can the system be said to be fully mature. But the capital market aspects were mature from the start, and that's a key consideration.

Another key consideration is that Australia has made several decisions that take it far down its path. In that sense, it is a highly developed system. We don't say that everything Australia has done is desirable—or, for that matter, undesirable. We leave that to social historians to judge. But we will draw attention to a number of developments from which we can draw lessons.

And finally, Australia's DC assets are the largest in the world, relative to the size of its economy. In absolute terms, America's DC assets in 2006 amounted to $5,444 billion, the United Kingdom's $623 billion, and Australia's $412 billion. But Australia's DC assets are 82 percent of its gross domestic product (GDP), ahead of Switzerland's 67 percent, the United States' 41 percent, and the United Kingdom's 26 percent.[1] In many senses, then, Australia is the world's most advanced DC society.

SOME FEATURES OF THE AUSTRALIAN DEFINED CONTRIBUTION SYSTEM

A little bit of history is useful to explain why the Australian system has grown up in the way it has.[2]

Prior to the mid-1980s, Australian plans were mostly defined benefit (DB). Roughly 40 percent of workers were covered, mostly public-sector and private-sector managerial workers. Benefits were traditionally expressed as lump sums because the tax system favored them. Prior to 1983 only 5 percent of the benefit was taxed, and with marginal income tax rates then peaking at 60 percent, that meant a maximum tax of 3 percent of the lump sum. In contrast, pension benefits were taxed as income. Lump sums became a no-brainer, and the system design stayed that way even after tax changes.

In 1985 a landmark settlement of an industrial issue resulted in a 3 percent superannuation award in lieu of a wage increase (which would have breached the wage guidelines then in place). This practice spread but produced uneven coverage. Then the Australian government legislated a minimum level of compulsory superannuation contribution starting on July 1, 1992, at 3 percent for smaller employers and 4 percent for those with payrolls exceeding $1 million. As initially planned, the minimum level increased to its ultimate 9 percent in mid-2002.

Today, Australia's overall superannuation system is seen as having three tiers:

- A government safety net that is unfunded and means tested.
- The funded DC "Super Guarantee," with its minimum 9 percent annual contribution.
- A voluntary but tax-privileged layer of personal savings.

This does not mean that DB is quite dead. The compulsory DC system permits DB as a substitute to DC, but the employer must demonstrate that its projected benefits are at least as rich as those likely to result from 9 percent DC. Most employers simply choose DC.

We do not attempt to describe the Australian pension (or "super," as they call it—short for "superannuation") system in detail. It changes frequently: For example, several changes were introduced effective July 1, 2007. And it often has one-shot or short-term features attached, for example, relating to contribution limits. We will not go into the details of all of these features here, and will concentrate only on those features that we believe contrast significantly with the American system.

Australian super is taxed differently from its American and British counterparts. In Australia, new employer contributions to a fund, and a fund's investment earnings, are taxed at 15 percent (a favored rate, being lower than the personal income tax rate for most taxpayers)[3]; then the benefit is tax-free, if taken at age 60 or later.[4] Employer contributions can be topped up by employees to a limit of $50,000 a year via pretax "salary sacrifice"; then after-tax contributions can be added to a limit of a further $150,000.[5] (In contrast, in the United States and United Kingdom, contributions and fund returns aren't taxed, but benefits are taxed as earned income.)

For low-income workers making after-tax voluntary contributions (which makes sense for those personally taxed at less than 15 percent), the government pays a match of up to 150 percent of the worker's contribution (varying with pay level, and with the match capped at $1,500 in any year) to encourage these workers to contribute.

A new government in 1996, despite its opposition to the Super Guarantee system, chose to retain it. But it added a new feature with its so-called "choice legislation." Since July 1, 2005, employees have no longer been restricted to selecting their investments from the choices offered by their employer. They have been permitted to direct their Super Guarantee contributions to any registered super fund.

As far as benefits are concerned, there is little leakage from the system before retirement. No loans are permitted. Benefits are, for the most part, locked in until a minimum age, which has been gradually increased. It used to be 55. Today, for employees born after June 30, 1964, it is 60.[6]

Workers still take their benefit in a lump sum. But this has placed a strain on the means-tested tier of the three-legged system. So, to encourage benefits to be taken in a series of systematic withdrawals, the government changed the tax system effective July 1, 2007, so that investment earnings on assets left in a super fund to finance a qualified income stream would be completely tax exempt: no 15 percent tax on investment returns on the balance left in the fund.[7]

CONSEQUENCES FOR COVERAGE

Today, participation exceeds 90 percent of workers, and close to 90 percent of superannuation assets are in DC rather than DB plans. So coverage has been dramatically expanded by the compulsory system. It is still not

100 percent, because those with extremely low incomes and the self-employed do not require automatic contributions.

In the United States, the new Pension Protection Act of 2006 (PPA) legislation created a safe harbor for employers who make auto-enrollment the default option, with an employee having to elect explicitly not to participate in the plan. But it is not compulsory for an employer to offer a DC plan. The absence of compulsion, combined with the opt-out provision, means that the United States is never likely to reach Australian levels of participation in a funded retirement system.

We say this not to recommend legislation—that is contrary to our purpose in this book. We say it simply as an inescapable conclusion.

CONSEQUENCES FOR ADEQUACY

It is far too early to judge conclusively whether the benefits from the Super Guarantee system will be adequate, because, as we mentioned before, the system will take decades to mature. This is simply the nature of any pension system. Meanwhile, though, we can say three things.

One is that the 9 percent minimum contribution rate is showing signs of becoming the 9 percent standard contribution rate, as far as employers are concerned. Few employers contribute more than 9 percent.

The typical employee contribution rate is 3 percent. So, typically, 12 percent of pay goes into the participant's super fund each year.

A second is that a lifetime contribution rate of 12 percent may be too low to generate a replacement ratio of 80 percent of final pay from age 65. In Chapter 3 we found that this replacement ratio required a base case contribution rate estimated at 16.8 percent—somewhat higher than 12 percent. And in Australia they think naturally in terms of retirement at age 60. We have seen an estimate that 30 years of contributing at 12 percent, together with investment returns exceeding wage growth by an average of 3.5 percent a year, would result in a typical after-tax lump-sum balance of around five to six times final annual pay—not nearly enough to provide 80 percent income replacement in retirement after age 60. (But the new 2007 legislation, encouraging benefits to be taken as an income stream, would help raise the after-tax replacement ratio.) Using a contribution rate of 12 percent and a retirement age of 60 in our own base case model produces a retirement income replacement rate of 42 percent.

In fact, a current theme for discussion in Australia, particularly in union circles, is whether the minimum 9 percent employer contribution rate should be increased to 15 percent.[8]

Nevertheless, the Australians do seem to be heading for a mature system that will be closer to providing adequate benefits than the U.S. system.

Our third observation is that targeted incentives to contribute can be effective. Over 1.2 million low-income Australians received a government match, which you will remember is up to 150 percent of the individual's voluntary contribution, at low levels of income. "Free money" works in Australia. With education, the idea of enrolling in order to get an employer "free money" match in the United States ought to work too, even though the typical U.S. match is not even close to 150 percent.

CONSEQUENCES FOR EMPLOYER ATTITUDES

One Australian industry veteran told us that he feels that employers stopped caring when compulsion was introduced. Perhaps that is too harsh a verdict. Certainly, employers offered the DC plans that compulsion forced them to do. Perhaps it was the "choice" legislation that took effect in mid-2005, permitting employees to direct their super fund money anywhere they chose, that really changed employer attitudes. What is certain is that the number of Australian corporate funds fell from 4,100 in 1997 to 289 ten years later.

One example of why this change occurred is provided by BHP Billiton, the world's largest mining company and then Australia's largest steel producer. In the late 1990s, BHP Billiton decided that making steel was no longer a core business. It is easy to see how they concluded that running a super fund is not a core line of business either, as most other Australian employers have also decided. Management time on noncore activities is reduced; so too are costs and fiduciary risk. In addition, DC funds are like retail financial products, so they need scale to offer comprehensive, competitive services.

Today, Australian retail funds do in fact capture about 30 percent of all assets. Industry funds (essentially funds covering employees in a particular industry) and public-sector funds each capture a little less than 20 percent, and corporate funds about 5 percent. (The remainder, about 25 percent, are funds with fewer than five members: so-called "self-managed" or "do-it-yourself" funds. They have large average assets per member, though they represent only 2 percent of all super fund accounts by number.)

So, for many employers, all they want is a direction as to where the employee's super fund money should be sent, just as it is necessary for them to know where the employee's net pay should be sent.

But "employers of choice" stay engaged. They use their market knowledge to choose best-in-class design and providers. They use their buying power to get good fees. They ensure best-in-class investment defaults. They consider auto-escalation of employee contributions (auto-enrollment being simply a fact of life in a compulsory system). And they facilitate education and advice through the workplace, to engage employees in the retirement savings journey.

This is a good place to draw attention to a very important feature of the Australian super scene: the involvement of unions. Industry funds are multiemployer funds, typically targeting members in a particular industry (such as MTAA Super and the motor trades industry; Cbus and the construction, building, and allied industries; Health Super and the health and community services industry; HOSTPLUS and the hospitality and tourism industries) or even geographical location (SunSuper in the state of Queensland). They are typically established by agreement between the representatives of employees (unions) and of employers (industry and trade associations), with a board that draws from both groups as well as from independents.

Unlike retail funds and commercial master trusts, industry funds have no profit motive—and proudly proclaim themselves the "new mutual companies," in an era when large mutual life insurance companies have become listed public companies. They provide services inexpensively, typically charging between $1 and $2 a week to each member for record keeping, benefit payments, and communication materials. (Investment management fees are charged directly to the funds.) They have expanded their offerings to insurance, home loans, and even cheap movie tickets. Some of the biggest industry funds now jointly own a bank and a financial planning firm. Passing on the benefits of scale is a key value. This is essential when they must compete with commercial organizations and provide such administrative services as internet access to benefit records and call centers.

LESSONS FOR THE UNITED STATES

We draw attention to three lessons. The first is that running a DC plan is clearly not a core activity for employers. Given a chance (particularly through "choice" legislation), most prefer not to be involved. This has the interesting corollary that employers who do stay involved have the opportunity to distinguish themselves from their competitors—in much the same way that, a couple of generations ago, the early adopters of DB plans could use them to attract and retain good people.

The second is the role that unions have very successfully carved out for themselves. In the same way that large employers can distinguish themselves from their competitors by continuing to be involved, unions have found a new dimension of valuable services to offer to their members.

The third lesson is that far fewer than 2 percent of participants choose to run their own investment portfolios. Two percent is the number of so-called self-managed funds, but they are really self-trusteed funds, with many invested in managed funds. These participants in the system are typically small business owners, high-net-worth individuals, and retired or soon-to-be-retired individuals with large sums to invest. We suspect that the proportion of truly self-managed accounts is not dissimilar to the very small proportion of participants in the United States who use a brokerage window. Personal expertise at that level of detail is rare.[9]

CONSEQUENCES FOR INVESTMENT CHOICES

The typical Australian super fund offers between 10 and 60 investment fund choices. Corporate funds (other than the very large ones) commonly offer only 3 to 5. Most investment fund choices are multimanager, diversified across asset classes, and involve active rather than passive management. Typically included are investment funds that might be labeled "conservative" (with 30 percent in equities and 70 percent in fixed income), "balanced" (50 percent/50 percent), and "growth" (70 percent/30 percent), perhaps with "high growth" (85 percent+ in equities) also offered. Single-sector funds generally are available but less used. The U.S.-style "brokerage window" is rarely used: Employees can go retail if they want to.

Roughly 70 percent of assets are in the default option for a typical single-employer or industry plan. And, typically, that option is the growth, or 70/30, allocation.[10]

These bare facts reveal several contrasts with the U.S. scene. Think first about the default option, which is the key to making a compulsory system successful. By and large, Australian participants have done far better with their 70/30 default than Americans defaulted into money market or stable value funds, and far better than if they had been themselves defaulted into Australian money market funds. A long-term perspective took hold right from the start: The Australian system was DBized, in that regard. The very recent American switch to target date funds as the default has not yet, however, crossed the Pacific to Australia. Australians therefore have yet to discover the way to get the beneficial long-term effects of a 70/30 allocation with the corresponding risk spread more sensibly over their working lifetimes.[11]

Australian super funds converged to multimanager investment funds very early. The benefit of diversifying risk across multiple managers is still not the typical American structure, particularly for medium and small DC funds. These often make record keeping the master, rather than the servant, of investment choice, a practice we mentioned in Chapter 9, and one we believe will change in America.

In that regard, too, Australia DBized its DC system, because multimanager arrangements dominated its DB system—just as they do in the United States. It would, we suspect, be difficult for an American sponsor of a DC plan, with a multimanager approach to investing its DB fund, to justify why it believes a single-manager approach fits DC.

Similarly with active and passive management. We mentioned in Chapter 9 the inconsistency of fiduciaries of both DB and DC plans in America using active management in DB and passive management in DC, a potentially uncomfortable posture to justify. Australian fiduciaries have typically avoided it, by large-scale outsourcing to active managers.

One commentator says that Phase 1 in the evolving role of investor education in Australia has been tried—and failed. It was to equip members to make good investment decisions. Phase 2 is an increasing emphasis on defaults; there has been good success here. We note that both of these statements also hold true in the United States, though Phase 2 is really only just starting. The Australian Phase 3, says this commentator, will be to get members to focus on the things they can influence: how much to save, when to retire—and here there is much more to be done, as in the United States. And Phase 4 will be to help members in the postretirement phase. This is just getting started, perhaps only fractionally ahead of the United States, if one of the strong messages in this book is heeded!

CHAPTER 13

Three Defined Contribution Plan Models

There are many kinds of retirement plans. We have distinguished between defined benefit (DB) and defined contribution (DC) plans. But there are also plans that are classified as hybrid in some way, and DC plans themselves can operate in different ways.

We have, for example, shown how the first American DC plans gave way to what we have called DC 2.0. We have discussed how the Australian DC system operates, in particular the areas of contrast with the American system.

It may be difficult to find semblances of order in all the activity that has taken place over the years in Australia and the United States, but we have found it much easier to understand how the pieces fit together by looking at the moving parts through three lenses, each corresponding to a model with a particular philosophy. We don't say that these models have guided a nation's approach or even an employer's approach, but the activity makes sense if one sees it through the lens of a particular model's approach (see Table 13.1).

THE BANK SAVINGS MODEL

In this model the idea is to save a little bit of money as a supplement to whatever else the participant may be doing to accumulate retirement assets. The participant is happy to see the account increase, with no risk of capital loss. No education is necessary. Reports show the progression of the account from one period to the next. At retirement the account value is taken in a lump sum.

What defines success? Essentially, no capital losses.

TABLE 13.1   Three Models of DC Plans

Model	Purpose	What Is Success?	Education Needed	Examples
Bank Savings	Supplement to other forms of retirement accumulation	No capital losses	None	United States' stable value investing; Japan's Post Office savings
Fund Supermarket	Grow savings through high returns	Every participant a successful investor	How to gauge risk tolerance, understand asset classes, and select investment managers	Australia's Superannuation; United States' 401(k)
Retirement Income	Postretirement income	Adequate income to retire on (from all sources)	Leave it to the experts (sponsors, trustees)	Some Dutch and Canadian plans

In the United States, small 401(k) plans that supplemented a DB plan usually reflected these characteristics. Even when DC supplanted DB as the main form of retirement provision, those participants in a "stable value" form of default investment option essentially got these characteristics, too.

Less recognizably, so, too, did participants in "cash balance" plans. These have always been called *hybrid plans* (and actually sometimes described in literature as a DB plan). But that's a misleading label. In its design a cash balance plan has nothing about it that is hybrid: It is pure DC, with individual accounts that are credited with contributions and an investment return that, for all the variations in its possible definition, is of a stable value nature. Participants have no choice. The only hybrid feature is that the sponsor is permitted to invest the assets in a fashion that does not match the credited return, and by investing more aggressively than the return suggests, is given the opportunity to earn more than the credited return, and use the surplus as a credit against future contributions. At least until new funding rules contained in the Pension Protection Act of 2006 (PPA), surplus could be anticipated in calculating minimum funding requirements, with the result that the fund value invariably was lower than the sum total of the individual's accounts. To a participant, therefore, this was not so much a hybrid plan as an underfunded DC plan with low returns and no investment choices—at best, a bank savings type of plan.

THE FUND SUPERMARKET MODEL

In this model the DC plan becomes the main vehicle for wealth accumulation, so a safe but small investment return is inadequate, and the focus therefore shifts to the investment return—how to grow savings through a high return—and its effect on the individual participant; hence the use of investment choice. Hence, too, the need for investment education, on how to gauge one's risk tolerance, how to understand asset classes, and how to select investment managers.

Given that choice is important in this model, reports to participants focus on the success of the participant's choices. Hence the need to show not only the progress of the account, but also to report the underlying investment return and compare it with benchmarks, both market benchmarks and peer benchmarks. And at retirement, the participant leaves the supermarket and takes the account value in a lump sum.

What defines success? Making every participant a successful investor. An impossible task, as we have seen, in the way it was initially attempted, but DC 2.0 learns its lessons from failure and focuses on autopilot provisions.

Australia's DC and the United States' 401(k) approaches, as largely practiced today, are examples of this model.

THE RETIREMENT INCOME MODEL

Our third model, which we feel is the most effective at providing sustainable income in retirement, is the Retirement Income Model. Here, DC can still be the main form of wealth accumulation, but the main focus shifts to postretirement income.

The auto features become particularly important, the goal being to replicate, as far as is possible in a DC environment, some of the desirable features of DB plans, with four in particular being important. In DB, everyone participates. In DB, contributions tend to be high. In DB, investment outcomes tend to be higher than in DC, reflecting the focus of a relatively small number of more informed decision makers. In DB, participants get longevity protection (i.e., the guarantee of postretirement income lasting for the rest of one's life). The first three of these features are just as important for the Fund Supermarket Model, but it is the fourth that marks out the Retirement Income Model and really fulfills the vision of DC 2.0 that we set out at the start of the book.

What defines success in this model? An adequate income to retire on, from all sources.

Hence reporting includes not only the much-appreciated transparency of a participant's account value (a transparency that DB never gave), but also the aspect of transparency in which DB has always been superior to DC: a projection of the likely postretirement income that the account value will generate. And education in this model can also show how this income integrates with various other sources of postretirement income: Social Security, any other employment-based plan, and other sources of savings or income. Eventually, if participants are to make informed decisions as to their risk tolerance, they need to be educated on the interaction of contribution rates, target returns, income goals, and risks.

In a sense, this short description of three ways of looking at plan design lies at the heart of the retirement plan solution promised in the title of this book. If the DC system is truly to meet its goal of providing secure income in retirement, then a conscious recognition of that objective would surely help. A reinvented DC system—DC version 2.0—should move beyond simply offering investment choices and toward the Retirement Income Model we have described in this chapter. This is the path to a more effective system.

AN EXAMPLE OF A PARTICIPANT STATEMENT
IN THE RETIREMENT INCOME MODEL

We make no attempt to create a thing of beauty or to be definitive or to comply with any particular set of laws or regulations. This is simply an example to show the kind of things that can be reported on usefully. In every section of the report, add any other similar identifying information you find useful.

XYZ Defined Contribution Pension Plan
Annual Statement prepared for [Employee Name Here]
as of December 31, 20XX

Part 1: Personal Identification
Name:
Address:
Date of birth:
Plan ID:
Hire date:
Current annual pay:
Beneficiary:

Part 2: What Your Account Is Worth
Value as of [previous date]:
Your contributions since [previous date]:
Company contributions since [previous date]:
Investment return since [previous date]:
Value as of December 31, 20XX:
Your current asset allocation is:

Note: If on a target date path, indicate current allocation and also say "and this will change as you approach retirement, in accordance with the 'Target 20YY Plan'"

Part 3: What Your Account Might Provide after Retirement
Your normal retirement date:

If, in the future, you earn exactly the same pay as your current pay and contribute at your current rate and the company also contributes at the current rate; if your asset allocation is as listed here; and if you buy a fixed-dollar life annuity at retirement at roughly the price available on December 31, 20XX:

There is a 50% chance that your annual income will be at least:
This is [x%] of your current annual pay.
There is a 75% chance that your annual income will be at least:
This is [y%] of your current annual pay.

Above is a standardized estimate to give you some idea, in advance of retirement, about the income your account might be able to generate, since the main purpose of this plan is to give you a source of postretirement income. Of course, this is necessarily an estimate and depends on making assumptions on many uncertain things. That is why we also give you some idea about the probability that the income will be achievable. Please see your plan document for further details. These estimates are based on assumptions about asset class returns (and the degree of uncertainty of those returns) made by [whoever takes responsibility for making these projections].

Part 4: Other Sources of Postretirement Income

Remember that this plan is intended to be one of many possible sources of income for you. Others are Social Security, other retirement plans you may be or may have been a member of, and personal assets. Though we cannot estimate what those sources will generate, we encourage you to find out about them so that you can take comfort in your preparations or take action if it appears that your preparations may not achieve all that you want them to.

Note: Here add a call to action: a tear-off postcard, details of how to go online to find more information such as the Social Security web site, and so on.

Appendix:

Note: Here add (a) all sorts of disclaimers, (b) details of the returns earned by the employee's account, (c) a statement along the lines of "since you joined the plan, the average annual investment return earned in your account has been x.y%."

CHAPTER 14

Collective Defined Contribution

As we contemplate the reinvention of the defined contribution (DC) system, it is in the ability to focus on postretirement income that we (in particular, the United States) have the furthest to go. The Dutch and Canadians show that there are imaginative ways to get there, "collective DC" being one approach that differs substantially from the Australian and American models. While it is the Dutch who are responsible for the name given to this approach, it is the Canadians who have been doing it for decades.[1]

Our purpose in this chapter is just to discuss the principles, rather than to present a treatise on how collective DC works. Indeed, though the principles can be stated briefly and simply, there is no shortage of ways to apply them, and they can be applied well or badly.

THE PRINCIPLES

The three financial principles are as follows:

- *Employers make defined contributions.* These plans originated in Canada, as multiemployer plans in industries where employers were often small and drew on a unionized labor pool to find workers for the jobs they contracted for. Every few years the employers' association and the union typically negotiated a contract under which workers were paid an hourly wage, with benefits financed via hourly contributions into benefit funds (including a pension fund) on behalf of each of the workers.

    Under this arrangement, the employers know what their total hourly wage bill amounts to. Even though the benefit contributions are formally made by the employers, the workers realize that the contributions really come out of their own pockets, because employers are typically indifferent as to the split between direct wages and benefit contributions; it is only the total hourly rate that matters.

A joint board of trustees, with representation from both employers and the union, collects the contributions and is responsible for all fiduciary aspects of running the pension plan.

■ *The payout formula is defined benefit (DB).* An actuary makes assumptions about future contributions, demographic patterns, and investment returns, and advises on a DB formula that can be sustained. Typically, this takes the form of deeming a certain number of hours of contributions to be equivalent to a year of credited service, resulting in a specified amount of monthly pension payable from a defined retirement age. The final decision on the benefit level is the responsibility of the joint board of trustees. Unlike traditional DC plans, in these multiemployer plans there is no accumulation of contributions and investment returns in individual accounts to determine benefit entitlement.

■ *Benefits paid reflect plan experience.* If the contributions won't support the benefits, the benefits must be reduced. Or, of course, a contribution increase can be negotiated, though that typically awaits the next round of bargaining. But it's the benefits that give way if long-term underfunding is suspected, rather than contributions being increased. That is what marks these plans as fundamentally DC plans, even though in their design they are true hybrids.

In the United States, these multiemployer plans operate with a distinctive twist when a participating employer leaves the plan. Under normal circumstances the joint board of employer and union trustees works as described in the previous paragraph. But if a participating employer leaves the plan when there is a funding deficiency, that employer must pay a proportionate share of the deficiency before leaving. For that employer, therefore, the plan becomes DB at the point of departure. We will not consider these plans further in this chapter.[2]

Some Consequences of This Hybrid Design

These plans are DC, but they get to the Retirement Income Model immediately. They pay postretirement income, not lump sums.[3]

As DC plans, they offer the employer finality in establishing what they cost. The hybrid transformation into a DB is aimed at offering workers predictability of postretirement income and individual[4] longevity protection, as in DB plans.

Workers enjoy portability of benefits across employers who are bound by the bargaining agreement. It doesn't matter which employers, or how many, they work for; their pensions build up in the same pot, as long as those employers are all part of the collective agreement.

Just as in DB plans, the actual security of the benefits depends on the relationship between the pension fund's assets and liabilities. In DB, the ultimate security of accrued benefits is dependent on the employer's ability to make up any deficit; in collective DC, it depends on the balance of negotiating power in the next round of bargaining. In both individual DB and collective DC, a cautious approach to actuarial assumptions enhances security, as does an investment policy that focuses primarily on attempting to match asset and liability characteristics.

As in DB, there are subsidies across groups of beneficiaries. The clarity of benefits depending on each individual's account is lost. DB's transparency of postretirement benefit and lack of transparency of preretirement benefit value both characterize collective DC, too. As with pure DB, no employee investment education is necessary. Workers make no investment choices. They do not require that expertise.[5]

The trustees are the investment fiduciaries, and to the extent that they decide on a mismatch between assets and liabilities, the absence of individual accounts gives them the freedom to consider nontraditional and illiquid asset classes.

Collective DC plans can be vulnerable to a decline in active membership, if it turns out that the inflow of contributions is lower than anticipated by the actuary. Individual DC doesn't have that vulnerability.

BROADER APPLICATIONS BY THE DUTCH AND CANADIANS

The Dutch have had industry-wide pension plans for decades. Their switch from DB to collective DC started after the painful combination of investment conditions that occurred in 2000–2002—falling stock market values that pulled assets down at the same time as falling interest rates that raised liabilities. As *Time* magazine put it: "… the country came up with a unique response. The Dutch funds are now no longer on the hook for providing a set income in retirement no matter what happens to financial markets—that is, they've gone DC—but they didn't shunt everything to individual workers. Risks are shared by all the members of a pension fund, and the money is managed by professionals."[6] The key is that while individual workers don't bear individual risk, as they do in DB, they do collectively share the entire risk.

Collective DC is contrasted not only with DB, but also with individual DC. Risk sharing across members, rather than individuals taking their own risks, is cited as a good thing, allowing members to "breathe easier," according to Jeroen Steenvoorden, director of the €4.6 billion collective DC plan for Dutch medical specialists.[7]

Collective DC can also be used in single-employer situations. According to *European Pensions & Investment News,* "Arcadis [a €600 million pension fund] was one of the first Dutch [company] pension funds to switch to a collective DC system [in 2005], and Armin Becker, director of the firm's pension fund, is seen by many as the father of the collective DC model."[8] Becker makes it clear in an interview that the pension fund had become so large relative to the company itself that the burden of a DB guarantee had become disproportionate to the company's profitability.

Collective DC applies to only a small proportion of the Dutch market, DB still being by far the most prominent form of retirement benefit. But a design pattern is beginning to emerge in single-employer collective DC: a target benefit based on a career average salary formula, benefits then indexed to price inflation, and a target overfunding cushion of 30 percent of liabilities.[9] Indeed, from an economic point of view, it can be said that the vast majority of Dutch pension plans are collective DC, in that even when the initial benefit level is DB and guaranteed, the indexing of this benefit to subsequent inflation is conditional on there being sufficient assets to provide it.[10]

In Canada, one of the most prominent pension funds of all is based on collective DC: the Ontario Teachers' Pension Plan. Its design—or, rather, its redesign—arose following a report entitled *In Whose Interest,* produced in 1987 by the Task Force on the Investment of Public Sector Pension Funds (Ontario), chaired by Malcolm Rowan, now retired, who held a number of senior positions in the Ontario government. Rowan recognized that the investment policy of a pension fund must be aligned with the economic interests of the stakeholders, and that for a plan to be a 50-50 partnership it is necessary for both gains and losses to be equally shared by sponsor and beneficiaries.[11] And that principle now underlies the plan design: "Collective" also includes the provincial government.

So when an actuarial valuation as of the start of 2008 revealed a shortfall (even in this well-managed fund) of $12.7 billion relative to assets of $108.5 billion, Teachers' CEO Jim Leech issued a statement that said: "Teachers' staff and board members have been working with the co-sponsors to help them identify the best solution for eliminating the shortfall." A reporter adds: "The options were not specified. They presumably include bigger contributions, smaller pensions or looser accounting rules." Leech explained the reason for the shortfall: "This highlights the continuing challenge of managing a mature plan. . . . Put simply, a declining proportion of the plan's members now bear increasing responsibility for keeping it fully funded. All defined benefit pension plans worldwide face this challenge."[12]

THERE'S MORE THAN ONE WAY TO SKIN A CAT

This chapter shows that there are many designs feasible that start with defined contributions and end up focusing on postretirement income. As DC systems around the world continue to evolve, the experience of collective DC in Canada and the Netherlands will be one experiment to which they will look for lessons learned.

Five

The Perspective of the Individual in Decumulation

Having looked at the question of retirement planning—and in particular the accumulation of assets during a working lifetime—from the perspective of the system, we now turn to the postretirement period and to a different perspective: that of the individual retiree. This change of perspective is necessary because the role of the individual is different and harder to manage after retirement. Throughout this book so far, we have taken the view that during the savings phase the needs of the many are best met by a system built around sensible, efficient default paths. If an employer has a defined contribution (DC) plan, then workers should (as a general rule) be put into that plan unless they actively elect not to participate. Unless they specify otherwise, their retirement assets should be in a growth-oriented strategy (even though that runs the risk of losses over some time periods), which gradually changes over time to reduce risk as the assets grow because that offers the most likelihood of competitive long-term returns. And so on. In short, employers should bake sound investment accumulation practices into their plan design.

But in the postretirement period, the link between the participants and the employer is substantially weaker: They no longer work for the firm. Plan sponsors have therefore traditionally paid much less attention to plan design features that affect the decumulation phase than to the features that affect the savings phase. But bearing in mind the 10/30/60 rule (which states that 60 percent of the total payout from a DC savings plan is typically earned *after* retirement), it is a phase that needs close attention. Plan sponsors can—and increasingly will—do more to ensure that their plan design is adequate to the task of managing the postretirement phase. But the individual has a role to play, too, even those who played little or no active role in the accumulation of their retirement assets.

The dynamics of decumulation center around three variables, or dials, as we will refer to them: spending, longevity protection, and investment. In this part, we will consider each of these in turn, addressing ourselves to the individual reader. We will finish the part with a description of new products aimed at decumulation. Then, when the individual's issues in decumulation are understood, we will turn in the next part to the role that the DC plan sponsor can play in helping the individual to cope with them.

This part is addressed directly to the individual approaching or already in retirement, and to financial planners. It will also provide background material for sponsors, since it forms the basis for the final part of the book, which is addressed to them.

CHAPTER 15

The First Dial: Your Personal Spending Policy

For personal plans, you need personal planning—and a new approach in decumulation.

People have different careers, different dreams. One can't tell people, "Here's how you ought to spend your money," and expect them to be grateful for the advice. Preferences are personal. One can say, "If you want to be able to spend $X after you retire at age Y, here's how much you ought to save." One can say, "Here are the risk and return characteristics of different asset allocations. Given your risk tolerance, here's the asset allocation policy that best suits you." Savings can be expressed in monetary terms; asset allocation can be expressed in percentage terms. But what you do with the rest of your money, the part you spend—that's personal. There are rules of thumb, there are averages, there are gurus who tell you what's the minimum that constitutes poverty-level spending. But preferences—those are intensely personal.

Most people have two simple motives once they retire: to continue to live in the lifestyle to which they have gradually evolved, and to leave something for their children—or more generally, to leave bequests. You might think that you can use the same analytic processes that helped you to formulate financial plans in the accumulation phase. But you would be wrong, for at least two reasons. Decumulation needs a different framework.

In the accumulation phase, while your planning horizon isn't precise, it doesn't matter much if you're off by a few years; if you initially think of planning to accumulate to age 65 and you actually go to age 62 or 67, it's not highly significant. But in decumulation, your planning horizon's uncertainty is supremely important; if you run out of money before you run out of life, it really matters a lot! In the accumulation phase, your focus was on building wealth, and you could think of the uncertainty of your end-of-horizon wealth as a good risk measure. In decumulation, cash flow is your new focus, and it's the uncertainty of the cash flow that you will receive that needs to be your new risk measure.

A better framework for decumulation analysis is to understand that you have essentially three personal policies you can formulate, as you make your plans for cash flow and bequests. One is spending policy: Should you draw down, each year, as much as you need to live the lifestyle you desire, or should you cut back to some extent? Another is longevity protection policy: To what extent should you buy a guaranteed lifetime cash flow stream (which we'll call an annuity) to ensure that you don't run out of money before you run out of life? The third is investment policy: How much risk should you take as you manage your remaining wealth in the decumulation phase?

Each of these policies, in a sense, gives you a dial you can turn up or down. The way in which the policies interact, and the order in which you should consider turning the dials, are the essential issues of financial planning in decumulation.

The first three chapters in this part of the book describe a planning process that anyone can go through, in considering how the dials interact. It is what the oldest of the authors went through after turning 60; it is what many financial planners use with their clients. Dallas Salisbury, president and CEO of the Employee Benefit Research Institute, says that 81 percent of Americans live from paycheck to paycheck; only 37 percent have ever constructed a budget; and most people don't start thinking about retirement until somewhere between 3 and 18 months prior to their scheduled retirement date. We hope that this part of the book encourages those who still have time to make an earlier start.

In this chapter, we focus on spending policy.

STEP ONE: HOW TO KEEP SCORE— THE CURRENT POSITION

Working with a financial planner always follows the same basic structure: First work out what you have, then set your objectives, then formulate a plan. The first two steps are essential precursors to any sensible plan, whether for accumulation or for decumulation, and we will briefly discuss these next. Note that while this structure applies to both accumulation and decumulation, we have seen that in many cases the accumulation phase passes with very little active involvement on the part of the participant. If the basic components of a financial plan are not in place by the time retirement approaches, they need to be crafted at this time. It is a complex undertaking, requiring all kinds of expertise. Even those who understand investing and longevity will find that they also need to understand taxes, the law, the

TABLE 15.1 What You Are Worth Today

Assets	(what you own)
– Liabilities	(what you owe)
= Net Worth	(what you are worth)

financial and insurance instruments that are available, and ideas in this planning space.

There are two aspects of the current financial position that are essential to quantify: what you're worth today, and what you have available to save or spend.

Table 15.1 deals with what planners call your "net worth": your assets less your liabilities, or what you own less what you owe.

For most people, this doesn't take long to establish. Most have only a few lines to fill out, unless your financial life is complicated. But it's instructive to put it all on one page and see what it nets out to. Of course, it's approximate because real estate and investments are often parts of it. And some of it is in tax-deferred savings, like a 401(k) plan, while much of it is instantly taxable. But it makes for a satisfying start.[1]

Table 15.2 shows the annual cash flow (or monthly, or whatever financial period you use for keeping track). This is where you identify your income from work or investments or other sources, and what you buy with it—what we'll call your spending pattern. It can be horrifying to see the difference between your income before and after tax. But let's move past that aspect without further comment. The reason to note both before and after tax is that most income is subject to tax, but some may not be. It is, unfortunately, the after-tax column that counts.

Note the use of the phrase "your spending pattern." What you spend money on will vary from person to person and family to family. And so will the way in which you classify it. There's no right or wrong way to

TABLE 15.2 What You Have Available to Spend or Save

Income From	Before Tax	After Tax
Work		
Investments		
Other Sources		
= Total Income		
– Spending		
= Available for Savings		

TABLE 15.3 Percentage by Category of Total Household Spending

	Age Groups			
	45–54	55–64	65–74	75+
Shelter	18.9%	18.1%	16.9%	19.4%
Transportation	17.6%	17.1%	18.3%	13.0%
Personal insurance and pensions	12.8%	11.3%	6.8%	3.0%
Food	12.7%	12.1%	12.6%	11.9%
Utilities, fuels, and public services	6.8%	7.2%	8.0%	9.4%
Other housing expenses	6.2%	7.3%	7.4%	6.7%
Entertainment	4.8%	5.2%	5.0%	3.8%
Health care	4.8%	7.0%	10.7%	14.8%
Apparel and services	3.8%	3.7%	3.0%	2.2%
Miscellaneous	3.7%	4.0%	4.1%	3.1%
Cash contributions	3.7%	4.5%	5.2%	10.6%
Education	3.0%	1.3%	0.7%	0.6%
Personal care	1.2%	1.2%	1.3%	1.5%

Source: Bureau of Labor Statistics, Consumer Expenditure Survey 2006.

classify it—do whatever makes sense in your own case. The Bureau of Labor Statistics regularly conducts a survey of American household spending.[2] The survey breaks out spending by age group and category. Table 15.3 shows how different age groups allocated their household spending based on the 2006 survey. Since the purpose of the calculations shown in Table 15.2 is to project what you're likely to spend once you retire, these classifications may be a useful guide.

How you classify your spending elements, and how much you spend on each, together constitute your current lifestyle. This is where many people will have a great deal of difficulty, not so much in identifying the elements as in assigning a number to each element. Those who use budgeting software will find that they have already done the bulk of the work just keeping track of their spending. For others, one way to proceed is to ignore the breakdown into elements of the pattern and take a much simpler aggregate approach. Assume your aggregate spending is equal to the full amount of your (after-tax) income, less whatever you save explicitly.

STEP TWO: WHAT ABOUT THE FUTURE?

This is where the going really gets tough: deciding in broad terms what you want to do with the rest of your life. Financial planners tell us that this is a subject that they find very challenging to talk to their clients about.

That's not surprising. Most planners come from a mathematical or a legal background; they're not psychologists or philosophers.

The basic concept is to ask yourself what you want to be or to do or to have 1 year from now, and 10 years from now. (One year and 10 years are approximations for the short term and the long term.)

The sorts of responses to the long-term question that come up at this stage of planning are along the lines of "to be financially independent at retirement," "to travel to some new place every year," "to leave a legacy for my children and grandchildren," "to leave money to my favorite charity." Again, these are personal decisions. And at this stage there's no need to quantify the answers. It's tough enough to identify and agree on the broad outlines.

If you want to do some really deep thinking, consider the following three questions, as posed by George Kinder in his book *The Seven Stages of Money Maturity*[3]:

- You have all the money you need. How would you live your life?
- You've just found out you have 5 to 10 years to live. How will you change your life?
- You've just found out you have 24 hours to live. What are your regrets?

The questions are profound. They force you to consider, in succession, what you want to have, what you want to do, and what you want to be.

Having done this groundwork for a spending plan, you're ready to turn to the question itself: figuring out what your plan for the future will cost.

STEP THREE: THE PROJECTED OUTFLOW—THE FIRST ATTEMPT TO QUANTIFY YOUR SPENDING PLAN

Go back to your current spending pattern—the expenditures for each element of your lifestyle. If you've been able to do something constructive about outlining your future, modify your current expenditures to allow for the changes in your future lifestyle. If you haven't been able to outline your future, then, in the absence of anything better, it's not unreasonable to assume that your current expenditure pattern will continue into the future. Either way, you now have a starting point.

Experts remind us that there should be some changes anyway. They tell us that we typically save less (if at all) after retirement. We tend to move into smaller homes and use smaller cars. But most of all, health care tends to cost much more after retirement.

There are scary stories and articles about health care. The Employee Benefit Research Institute estimates that a couple retiring in 2008 at age 65 without employer-sponsored health care needs to have saved $194,000 to cover future health care costs, covering Medicare Part B (general medical care including limited home health care) and D (prescription drugs) premiums, Medigap Part F premiums (to supplement Part B), and out-of-pocket expenses for copayment and cost-sharing items. That amount gives the average couple a 50-50 chance of having enough money for health care until they both pass away. For a 90 percent chance of adequacy the amount increases to $305,000. A couple with higher-than-average use of prescription drugs requires even more.[4] Most people in their preretirement state know little about this, and clearly need to understand much more.

This big number includes nothing for the cost of long-term care, meaning the chance that some serious illness will require either in-home care or nursing-home care for some time. Medical expenses tend to be concentrated at the end of life. Expenses in the final year of an individual's life are, on average, five times as high as in a nonterminal postretirement year, and 30 percent of the final year's expenses occur in the very last month.[5] Budgeting for this is both frightening and expensive. Most people don't. At most, they keep an emergency fund in case they need money for something unanticipated. One way to at least get an estimate of what's involved is to get a quotation from an insurance company about the size of the premiums necessary to insure against the costs of these events.

Coming back to what the experts say about postretirement spending, take that only as a very general guide. In fact, people seem to move through postretirement phases.[6] In the early phase, they tend to be more active and are likely to travel, explore personal interests, or even go back to school. During the middle retirement years, they tend to slow down and sometimes downsize their residences. In the late retirement phase, they typically limit their activities, and their expenses are increasingly driven by medical and health care costs.

Now let's assume you have made a rough projection of your future spending pattern. Congratulations! You have, in effect, created your very own "spending plan." We deliberately glorify this with a special name. It isn't only endowments and foundations that have spending plans. It's important for you to have one, too. It's just as important to have a spending plan for your postretirement years as it is to have a saving plan for your preretirement years. Of course, it's not essential, in the sense that it's still possible to have a happy retirement with no planning at all. But if you're going to plan, then an explicit spending plan is a part of the process.

It won't stay constant. Nothing does. But it's a start.

STEP FOUR: HOW LONG WILL YOUR ASSETS SUSTAIN YOUR SPENDING PLAN?

This formulation of your spending plan is only a start, in the sense that you're likely to have to do several variations of it before you settle on a final version. Why? Because it needs to be reasonable in the context of the actual assets you've accumulated. Remember all that early work to establish your net worth and your saving? That, too, needs to be projected, along with the investment returns they generate, to see if you have sufficient assets to decumulate for as long as you need (a period we'll discuss shortly). And because investment returns are uncertain, you should make multiple projections of the possible investment outcomes for your assets.

In fact, your wealth consists not only of these accumulated assets. You may also have wealth in a preannuitized form: Social Security, lifetime income from a defined benefit (DB) pension plan or a lifetime annuity, and so on. Most people don't think of this as wealth. We're accustomed to thinking of wealth as a lump sum. But it's at this stage of the planning exercise that the value of guaranteed lifetime income becomes apparent: You don't have to worry about outliving these sources of income because they'll go on as long as you live. And Social Security has the added benefit of increasing in the future in line with inflation.[7] Yes, all of that is truly a part of wealth, even if it comes in an annuitized form rather than in a lump sum.

All of this will give you not only a range of possible investment outcomes, but also a range of possible decumulation paths. For most of us, the projections will show that our assets will eventually run out. If they run out at some incredible age, like 120, that means in practice that longevity isn't likely to be an issue. If they run out at an early age (75? 80?) longevity could be a very serious issue. In between? Then we have choices about how we simultaneously manage our longevity and investment risks. That's an absolutely fundamental issue, which we will discuss later.

But for now, let's return to these projections. You will need to find out what you can reasonably expect from Social Security and your employment-based pension plans. Finding out is a learning experience in its own right. What we have discovered, as we studied this subject, is how poorly many people understand their plans. This is what the Employee Benefit Research Institute (EBRI) says[8]:

> *Many workers are counting on benefits that won't be there ... Only 41 percent of workers indicate they or their spouse currently have a defined benefit plan, yet 62 percent say they are expecting to receive income from such a plan in retirement.*

Similar misunderstanding is rife in connection with long-term care coverage. The EBRI again:

> *One-quarter of workers and more than one-third of retirees report they have long-term care insurance (separate from health insurance, Medicare and Medicaid) to help pay for care they might need in a nursing home, assisted living facility, or at home. But only 10 percent of Americans age 65 and older are estimated to have had private long-term care insurance in 2002, suggesting that many are counting on coverage they do not actually have.*

All of that suggests that it'll be time well spent, finding out about your benefit plans.

Before you can complete your projections, you need to formulate a rough investment plan. At this stage, it isn't necessary to go into detail. What you're looking for is an investment return to include in your projections. Some planners do what they call "Monte Carlo" projections, involving hundreds or thousands of runs. That could be useful at the stage when you're customizing your investment plan (which we'll discuss in Chapter 17). For now, it's enough of a start to use some estimates of high, low, and medium returns. You can customize the work later. Your goal at this point is to complete the projections to get a range of ages at which your wealth is projected to run out.

CHECKPOINT: IS THERE A GAP TO BE BRIDGED?

What's a safe age to project running out of money? For a first approximation, remember that you can buy a lifetime income annuity for a cost that's somewhat more (as we'll explain in Chapter 16) than the wealth you need for your projections to suggest that it will last as long as your life expectancy. (For a couple, of course, this is the second-to-die expectancy we discussed in Chapter 2.) So, if you have that amount of wealth, you can insure the continuation of your cash flow for as long as you live. First approximation, then: let's say something like 20 percent longer than your life expectancy.

Suppose you are making these projections while you're still in the accumulation phase. And suppose you find that when you project decumulation, you are likely to run out of money earlier than you would like. Then, as we explained in Chapter 3, you have essentially three choices during your remaining accumulation years, and one choice that is focused exclusively on your postretirement years. You can save more, retire later or take more investment risk (all of which can be done before retirement), or spend less after you retire. Let's focus on this last option.

Most people avoid cutting back on spending until it is absolutely essential. They think, "I can always cut back on my lifestyle in retirement if it looks like I might use up all my savings." That was the attitude of more than 80 percent of workers surveyed, according to the EBRI.[9] This may be part of a general pattern of overconfidence. In 2007 the EBRI reported:

> ... *One-quarter of workers are* very *confident about their financial security in retirement (27 percent), while more than 4 in 10 are* somewhat *confident (43 percent). However, at least some of those who say they are* very *confident may be overconfident: 24 percent of* very *confident workers are not currently saving for retirement, 43 percent have less than $50,000 in savings, and 37 percent have not done a retirement needs calculation.*

There is evidence, however, that individuals are becoming more realistic in their attitudes toward retirement readiness. In 2008, the EBRI reported that "the percentage of workers *very* confident about having enough money for a comfortable retirement decreased sharply, from 27 percent in 2007 to 18 percent in 2008." Nevertheless, the EBRI goes on to report: "the percentage of workers attempting a (retirement) needs calculation (in 2008) ... is statistically unchanged from 2007."[10]

McKinsey & Company said that 32 percent of their surveyed baby boomers "hold that they can just reduce their retirement spending.... But here again, reality paints a starkly different picture: only 10 percent of retirees say they have been able to significantly reduce their expenditures."[11] That's why we suggest that you consider now (if you have a gap that needs to be bridged) a sort of "spending plan for essentials."

You can get input from experienced planners as to what things typically are deemed to be essentials and what things are deemed to be the discretionary part of a lifestyle. And you can take this into account in deciding what spending pattern, for you, constitutes the bare minimum that you can contemplate.

If you find in your decumulation years that you really do have to make your assets stretch further, formulating this essentials spending plan will give you guidance as to where the reductions can come from.

We mentioned that you can also reduce the need for funds by starting to decumulate gradually and postponing the date when full-blooded decumulation starts.

McKinsey reports that almost half of baby boomers expect to work past 65.[12] They point out, though, that among current retirees, only 13 percent actually did so. Of course, times may be changing. Birth rates around the developed world have been low for many years, and longevity has been increasing, with the result that the ratio of retirees to workers is rising; society may therefore find it very convenient to accommodate 65-year-olds who want to retire later, or work part time for a while. But even if society changes in this way, an individual shouldn't take it for granted that a planned postponed retirement will happen. The EBRI notes that "... a large proportion of retirees leave the work force earlier than planned (51 percent in 2008). Many ... who retired early cite negative reasons for leaving the workforce before they expected, including health problems or disability (54 percent), changes at their company, such as downsizing or closure (33 percent), and having to care for a spouse or another family member (25 percent). Others say other work-related reasons (22 percent) or outdated skills (14 percent) played a role."[13]

To sum up: There are many ways in which to try to bridge a gap that leaves you feeling uncomfortable. Test different contingency plans, play with the numbers, decide what you'll do if the need arises—and monitor your situation regularly, to see whether, as time marches on, you're moving away from your problems or deeper into them. It's impossible to overstress the need for looking at this dynamically. You can't plan and then put away your plan. Too many things change. You need to react to those changes.

NEXT UP

After these projections, you should now have three clearly defined ideas:

- An idea of how much your proposed, desired lifestyle will cost; the cost of a scaled-down lifestyle that considers only the essentials of life; and which elements of your spending will be the first to be decreased if you have to cut back. Where you eventually end up, at your desired lifestyle or somewhere short of it, is your spending policy.
- An idea of a range of time at which your wealth is projected to run out. Whether and to what extent you hedge the possibility of it running out before your life runs out will constitute your longevity protection policy.
- A first range of estimates of the investment returns you might earn in the future. Tightening this up will result from your investment policy.

We turn next to longevity protection.

CHAPTER 16

The Second Dial: Your Longevity Protection Policy

Spending policy—how much of your accumulated assets you decide to spend each year—was our first postretirement dial. The second concerns longevity—how long you live. At first sight, this may not look like a dial at all: Retirees have a high level of control over the spending dial and a fair degree of influence on the investment dial (we cannot control investment markets, but we can control which assets we invest in), but we do not have a great deal of control over how long we live (and the control we do have, we use to prolong our lives, irrespective of the financial consequences). There are, however, two ways in which the impact of life expectancy on retirement planning can be managed. The first we have already mentioned: We can reduce the length of time for which our assets need to last, by postponing the date of retirement. The second is through the purchase of an investment—an immediate annuity is the simplest example—which protects against the financial consequences of an unexpectedly long life. It is this question of longevity protection on which we will concentrate in this chapter.

HOW AN IMMEDIATE ANNUITY WORKS

In Chapter 5, we said that you can buy an immediate lifetime annuity from an insurance company for somewhat more than the cost of having enough wealth to be able to draw down the same cash flow for a period equal to your life expectancy. Give the insurance company a lump sum of that amount, and they will guarantee that you will receive the cash flow for as long as you live, no matter how long that may be. How can they make that guarantee? Where do they get the extra money from, if you do indeed live past, say, age 100?

The quick answer is that the insurance company pools your longevity experience with that of its other annuitants (i.e., the people who purchase annuities). It knows that while some annuitants will live much longer than the average, others will live less long. As long as the overall group experience is broadly in line with their forecasts, they will be fine.

Here are the details of how it works. Suppose there are a lot of people your age and in roughly your state of health. Let's suppose that all of you together buy annuities under which the total expected first-year payout is $100,000. The insurance company projects what proportion of the purchasing group it expects to be still alive after one year, two years, and so on, and from that it projects how much the required $100,000 payments will decline each year. The resulting payout curve for the insurance company will look something like the one labeled "standard longevity" in Figure 16.1. The insurance company then calculates how large a total lump sum it will require to finance these payments, assuming that the assets are invested in fixed-income investments.[1] It adds something for its expenses, for the possibility that it has underestimated the group's longevity, and for a profit margin. Then it charges each member of the group his or her proportionate share of the total lump sum.

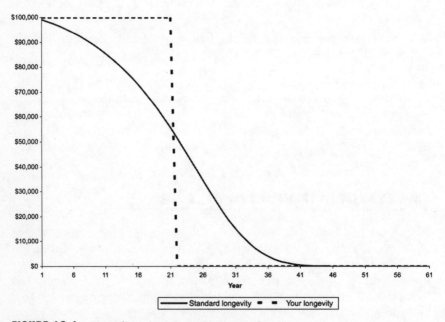

FIGURE 16.1   Immediate Annuity = Longevity Swap

You will receive your proportionate share of the $100,000 a year, a dollar amount fixed at the start, for as long as you live, which in Figure 16.1 is assumed to be 22 years. If you live for a shorter period, the line labeled "your longevity" would fall to zero further to the left. If you live longer than 22 years, that line would continue straight up to some point further to the right, before again falling to zero.

The insurance company doesn't particularly care how long you survive. It expects that, with a sufficiently large group of purchasers of these contracts, and a margin built into "standard longevity" by shifting the curve further to the right than it actually expects, and its expense and profit loadings, it will make a satisfactory profit over the long term. In effect, those who die early subsidize those who die late and generate profits for the insurance company. That's where the money comes from, to pay those who survive a long time.

One way to look at this is as a swap—or exchange—with the insurance company. You're swapping *your* longevity for the *average* longevity built into whatever standard table the insurance company is using. You pay a lump sum to the insurance company equal to the present value of payments over the standard longevity, and you receive periodic (typically monthly) payments for your own longevity, whatever that turns out to be. The concept of a swap is well established in financial markets: For example, it is common for companies and banks to swap fixed interest rate payments for variable interest rate payments—which is known as an interest rate swap—or streams of income in one currency for another. So there's nothing too unusual about the idea of a longevity swap, exchanging fixed longevity for variable longevity.

Because you pay your lump sum in advance and receive periodic payments later, you also expose yourself to counterparty risk: the risk that the insurance company doesn't survive long enough to meet its obligations to you.[2] In this chapter, we are going to ignore the risk that the insurance company expires before you do.

THE BENEFIT OF BUYING A LIFETIME ANNUITY

The benefit of buying a lifetime annuity, of course, is the longevity protection. It is possible to calculate roughly how big a benefit this is.

Suppose you know how much you propose to spend each year for the rest of your life (and, to simplify the illustration, suppose this amount will stay constant forever). You can make a best estimate of the return you'll receive from, let's say, an investment in fixed income. Knowing your life expectancy, you can calculate the lump sum you would need to have today, in order to decumulate over a period equal to your expectancy. For example, a 60-year-old American male may calculate his average life expectancy as 22 years, and find a 6 percent return to be available on fixed-income assets, and from that calculate that a lump sum of $12.04 would be needed for each dollar of income for the 22 years.

Of course, if $12.04 is all he has, it's pretty much a 50-50 proposition whether his life or his capital will expire first. If he outlives the 22-year average, the money runs out. That's not much comfort. So suppose he wants no more than a 1-in-100 chance of outliving the stream of income. Now we need to consult the life expectancy table, and we find that this means we need an income stream that lasts not for 22 years, but for 40 years. The required sum is no longer $12.04, but rather $15.05, an increase of 25 percent. That extra sum is needed because one individual is unable to average out the long- and the short-lived experience that a group will have, so to get to 99 percent confidence of not outliving the income stream, a large extra buffer is needed in reserve.

To reduce the odds of outliving the income stream from 50-50 (i.e., based on the average life expectancy) to 1 in 100, the increase in the capital required is not always 25 percent. It varies with age and with the fixed-income return assumed. For example, if our 60-year-old male wants the income stream to increase each year in line with price inflation, then he needs to base the calculation on the rate of return that is available net of inflation (this is referred to as the "real return"). At a real return of 3 percent, the premium for longevity protection (i.e., the cost of a 40-year payment stream compared to a 22-year payment stream) jumps up to 45 percent. And if he wants 100 percent protection against longevity (so the money needs to last indefinitely), an income of $1 rising in line with inflation would cost $33.33, which is more than double what the same income would cost, lasting only for the average life expectancy.

It's clear that the ability to do a swap with an insurance company, and pay only enough to decumulate over your expectancy, is potentially a very valuable feature.[3]

SHOULD EVERYONE BUY AN IMMEDIATE ANNUITY?

It might appear from our analysis that an immediate annuity provides some advantage for everyone; that we should all implement a personal longevity protection policy of hedging 100 percent of our longevity risk. Not so. For example, if you know you're not in good health, then longevity protection is much less likely to be something you really need. You don't want to increase the chance that you will be one of those who subsidize the longer lived. That's obvious. And in fact, insurance companies know that only those in good health will buy immediate annuities. That is why they build longevity into their standard longevity tables, which is much longer than that experienced by the population as a whole. It is also why they don't bother to perform medical tests on individuals applying to buy annuities.

But should anyone in good health refrain from buying an immediate annuity? Actually, yes. It turns out that, if you can afford it, it is more valuable to put off buying the immediate annuity as long as you can. Of course, that raises a couple of questions. What does "if you can afford it" mean? We will answer that in the next chapter. And how does an immediate annuity become more valuable to you if you purchase it later?

The answer to that second question follows from what we have just shown about the value of swapping your own longevity for the average longevity. The older you get, the more spread out the longevity curve becomes. As we saw, a 60-year-old male needs 22 years of income to cover the average life expectancy, but 40 years (almost twice as long) to reduce the odds of outliving the income stream to less than 1 in 100. At age 70, he would need 14 years of income on average, but 35 years to provide the same longevity protection—the ratio is now *more* than double. And that ratio keeps getting bigger the older you get.

Economists have refined this concept by adjusting for the fact that in reality an individual would not spend a fixed sum for 22 years, if they found themselves to be running out of money by doing so. Rather, they would reduce their spending, and suffer a reduced standard of living as a result. This requires some further assumptions and calculations—which we will not go into—about how much of a problem this reduction in standard of living would be (or, in technical terms, what is the utility attached to different levels of income). The resulting refinement of the analysis we have shown produces something known as *annuity-equivalent wealth* (AEW).[4] It measures the value of being able to annuitize by asking: If there were no annuity market, how much more money would you need in order to feel equally happy about your spending pattern? And AEW, as one would suspect, gets bigger as you get older.

All of this is just a way of saying that the older you get, the bigger the *proportionate* value of hedging longevity risk, and the happier you are to have the ability to buy a lifetime annuity. Annuities therefore become more valuable to you as you get older.

And that's why we said, earlier, that you should wait as long as you can before buying an annuity. It gets cheaper, and the longevity hedge is more valuable. Before we turn, in Chapter 17, to defining "as long as you can" and telling you how to decide what proportion of longevity risk you might want to hedge, let's take a look at why so few people actually buy immediate annuities—far fewer than ought to, in fact.

REASONS WHY SOME PEOPLE DON'T LIKE TO BUY IMMEDIATE ANNUITIES

In practice, the number of immediate annuities sold in the United States is quite small. People simply don't seem to want to buy them, whatever we and the economists may say about their value.

One reason is simply the way in which people look at them. They don't frame the question in terms of longevity swaps, but they do see the large lump sum they have to pay, and they compare it with the annual income they receive. It's not valid to compare a lump sum with an annual cash flow, but people do it anyway. There's an element here of what we called hyperbolic discounting in Chapter 10. We feel the cost immediately, but deeply discount the future benefit. Meir Statman eloquently recounts the regret of an annuity-purchasing friend, quoting him as saying, "Yesterday, I was a millionaire. Today, I'm living on $79,700 a year."[5]

A second reason is a loss of control. The lump sum is gone, the insurance company has it, and the deal is irreversible. Milevsky and Young[6] remind us why, before buying a lifetime annuity, it is always worth thinking hard about it to make sure you really want to do it. Because the purchase is irreversible, in making the purchase you are giving up the option to keep your portfolio flexible and the chance that a high return will reduce your need to lock in longevity protection. This is not a tradeable option, of course; but it is a real option nonetheless. This makes it clear that a lifetime annuity purchase is a last resort, not entered into lightly. (We expand on this idea in Chapter 17.)

A third reason is that the purchaser, in hedging longevity risk, enters into a new risk: that of dying early, of losing life and capital together. Remember that we said that it's those who die early that subsidize those who die late, among annuity purchasers. Some prospective purchasers think, "I want longevity protection, not a gamble!"

A fourth reason is that the lump-sum purchase price effectively becomes a fixed-income investment. Because of the way insurance companies calculate the lump sum, in effect the purchaser, while buying longevity protection, is also committing that amount of money to a fixed-income investment. If this is all or a large chunk of the wealth the purchaser has left, the idea of such a large proportion in fixed income may not appeal.

Finally, it may be unnecessarily capital intensive. By this we mean that most of us really don't want longevity protection until we are already winners in the longevity stakes, that is, until we have outlived our expectancy. It's not when we're 60 or 65 that we feel worried about outliving our wealth; it's when we're 85. Receiving the first 20 or so years of annuity payments does not give us the feeling we're getting longevity protection; it is the later payments that make us feel grateful we bought the annuity. So why buy a lifetime of payments that start at 60 or 65? Why not buy payments that start at 85? That second set of payments costs much less—that's what we mean by saying that buying an immediate annuity at 60 or 65 may be unnecessarily capital intensive.

FORTUNATELY...

It should now be clear that guaranteed lifetime income streams are, in themselves, potentially extremely useful instruments for a large segment of the retired population, but the traditional lifetime annuity has some undesirable features that come with it. Fortunately, as we will see in Chapter 18, we are just starting a period of considerable innovation in the design of financial products aimed at the decumulation market. These new products are specifically targeted at the objections we have listed.

APPENDIX: MORE ON ANNUITY-EQUIVALENT WEALTH

The economists' concept of AEW is a valuable one, though little known outside the circles of those who write about it. Here we will explain the concept in more detail, while omitting the heavy-duty mathematical equations and calculations that accompany it.

AEW measures the value of being able to annuitize by asking: If there were no annuity market, how much more money would you need in order to feel equally happy about being able to stick to your spending plan? AEW expresses the answer as a ratio, like 1.25, meaning that if there were no annuity market in Country B, you would feel equally content there if you had 25 percent more money than you had in Country A, which has an annuity market. Here is how the calculation is done.

Suppose in Country A you could buy a lifetime annuity for some lump-sum amount X, and thus lock in the spending plan that you are happy with. The amount X depends on your age. But whatever your age, it gives you satisfaction ("utility," as the economists call it) to know that you won't have to depart from your spending plan, no matter how long you live.

Now suppose instead that you live in Country B, which has no annuity market, and you have the same amount X. What would you do? You would start by wanting to spend at the planned level, but you would find it wise to set aside a little capital just in case you live a long time. That reduces your spending a little bit. This reduces your utility. How much? It varies from person to person. Economists use a complex formula to estimate the "disutility of changing the consumption pattern"—we won't attempt to explain the formula. The longer you survive, the more you have to gradually cut back on your desired spending pattern, and so the more your utility is reduced. Therefore, the absence of an annuity market in Country B leaves you with a lower utility than you would have had in Country A.

Ah, but suppose you started off in Country B with more money initially—an amount Y, bigger than X. Then you would be able to set aside small amounts of capital each year and still stick with your desired spending plan. Terrific! How much bigger than X would Y have to be, to restore your initial utility? That's what AEW measures.

Of course, AEW would vary from person to person, depending on the person's tolerance for consuming less than the desired amount. For someone who feels that reductions in consumption are not terribly important, AEW would be not much bigger than 1. For someone who felt really upset at having to spend less than planned, AEW would be bigger. Call the degree of being upset the person's "risk aversion."

Here is the point: For a given spending plan, and for a given risk aversion, AEW increases with age. In other words, the value of having the ability to buy a lifetime annuity increases as you age.

Why? An (almost) intuitive explanation is that it becomes more and more valuable, as you age, to be able to swap your own longevity for the average longevity. And that is because the older you get, the more spread out the longevity curve becomes. You can see this visually in Figure 2.4 in Chapter 2. The further you go to the right, the flatter and flatter the right-hand tail becomes. So in Country B, with no ability to buy a lifetime annuity, as you age, you have to set aside proportionately greater amounts in order to hedge your longevity by yourself. And so, living in Country B reduces your utility more and more, the older you get. To put it another way, living in Country A and being able to hedge your longevity by buying a lifetime annuity becomes increasingly attractive, the older you are.

That is what we mean when we say that a lifetime annuity becomes more valuable to you as you get older.

CHAPTER 17

The Third Dial: Investment Policy

Nobody can control the returns that are available from the investment markets. But we can control the amount of our assets that we invest in each type of available asset class. This is called *asset allocation:* For example, one often hears about a "60/40 investor" which is shorthand for someone who allocates 60 percent to various types of equities and 40 percent to various types of fixed-income investments. We discussed in Chapters 3 and 4 the importance of investment policy prior to retirement; in this chapter, we will examine some aspects of investment that take on particular importance *after* retirement, in the decumulation phase.

Traditional discussion of investment policy deals with financial assets. In decumulation, it is important to broaden the perspective and think in terms not just of financial assets but of all kinds of assets. In particular, think not just of the allocation of financial assets across different asset classes, but of the allocation of wealth across three types of assets: liquid financial assets (such as cash, stocks, and bonds), annuities (particularly those guaranteeing lifetime cash flow), and other assets such as home equity. While some retirees may not have home equity, and many have preannuitized wealth that cannot be converted to a lump sum, it is nevertheless often possible to control the allocation of wealth across these three broad types in decumulation. How they are best deployed is the focus of the rest of this chapter.

A REMINDER OF OUR GOALS AND OUR CHOICES

We first need to remind ourselves about two sets of facts. One concerns our goals, the other concerns the choices we have.

Essentially, we all have two goals. One is longevity protection: to have our assets last at least as long as we live. The other is the bequest motive: to leave something for others after we are gone.

There is a constant tension between the two goals. The more you focus on longevity protection, for example, the less you have to care about bequests. In the extreme, if longevity protection is your only goal, you want to make sure you have enough for your lifetime's spending, and if, in the course of ensuring that, you have to buy an annuity with all of your remaining assets, so be it. At the other extreme, if you don't care at all about longevity protection and insist on preserving your ability to make bequests, then you may have to sacrifice your standard of living. And in between (which is where most of us live our lives), we want to do a bit of both. We are prepared to contemplate some reduction in our standard of living, if that's necessary to both protect against longevity risk and leave something for bequests.

A FRAMEWORK

Now let's review our choices, in the sense of the assets we can choose to invest in. Essentially, there are four broad types, as shown in Table 17.1.[1]

Remember that, in decumulation, there are two sorts of risk: investment risk and longevity risk. Those two risks dictate the two axes of Table 17.1.

Start with the lowest row of Table 17.1, and think about what we are all familiar with, the assets that we consider when we think about investment in isolation, unconnected to questions of longevity. In that case, the sort of asset that is considered risk free might be Treasury bills, as an example. The sort of asset that is considered risky might be equities, as an example. Of course, there are other assets, too: bonds, Treasury inflation-protected securities, real estate, and so on. Table 17.1 is a simplification to present the choices in conceptual terms, with "risk free" and "risky" as the relevant characteristics.

From a longevity protection perspective, all of these assets are risky because they provide no longevity protection. So, for decumulation purposes, we need to add a new dimension: assets that are risk free as far as longevity

TABLE 17.1 Basic Asset Types to Consider (Examples Shown for Each Category)

		Investment Characteristic	
		Risk Free	Risky
Longevity Protection Characteristic	Risk Free	Conventional lifetime annuity	Variable lifetime annuity
	Risky	Treasury bills	Equities

is concerned. And, of course, these are conventional lifetime annuities.[2] The payout might be fixed in nominal terms or in inflation-indexed terms, but the main point here is that it creates freedom from longevity risk for the purchaser. The final asset type, then, is the sort of lifetime annuity that is risky from an investment perspective. This might be a lifetime annuity linked to the return on a fund, for example. These are difficult to find,[3] but (as we discuss in Chapter 18, on product innovation) the principles are well known and they might find favor at some future time. The characteristic of this fourth asset type is that it provides lifetime cash flow, but the level of the cash flow is uncertain and varies with the return on some risky type of asset.

How should you decide on the allocation of your assets across these types? That is the fundamental question we will deal with. But first, let us bring housing wealth into play.

TAKING OWNER-OCCUPIED REAL ESTATE INTO ACCOUNT

Until now, we have been vague about which of your assets we are referring to when we say that you ought to have an investment plan. In particular, we have not drawn special attention to the asset that, for most people approaching their decumulation years, represents the biggest portion of their accumulated wealth: the home they own and live in.

The Employee Benefit Research Institute (EBRI) says: "Quantifiable data from the 2004 Survey of Consumer Finances (conducted by the U.S. Federal Reserve Board) found the median (midpoint) level of household assets of Americans is $172,900. This includes the value of the primary home, which had a median value of $160,000 for those who owned a home."[4]

Of course, financial assets (like stocks and bonds and bank accounts) tend to increase with age, so that by the time a couple approaches retirement, the accumulation is probably much greater than the EBRI's number, which is the median for the whole population. But even then, housing wealth dominates. In a comprehensive paper on the role of housing wealth in decumulation, Sun, Triest, and Webb (ST&W) use this as a base case: "We assume that the household has the mean amounts of financial and housing wealth for the median 20 percent of married couples turning 65 between 1994 and 2000: $90,667 and $101,333 respectively...."[5] The numbers may be out of date, but the importance of the primary residence is obvious.

Yet few papers deal explicitly with owner-occupied homes. Some deal with financial assets only. Others refer to the fact that retirees sometimes downsize. But few integrate this important asset into formal planning. We think it is essential to do so. ST&W do so. While their paper itself is technical, it reaches interesting conclusions. So our discussion will follow ST&W.

If you own your home, think about what it represents financially (in addition, of course, to its emotional content). It negates the need to pay rent for the rest of your life. That makes it a lifetime annuity indexed to the rental cost of housing. That is a large part of its value. And the rest of its value (the "reversionary interest," as ST&W call it) becomes available for bequests. It is this reversionary interest that can also be tapped into, by the owner, by means of what is called a *reverse mortgage*.

This is where you can borrow against your home equity, receiving (at your choice) a lump sum, a lifetime income, or a line of credit. Of course, you owe interest on the amounts you receive. But you never actually pay the interest; it gets added to what you owe. When the final owner-occupier dies, the home is sold and the lender takes whatever is owed, but this cannot exceed the sales proceeds. If the sales proceeds are bigger, the balance goes into his or her estate for bequests. That's how it works.

The amount you can borrow depends on your age and on current interest rates. The younger you are, the less you'll be able to borrow, because the home equity value has to support a lifetime of payments (if you choose the lifetime income) and of interest accruals. Similarly, the higher current interest rates are, the less you will be able to borrow, because interest is likely to add up faster.

Few people make use of this product. Most are put off by the high initial charges that come with it. Yet, even taking those charges into account, it can be useful in a number of situations. What are those situations?

Obviously, the greater the financial assets you have, the less the need for tapping into your home equity. But you may find (as you do your projections, or as you monitor the situation periodically during your decumulation years) that you are worried about running out of money. And you don't want to sell your home and move. That is when the option of taking out a reverse mortgage is worth considering.

If you are going to take a lump sum, say ST&W, take it as early as possible. But should you actually take a lump sum, or is a lifetime income preferable? That depends on how much of a risk taker you are. If you are very risk averse, it's better to spend down your financial wealth first, then take out a reverse mortgage in the form of a lump sum—and buy a lifetime annuity with it. Either of those approaches (the lump sum or the lifetime income) is superior to taking a line of credit when your financial wealth is exhausted, because a line of credit gives you no longevity protection and gives you less lifetime income than the other approaches.

So, for the rest of this chapter, we will assume that, if it turns out to be necessary, your assets under consideration include the proceeds of borrowing through a reverse mortgage.

In fact, even if you don't ever need to borrow, ST&W point out that the reversionary interest in your primary residence should affect the way you invest your financial assets. Why? Because you should consider the reversionary interest an asset in its own right, adding it to your asset portfolio. Your financial assets therefore constitute a smaller proportion of your total asset portfolio than if you ignore the reversionary interest. And so you can invest that financial wealth more aggressively.[6]

MANY RULES OF THUMB ARE JUST PLAIN WRONG

It is almost impossible to overstate the importance of investment policy in this phase of life. Remember the breakdown we derived in Chapter 4: Each dollar decumulated consists of approximately 10 cents of original savings, 30 cents of investment return during the accumulation phase, and 60 cents of investment return during the decumulation phase. This drives home not only the importance of investing your assets sensibly; it also drives home the importance of the return you earn in the decumulation phase.

We have had this confirmed anecdotally many times. For example, a former colleague of ours who retired about 10 years ago has observed: "I don't know how it happens, but we've spent everything we had 10 years ago, and yet we still have almost as much as we started with." The explanation is, in relative terms, that the colleague and her husband had spent the 40 cents that their original savings and preretirement investment returns amounted to; and now, in retirement, the remaining 60 cents were kicking in and they had earned almost 40 cents of those decumulation returns. This is what happens when an investment strategy has its planned effect. The pleasant surprise becomes an unpleasant one in times of falling markets, or if the investment strategy fails.

There are many rules of thumb for investment policy in the decumulation phase of your life, not all of them sound. One is that your equity exposure, as a percentage of your financial assets, should be 100 minus your age: 35 percent at age 65, 20 percent at age 80. Another is that, whatever your current equity exposure, you should reduce it in retirement.

Neither of these rules makes financial sense. But that is not the received wisdom. "Half of all advisors always or usually recommend an asset allocation change upon a client's retirement,"[7] according to Mathew Greenwald & Associates, Inc., a firm that does numerous surveys in this field. And the change is typically to make the equity exposure glide down after retirement, continuing in the decumulation phase what happens at the end of the accumulation phase.

It is easy to show why that is misguided. Most retirees' assets build through their working lives, particularly in the 10 years leading up to retirement; then the assets peak at retirement and start to decline. In the accumulation phase, this leads to the justifiably popular target date approach to investing, described in Chapter 8. For most of us, our assets then start to decline, as we start to decumulate. To maintain a constant dollar risk exposure in decumulation (and remember, that is more or less the basis behind the target date approach in accumulation), we would need to *increase* our equity exposure as our wealth decreases. To maintain a constant proportion of our remaining cash flow at risk, we would need to *preserve* our equity exposure as a constant through decumulation. There is no reason other than fear itself that calls for a *decreasing* equity exposure as age increases.

But much more important, these rules of thumb take no account of the relationship between a retiree's spending plan, wealth (both preannuitized and nonannuitized), and life expectancy. Just as we believe that everyone ought to have a customized spending plan, we also believe that everyone ought to have a customized investment plan that is a part of a broader wealth allocation plan. For this, we introduce the concept of wealth zones.

FOUR WEALTH ZONES

What does your total wealth amount to? For retirees, it is probably more useful to rephrase the question: What does your total wealth enable you to do? The more you have, the more flexibility you have in your lifestyle and in your ability to leave bequests to others. We take that simple thought as the basis for defining four wealth zones, as follows:

- **Zone 1:** This zone is where you are working to build up enough money to buy a lifetime annuity for your "essentials" lifestyle (the bare minimum lifestyle that you can tolerate, as we discussed in Chapter 16). Call this the "essentials zone."
- **Zone 2:** Here, you have enough for the essentials, but are now concerned with ensuring you have enough additional money to buy a lifetime annuity for your desired lifestyle. Call this the "lifestyle zone."
- **Zone 3:** For most of us who get this far, this third zone is everything else we have. Once you have your own needs—and wants—covered,

you have moved beyond the zone where you are saving for yourself; you are saving for others. So let's call it the "bequest zone." Now, there will still be the wealthy or frugal few who have money slurping over into....

- **Zone 4:** So much money that you never actually decumulate. You keep accumulating assets. That is because you can live your desired lifestyle out of investment returns alone, so there is no need to tap into capital. Call this the "endowed zone."

The key to defining your position is to find out the highest zone into which your wealth allows you to climb. Are you in the third zone of wealth, or only the second? Or are you among those in the top zone? That is the fundamental point. It is not necessary to divide the money physically into several slices, nor will it turn out to be necessary to find different investment policies for different slices. All we are doing here is defining different breakpoints, to see which zone your aggregate wealth puts you into.

It is clear that where each zone begins varies from one person to another. And the wealth in each zone also varies according to what each person wants to do. The spending plan (whether for essentials or for the full desired lifestyle) is an essential determinant. The same amount of money that is enough to leave one person content that their desired lifestyle is fully covered—putting them into the bequest zone—may leave somebody else concerned that they do not even have their basic needs assured, putting them in the essentials zone. That is why we emphasize the importance of personalized spending and investment plans after retirement.

Note also that there is a base of preannuitized assets that comes into play here. By this we mean Social Security and any defined benefit (DB) pension assets that may exist.[8] In years gone by, when DB plans were at their peak, many retirees found that, with Social Security and their DB pension, they had more than enough to live as they desired. That meant they were automatically lifted beyond the first (essentials) and second (lifestyle) zones. All their financial assets automatically became available for bequests, and since they never needed to touch this money for their lifestyle, it automatically got them into the endowed zone, no matter how small these assets were.

Today, this base of preannuitized assets is in relative decline, and as defined contribution (DC) becomes a generation's main form of retirement provision, more and more people will find that they need their DC and other assets to lift them beyond the essentials zone and the lifestyle zone; and many may not have enough to climb any higher than that. That will affect the flexibility they have to achieve their lifestyle and bequest goals.

HOW YOUR WEALTH ZONE DETERMINES YOUR CHOICES

We assume that you are in good health; otherwise, our discussion of longevity protection is irrelevant.

In the Essentials Zone

If you are in this zone, then you don't have enough money even for the essentials of life.

As you reach the top of this zone, then you have just enough for the essentials of life—provided you buy a conventional lifetime annuity. You have nothing extra for bequests. If you do not buy a lifetime annuity, then you can't even be sure of longevity protection. Therefore, the only chance you have of fulfilling either of the two goals (longevity protection and bequests) is to focus entirely on longevity protection and buy a conventional lifetime annuity.

That, at any rate, is the theoretically optimal solution. But it assumes that you know exactly what your spending will be from year to year. And in practice nobody really knows that. In particular, the incidence and size of health care expenses are unknown. We think that most people in the essentials zone are likely (sensibly) to hold an emergency cash reserve before thinking of anything else. And then they will rely on some form of social assistance, barely having enough for the essentials of life. Social assistance becomes the source of longevity protection.[9]

Sadly, in the essentials zone, you do not have the luxury of choice.

In the Lifestyle Zone

Now you have enough for the essentials, but not enough to ensure that you can live your desired lifestyle. Yet that means you do have a little bit of flexibility. Remember that in Chapter 16 we said you should delay buying an annuity as long as you can. Now we will discuss the question of when "as long as you can" runs out. It depends on how much risk you are willing to take, as you balance your wealth and your spending. In this context, risk tolerance also means your tolerance to reduce your standard of living, if the risk does not bring the reward you hoped for.

If you are totally risk averse, then you focus on maintaining the best living standard your (inadequate) wealth can buy, ignore the bequest motive, and buy a conventional lifetime annuity right away. This guarantees that you can live something between your desired lifestyle and your essentials lifestyle (depending on how far into this second zone you have climbed), no matter how long you survive.

If you are willing to tolerate some risk, then you can extend your choices. It also matters what sort of risk you're willing to tolerate.

Suppose you don't care at all about the bequest motive. Then your sole focus is on longevity protection. But why would you take any investment risk at all? Because you would like to see if the risk increases your assets to the point where you'll have enough money to live your full desired lifestyle. What is your course of action? Two choices, really.

One is to buy a conventional lifetime annuity to cover the essentials (thus locking in the essentials lifestyle), and invest the rest in something risky—either traditional risky assets or a variable lifetime annuity. In both cases you will hope that the risky asset performs well and enables you to eventually live your full desired lifestyle. If you select the risky asset rather than the variable lifetime annuity, then you will also monitor its value periodically to see if it has expanded to the point where you can buy a conventional lifetime annuity to guarantee that your desired lifestyle is now fully protected.

The other choice is not to buy a conventional lifetime annuity at all. You buy either a portfolio of traditional risky assets or a variable lifetime annuity, and hope that the risky assets perform well enough for you to lock in your desired lifestyle. If you select the risky assets alone, then you will periodically monitor its value to see whether it's approaching a floor value or a ceiling value. The floor value is that you should never allow it to fall below the bottom of the lifestyle zone, that is, the amount required to lock in your essentials lifestyle with a conventional lifetime annuity. The happy ceiling is reached at the top end of the lifestyle zone, that is, when you have enough to lock in your desired lifestyle with a conventional lifetime annuity.

What if you really do care about the bequest motive?

Then your choices are essentially the same as discussed earlier in this section. But you won't buy any of the variable lifetime annuity, because no matter how well the risky asset does, there is nothing that outlives you.[10] So your risk exposure is confined to the traditional risky asset; and if it performs well enough to exceed the amount you need to lock in your desired lifestyle with a conventional lifetime annuity (i.e., your wealth overflows from the lifestyle zone into the bequest zone), then you will have something left over for bequests. Or, even if you never get to that point, you might choose to lock in some lifestyle below your full desired lifestyle, and leave the rest for bequests. That depends on the relative strength of your bequest motive versus your desire to live your full contemplated lifestyle.

In the Bequest Zone

Now you have the luxury that you could *ensure* longevity protection as well as contemplate bequests.

You have the freedom to think about investment in isolation, ignoring (for the moment) longevity protection considerations.[11] You can do this as long as you remain in the bequest zone, because then you know you have enough, if you ever so desire, to trigger the purchase of a conventional lifetime annuity to lock in your longevity protection, using the money in the essentials and lifestyle zones. That potential purchase amount therefore becomes a floor below which you will never allow your assets to fall. Your asset allocation, using traditional assets alone, will reflect your risk tolerance, which in turn will be determined by two sets of considerations: Your desire to ensure that, as you periodically monitor your future position, you never drop out of the bequest zone, and your bequest motive.

Those two desires, as mentioned before, are in constant tension, and the tension is particularly acute in the bequest zone. It shows up very strongly if your asset portfolio has the misfortune to start off with a series of disappointing returns, threatening to move you out of this zone. Undoubtedly, you will then reassess not only your asset position but also your risk tolerance and the relative strength of your bequest motive. You will probably find yourself changing your asset allocation, to become much more defensive. (Equally, if you have the good fortune to start with a series of high returns, you will probably find yourself changing your asset allocation to take more risk.) In short, being in the bequest zone makes you realize very strongly the impact of sequential risk and the need for a dynamic process to reevaluate your situation periodically.

There is also another powerful reason to monitor your position periodically. Annuity purchase prices are sensitive to movements in interest rates, so the breakpoints between the zones change when interest rates change. You could therefore find yourself moving between zones even if your assets don't fall in value. All of which reinforces the notion of a dynamic process.

What if you are extremely risk averse? You would probably buy a conventional lifetime annuity to lock in either your desired lifestyle or your essentials lifestyle. The stronger your bequest motive, the lower the lifestyle you would lock in. If you lock in your desired lifestyle, that will exhaust your essentials and lifestyle zone money. What is left then becomes an investment-only issue, with bequests as your sole focus. If you lock in your essentials lifestyle, then that exhausts your essentials zone money, and you will manage the rest with an eye to maintaining longevity protection and never dropping out of the bequest zone. Again, the competing tensions, the exposure to sequential risk, and the need for a dynamic strategy are all apparent.

Finally, as we end this discussion on how long it makes sense to postpone the purchase of longevity protection, we repeat the reminder from Milevsky and Young[12] to think hard before you commit yourself to the irreversibility of a lifetime annuity purchase. And we mention one other consideration regarding the timing of an annuity purchase, and it relates to the level of interest rates. In effect, buying a conventional lifetime annuity creates a fixed-income asset, with the interest rate locked in forever. When interest rates are historically high (or if you believe they are at a peak), this makes the purchase attractive; when interest rates are historically low (or you believe they are at a trough), it makes the purchase unattractive.

In the Endowment Zone

Now you have the luxury of not having to worry at all about longevity protection, because you are continuing to accumulate money. Your entire focus can now be on bequests. Lifetime annuities are therefore irrelevant to your purpose, and the only assets you will consider are the traditional risk-free asset and the traditional risky asset. How much of each you hold will depend on your risk tolerance. While this is hardly a trivial problem (particularly because of the amount of money you have), it is trivial from the perspective of decumulation because longevity protection is automatic, and therefore there is zero motivation to worry about that particular aspect.

BEQUESTS

Certainly, anyone in the bequest or endowment zone ought to be thinking seriously about bequests, because they have enough to outlive their wealth; and many in the lifestyle zone will have a bequest motive, too. In our research on attitudes toward giving, we found three angles compelling. In our case, they all relate to our children.

One angle relates to how much one should leave to children. The most famous quote in this context comes from Warren Buffett: "... enough money so that they would feel they could do anything, but not so much that they could do nothing."[13] Less well known is how Buffett quantified it: a few hundred thousand dollars, for a college graduate. That was 20 years ago. Since then the cost of living has doubled. In any case, most people are not able to leave even Buffett's limited amount to their children; it's his philosophy, not the amount, that encapsulates wisdom.

We have heard a wonderful and practical way to think about an amount. Charles W. Collier, senior philanthropic adviser at Harvard University and author of *Wealth in Families*,[14] talks to wealthy alumni who give something back to the university but have challenges about how much they should first reserve for their children. Collier suggests that the parents might ask their children: "What work is going to be meaningful to you? How much money do you need from us to live a worthwhile life?" This can bring out the best in the children, who have a chance to formulate goals (often socially conscious ones); and it is the starting point for estimating how much money that requires. Interestingly, this will result in different *amounts* for each child, but equal (and enormous) *satisfaction* for them. Of course, this requires a certain type of family culture for it to work. It would be disastrous, for example, in a family in which the children can't wait to fight over their parents' estate.

A second angle relates to estate taxes. Many countries have the custom of levying tax if the estate is left in one way but not if it is left in another way. It's as if the estate will be taxed if the money is in one pocket but not if the money is in another pocket. Naturally, it then makes sense to think in terms of transferring money from one pocket to the other. One frequent device for this purpose (in the United States, at any rate) is an insurance policy, since insurance proceeds can be structured to fall outside the estate.

We think the best way to look at this question is to regard the policy as an investment. After all, if the pace at which the money builds up in the policy is slow relative to the pace at which it would otherwise build, then there is an opportunity cost to the policy. At some stage, the opportunity cost could exceed the saving in estate tax. Is this likely to happen? If so, how far in the future?

The third angle relates to the timing of bequests. Buffett, again, is famous as having made a mind-bogglingly generous gift to the Bill and Melinda Gates Foundation, to be donated (and spent) in periodic amounts, so long as either Bill or Melinda Gates is alive. This inspires the notion of giving now, rather than having recipients wait until someone dies. One of the authors has grown-up children, with an expectancy of their having to wait 30 or more years to inherit anything. Why make them wait that long, when something gradual through their working lifetimes would be much more useful?

He and his wife sat down with their kids and brought them into their thinking. This was the first time they had ever had a family discussion of this nature. It was heart-warming and brought the family even closer together. They included the "meaningful work" question as an ongoing issue. (The kids had never given it much thought. That will have to develop in the future.) The parents have, so far, found one ongoing way in which they can do something for the kids now (helping them with part of the cash flow to purchase modest homes now, when their own cash flow is under stress from all the traditional demands and desires of being in the early years of their careers), and that is very satisfying. It avoids, for example, one possible regret that might result from a consideration of the third question posed in the section entitled "Step Two: What about the Future?" in Chapter 15. You'll remember that question: "You've just found out you have 24 hours to live. What are your regrets?" "I wish we had helped the kids earlier in their lives, instead of making them wait until we both die" need no longer be a deathbed lament.

This discussion had an amusing note, too. (And it's not just the fact that it is has now gone into family lore as "Dad's decumulation talk.") The author's wife was evidently concerned that he might want to lead the discussion and conduct it in business fashion rather than as a father because, without saying a word, she handed him a cartoon. It shows a family sitting around a kitchen table. The kids are so young that one head is barely visible above table level. The father is saying, "Before we begin this family meeting, how about we go around and say our names and a little something about ourselves." The author correctly interpreted this as a warning, and his family reports that he behaved himself.

CHAPTER 18

Product Innovation with Decumulation in Mind

This chapter looks at the types of investment products that are starting to become available to fill the gaps we've identified. The first gap is the lack of a popularly accepted means to convert a sum of money into a lifetime income: As we described in Chapter 16, the lifetime annuity achieves this goal, but the way in which it does so has meant there has been in practice relatively little demand for these products. The second gap—described in Chapter 17—is the lack of a way to address simultaneously the problem of longevity protection and the problem of investing your accumulated assets.

These are big gaps. There is a huge amount of wealth that is shifting its focus from accumulation to decumulation, as the Baby Boom generation reaches retirement age. Unsurprisingly, the financial community is responding with a flurry of innovation, designing products to fill these gaps that they hope will win greater popular acceptance than traditional lifetime annuities have been able to. At this early stage, it is hard to tell which new features or products will prove to be the most appealing. Hence the rash of product innovation. Let battle commence!

In this chapter, we will describe some of the new products under six broad headings. The products that we will describe are not all available in every country, or necessarily widely available in any one country. But their features are well known and understood, having in most cases been discussed in financial literature; it is these features, or some combination of them, which will form the basis of how the decumulation challenge is met in the future.

VARIATIONS ON THE LIFETIME ANNUITY

The first category of product to consider is the various mutations of the basic lifetime annuity itself. This is a product focused on providing longevity protection. That is what it does, in its purest form. But several flavors of this basic product exist.

For example, consider the joint-and-last-survivor annuity, which pays an income while at least one of two partners is alive. That's the longevity protection aspect. But it is equivalent to a lifetime annuity while both are alive, followed by a continuation (typically, at a lower cash flow rate) to the survivor. In that sense, it provides lifetime protection to the first to die, followed by a bequest (converted to lifetime income) to the survivor.

Another variant is the lifetime annuity that guarantees to pay for at least 10 years (or some other period—for our analysis, the period isn't relevant), even if the annuitant dies during that period. Again, that provides a lifetime income, along with a bequest (in the form of ongoing cash flow to the named beneficiary) if death should occur within the first 10 years. The size of the bequest thus declines over time. Another variant is the "return of purchase price" annuity, in which, if death occurs before the lifetime income payments add up to the purchase price, the balance of the purchase price is paid to the named beneficiary.

From an investment perspective, each of these variants can be seen as the purchase of a security (the lifetime annuity) together with a put option (triggering further payments on death, under terms agreed to at the outset). The more likely it is that the put will be exercised, the more it costs, and the smaller the lifetime income that the rest of the combined purchase price secures. Or one can look at it from a longevity perspective: The more likely it is that the bequest will be triggered, the smaller the lifetime income that the rest of the combined purchase price secures.

These variants are clearly designed to address the concern of some annuity purchasers who say "I want longevity protection, not a gamble," fearing the early loss of life and capital simultaneously. But when it comes to addressing the other four concerns that we identified in Chapter 16 (the income that looks puny alongside the annuity purchase price, the loss of control of capital, the 100 percent fixed-income investment strategy, and the capital intensiveness), other product designs are needed.

LONGEVITY PROTECTION PLUS LONG-TERM CARE INSURANCE

One new product combines the desire for lifetime income with the desire to buy insurance against the unpredictable spikes in spending required for long-term care. It pays out a lifetime income as well as whatever is required for long-term care (the latter benefit amounts being subject to limits, of course, exactly as with long-term care insurance).

Of course, both of the components of this bundled product can be purchased separately. But the combination adds a new feature. A stand-alone long-term care policy does not have a guaranteed premium rate; typically, the premium can be increased at some future date, if economic conditions require the increase. The new bundled product effectively comes with a guaranteed built-in premium, because the cash flow provided by the product stays constant throughout, regardless of economic conditions. As with all bundled products, however, it is not immediately clear what other sacrifice is built in, in exchange for the guaranteed premium. You can get some idea of the cost of the guarantee by comparing the bundled cost with the separate cost of a traditional immediate annuity and a long-term care policy.

This type of product deals specifically with the long-term care aspect of the concern over loss of control of capital that comes with a traditional lifetime annuity: For many, fears over being unable to meet long-term care costs are a major drawback of the traditional annuity.

GUARANTEED MINIMUM WITHDRAWAL BENEFITS

The third category of product that is vying for control of the decumulation market labors under the cumbersome name of guaranteed minimum withdrawal benefits (typically abbreviated to GMWB). This product fits in a hitherto thinly populated cell of Figure 17.1: the one that is risk free as far as longevity protection is concerned and risky as far as investing is concerned.

Here's how it works:

You pay a lump sum to an insurance company. The insurance company invests it in a commingled fund with a prespecified investment philosophy. You choose the fund from an available line-up. There may be one or more managers of the fund, and the insurance company may or may not be involved in fund management. The important point is that the investment vehicle is not purely a fixed-income vehicle, but lets you implement an investment program that reflects your desired level of investment risk.

Periodically (monthly, quarterly, annually—as agreed in advance) you receive a distribution from the fund. The distribution may be constant or vary with the return on the fund. If you want to, you can withdraw more than this basic distribution amount, and the characteristic that is of crucial importance is that, provided you do not withdraw more than a specified maximum amount every year, the insurer guarantees that that amount will continue for the rest of your life. That holds even if the remaining value of the investment declines to zero. In effect, therefore, there is a lifetime cash flow guarantee. If you withdraw more than the maximum, the longevity protection is not lost, but the guaranteed cash flow is reduced.

In some of these GMWB contracts, investment experience is reviewed periodically and, if the experience has been favorable, the guaranteed level of lifetime income is reset upward (and so cannot be reduced subsequently if future investment experience is poor).

In addition to getting the guaranteed lifetime cash flow, you remain the owner of the remaining investment in the fund. This means that the balance of the account is available to your estate or a named beneficiary. It also means that you have not been forced to annuitize the investment irrevocably, and retain the ability at any time to terminate the investment.

Those are the essential financial features. We have no doubts that many variants of the basic GMWB design will be offered, with other features added.[1] The products will undoubtedly have different names and different acronyms.

When we look at GMWB products in the context of the various weaknesses of traditional lifetime annuities, as described in Chapter 16, we find that they address, to a large extent, all of them. First, there is no need for a myopic comparison of lump sum versus annual cash flow, because the buyer owns both. Second, there is no loss of control, because the purchase is reversible. Third, life and capital can't be lost together, because the buyer owns the balance of the account. Fourth, it's no longer effectively a fixed-income investment. And fifth, it's not unnecessarily capital intensive because there is no annuity purchase at all.

Is there a catch? Not necessarily; it's just a combination of features. But we do not believe that our analysis necessarily points to GMWB products as being the right decumulation product for everyone: There are at least two considerations that need to be made in each individual case. First, are the features exactly what we've described? Or are there variations that bring back one or more of the negative features? Second, what's the price of the features? If each aspect is priced separately and you have the choice of electing it or not electing it, then you can make an informed choice. But if the features are bundled together for a single high price, then it's a take-it-or-leave-it package and your ability to judge if you're getting good value for the package is seriously diminished.

It's not our purpose to describe every variant of this family of products. We simply want you to understand what's possible, how to check which of the five negative features are addressed, and to realize that pricing a complex product isn't easy.

THE LONGEVITY POOL

In this variant nobody underwrites the longevity element.[2] Instead, the purchasers of a mutual fund share the longevity experience among themselves. When members of the group die, their units stay in the fund and increase the value of the units of the survivors, constituting a "mortality credit" to the others. New members are admitted to the group via a purchase price that anticipates longevity; whether the mortality credits are bigger or smaller than anticipated has an effect, because no insurance company underwrites the actual experience. The design of this sort of product can accommodate a lifetime income that increases, in which case the starting amount will be lower than if a constant dollar payout is selected, or a payout stream that reflects the return on the risky portfolio.

Unlike the GMWB products, in this case the purchase is irreversible, because (as with traditional lifetime annuities) the early deaths subsidize those who live long. In exchange, there is no insurance company loading for longevity guarantees and profits.

Compared to the traditional lifetime annuity, the advantage of the longevity pool is that it offers longevity protection without forcing a 100 percent fixed-income investment strategy.

ADVANCED LIFE DEFERRED ANNUITIES

Advanced life deferred annuities (ALDAs) are designed for retirees who have enough money to decumulate for some time, and hence don't want to pay for longevity protection in the first few years, nor do they want to risk losing life and capital together. So, in exchange for a lump sum paid today, the insurance company makes no payments until a certain advanced age (perhaps 80 or 85 or even 90); that's when a preagreed level of cash flow commences, and is guaranteed to continue until the buyer dies.

Because no payouts are made until the advanced age is reached, the cost of this annuity can be dramatically lower than that of a traditional immediate annuity.

What happens if the buyer dies during the deferral period? The design of an ALDA can accommodate either no payment at all or some specified payment (for example, a return of the initial lump sum). The smaller the death benefit in the deferral period, the lower the cost of a given amount of cash flow from the advanced age.

This type of product is aimed at reducing the objection that a traditional lifetime annuity is unnecessarily capital intensive, because the unwanted protection in the early years is not a part of the payout stream. For this reason, an ALDA is sometimes called *pure longevity insurance* because it offers that protection in a pure form, paying out only if longevity really is long.

PURE DECUMULATION PRODUCTS

The sixth and final category of product that we will consider in this chapter is one that is a pure drawdown product, with no longevity element at all. But its design incorporates features that are meant to appeal particularly to second and third zone decumulators, perhaps even fourth zone (in the classification we introduced in Chapter 17). These decumulators want to preserve their flexibility and not buy a lifetime annuity unless they are in danger of dropping into a lower zone. They want to decumulate at a rate that fits their spending plan. And they want a dynamic approach to investing, taking sequential risk into account. In other words, if the portfolio starts by performing well, then it is desirable to increase risk in search of a higher return; but if it starts out badly, then it is desirable to reduce risk, so that the bequest motive is not undone. That way, there is likely to be enough money at the end of some specified period to actually buy a lifetime annuity, if in old age that turns out to be necessary. And the dynamic approach continues throughout the specified period.

Pure decumulation products have many variations, among them: the term of the investment; a choice of starting decumulation rate; whether the ongoing decumulation amounts are fixed in dollar terms or vary with inflation or with the fund's return or are designed to exhaust the fund over the specified period; and of course the fund's investment philosophy. For products that do not explicitly exhaust the investment at the end of the horizon by varying the amounts paid out, there is typically a secondary objective of preserving some proportion of the initial invested capital; but how much credibility is attached to the secondary objective by the public remains to be seen, because it is not guaranteed and the public doesn't yet have any experience of observing how often the secondary objective is attained.

Again, it is not our purpose to describe every variation of this family of products. Our focus is to see which of the negative features of traditional annuities it addresses. And those are, as with the GMWB family, all of them: There is no myopic mental transfer from a lump sum to an income stream amount, no irreversibility, no loss of capital when life is lost, no restriction to a fixed-income contract, and no unnecessarily capital-intensive payment for longevity protection. Having said that, there is one important and potentially desirable feature that these products lack: There is no longevity protection. Pure decumulation products are a convenient way to decumulate, but are not a direct replacement for the traditional annuity, if longevity protection is required.

Because there is no longevity protection, it is easier with this family of products to assess whether the charges are reasonable value for what you get, than for products that bundle the investment and longevity protection charges.

WHICH TYPE OF PRODUCT IS BEST?

Each of the six types of product we have listed accentuates certain desirable features, and charges you for them. Which problems the buying public most wants to solve, and therefore which features the buying public will like most, have yet to become clear.

We think of the situation as rather like the desire, perhaps 15 years ago, for the miniaturization of electronics. We have seen a frenzy of miniaturization: phones, cameras, positioning devices, music players, e-mail and web-surfing devices, full-blooded computers, TVs—the list goes on. Time has shown that the one essential device that the public wants is the mobile phone. That now dominates the field of miniature electronics, and the other devices, while they have a stand-alone existence, have often become add-on features on mobile phones. That sort of dominance may well develop in the field of decumulation products, with one winner, and the others then becoming add-on features. But the winner is not yet evident.

There is another lesson from electronics. The mobile phone went through a number of iterations before it became a must-have product. It once used to be more like a luggable brick. Its dominance would have been hard to predict at that stage. That, too, may happen with decumulation products. Just because a particular family of products does not conquer the world immediately doesn't mean that it might not eventually win, with tweaks and streamlining. It won't necessarily be something completely new that wins.

The Plan Sponsor's Role

In this final part of the book, we look at the defined contribution (DC) plan sponsor's objectives and responsibilities. What does the sponsor want the plan to achieve? How can the plan meet those goals more effectively? What are the responsibilities that must be executed?

There are, in effect, two levels of answers to questions of this sort. There's the "bare minimum" answer, which is predicated on the attitude that you're in the business of providing a DC plan, whether or not you wanted to be, and there are some things you simply have to do in order to satisfy the legal requirements that exist and to avoid making a mess of things. You may not have the time or the money or the inclination to do more than the minimum. We would guess that there are many employers who think this way. This part may be of little interest to them.

There are also sponsors who would like to do more than the minimum. If you are one of them, then it is to you that we address these chapters. Our text is pitched at the "best practice" level of answers to the questions, so that you can see what best practice is and decide how far you want to go in that direction. That's consistent with our approach to the whole book: There are ways to do things better; here they are. It's not legally required that you do this, but as DC 2.0 takes root and gradually becomes judged by the higher standard we discussed in the first chapter, these best practices give the retirement system as a whole its best chance to be successful.

We start with governance: the establishment of a decision-making structure for the plan. Then we move to fiduciary responsibility, that is, the legal angle. (This is where the gap between minimum standard and best practice really involves taking on responsibility voluntarily.) Then we discuss how to create metrics that help you keep track of how successful your plan is. And, finally, we visit what is almost terra incognita in the United States: The decumulation phase, where your minimum responsibility is to do absolutely nothing, but where your retirees probably could use a lot of help.

CHAPTER 19

Defined Contribution
Plan Governance

In contrast to management, which is about running a business, governance is about seeing that it is run well. So you would judge management by results and governance by process.[1] It is self-evident that a better process is more likely to lead to better results. More formally, governance is the process of making, implementing, and evaluating decisions related to an area of responsibility. It is defined by the decision structure: What are the decisions that have to be made, who has input, who makes each decision, who implements it, who monitors it in action, who evaluates it.

Governance principles have been around, in some form, for as long as decisions have been delegated. There is no need to reinvent them for defined contribution (DC) plans; they have to be adapted to the DC context and applied. Over the course of the authors' careers we have observed a dramatic change in the scope of the governance principles applied to DC and the consistency of their application. But there is room for improvement, not so much in the principles themselves as in their implementation.

In this chapter, we draw together governance threads from other parts of the book. We also use the story of how American DC plans have evolved, to illustrate the principles. Our discussion focuses on investment aspects rather than record-keeping aspects.

THE PURPOSE OF DEFINED CONTRIBUTION
PLAN GOVERNANCE

The purpose of DC plan governance is to provide for the oversight, administration, and management of the plan. Plan sponsors and fiduciaries have a variety of responsibilities to the plan and to the participants. Sound DC plan governance helps ensure that these responsibilities are met. It is not our goal to provide a complete list of these responsibilities. There are many readily available sources of this information, including plan advisers, consultants, and ERISA (Employee Retirement Income Security Act of 1974) attorneys.

Some of the basic elements of good DC plan governance include:

- Naming persons or entities as responsible parties (who).[2]
- Listing the specific responsibilities of each party (what).
- Written procedures relating to plan management (how and when).
- Evaluating the plan and plan management against appropriate performance standards.
- Documenting the activities of plan management.
- Making changes to the plan and plan management when needed.

While the rest of the chapter discusses aspects of governance and fiduciary responsibility from the perspective of you, the appointed fiduciary, before we get there we want to make a few remarks on an infrequently discussed topic: the responsibility of appointing fiduciaries. Fiduciaries are typically appointed by a CEO or board or board committee. Those who appoint a fiduciary are themselves fiduciaries under ERISA; so the act of appointing a fiduciary is itself a fiduciary act that carries with it the duty of prudence and the duty to monitor.

Often, the appointing fiduciary creates a charter describing the general organizational structure and the duties of the appointed fiduciaries. Regardless of who drafts the charter, it should be approved by the appointing fiduciary and accepted by the appointed fiduciary. Typically, this includes the responsibility to review the plan document as it relates to the appointed fiduciary's responsibilities because one governance issue is the responsibility to administer the plan and manage its investments in accordance with the documents that control the plan.

The appointing fiduciaries have the responsibility to prudently monitor the activities of the appointed fiduciaries. Correspondingly, the appointees can assist the appointing fiduciaries by providing them with regular reports on their governance activities and their results.

RISK MANAGEMENT

Risk management is a critical part of DC plan governance. Risks are defined in the context of specific objectives. An objective may be to cause an outcome such as "have greater than 90 percent eligible participation in the plan," or to prevent an outcome such as "not incur plan-related fines or penalties from regulating agencies." Risk management in turn is customized to the risks associated with the plan's objectives. Proper DC plan governance (including the embedded risk management) must therefore flow from the plan's objectives. Without clear plan objectives, plan governance has no foundation.

A DEFINED CONTRIBUTION PLAN'S PURPOSE AND OBJECTIVES

Defined benefit (DB) plans define an outcome (the benefit); DC plans define a tactic (the contribution). The purpose of a DC plan, however, goes beyond the mere making of contributions, and it has objectives that go beyond the collection of contributions. Sponsors typically do have a purpose in mind for their DC plans, but often it is not written down or articulated clearly for those charged with the plan's governance. But plan governance can only be as good as the articulation of the plan's objectives. We sense that the true objectives of many DC plans in America are changing. As the objectives change so must the governance built around these objectives.

Three changing objectives illustrate our point: from benefiting a few to benefiting many, from a focus on supplemental savings to a focus on income replacement, and from lump-sum distributions to sustainable income.

From Few to Many

We noted in Chapter 1 that America's 401(k) plans have moved from being a vehicle for tax-deferred savings for a few high-paid employees (or, at any rate, for those who could afford to make deferrals) to being designed to meet the needs of the whole workforce. The few tended to be a limited number of motivated employees who were reasonably experienced personal investors, wanted to select investment vehicles themselves, were vocal in driving changes in the plan's line-up of investment funds, and traded in and out of them frequently.

With the focus now on the many, who are unlikely to become proficient investors despite the investment education provided by the sponsor, the corresponding changes in governance arrangements are to focus on the default option; to limit the number and type of investment choices to those that are likely to result in reasonable outcomes; and to stop reacting to the needs of the vocal few by including all their demanded fund choices, and instead simply offer them a mutual fund or brokerage window, with a fee borne by those few participants rather than by the sponsor or by all participants.

In effect, a new plan purpose and new objectives drive governance changes.

From Supplemental Savings to Income Replacement

In the early 1980s, many DC plans came into existence as savings plans that were supplemental both to a DB plan and to Social Security. Fast-forward to today and many of those DB plans are closed to new entrants or even to new accruals, and Social Security is acknowledged in its trustees' annual reporting to contributors to have an unsustainable combination of benefit and contribution provisions.[3] In many cases, the objective of the 401(k) has shifted from a supplemental savings plan to an important source of income replacement in retirement.

The corresponding change in plan governance is to change the design and evaluation criteria for plan investments. Rather than focusing on growing an initial investment over time, focus on converting a stream of contributions into wealth over a period of time. This explains the shift toward target date funds in recent years. But few plan sponsors or DC practitioners have adopted fund evaluation metrics for target date funds—something that is needed in the industry today.

From Lump-Sum Distributions to Sustainable Income

As we will discuss in the final chapter of this book, most DC plans do not provide any form of retirement benefit other than a lump-sum distribution. It is an area of considerable debate, as to whether providing sustainable income at retirement is a sensible (or even desirable) plan objective for an employer. It is unclear what most DC plan sponsors will decide on this question.

Investment product manufacturers seem very interested in promoting this idea; it is less clear if this interest is just as high among plan sponsors. But if plan sponsors do decide to make sustainable income a formal or informal plan objective, it will change aspects of their plan governance. They would need to create investment policy statements covering investment vehicles for sustaining income in retirement, with corresponding criteria for selecting, evaluating, and, if necessary, replacing these products. Moreover, whenever the change in objective occurs, plan governance must change at the same time: Novelty or lack of clarity about how to evaluate new investment types is not a good excuse for a delay in modifying plan governance.

FIDUCIARY DUTY

Governance is the responsibility of plan fiduciaries. A fiduciary is someone who has the responsibility to act on behalf of another in a position of trust or confidence. Fiduciaries of DC plans in America are held to standards established by ERISA. There are two aspects in particular of these fiduciary standards that have a subtle yet profound impact on DC plan governance.

Exclusive Benefit of Participants

Sponsors of retirement plans qualifying under ERISA, and fiduciaries they appoint, are held to what has come to be known as the "exclusive benefit rule." Section 404(a)(1) of ERISA states that "fiduciaries must discharge their duties with respect to the plan solely in the interest of participants and beneficiaries."

This seems clear: As a fiduciary, you make decisions that are best for the participants, and your personal interests should not affect your decisions, even secondarily.[4] Let's walk through an example of how the fiduciary's interests and the participants' interest might be in conflict, and the way to resolve the issue.

In the early days of 401(k) plans, many plans did not allow their employees to choose where their account was invested. Slowly, employers began to offer investment choice to their participants. At first the choices were few, but over time the number of choices grew to dozens and in some case hundreds. According to the Vanguard Group, in 2006 the average number of investment choices offered in a 401(k) plan was just over 20. In addition, 15 percent of plans offered more than 26 investment options to their participants.[5] Why so many choices? Our experience in working with DC plan sponsors over the years suggests that the primary reason is to respond to participant requests for more and varied choice. We saw in Chapter 8 that one result is that DC investment returns trail DB returns.

Many plans are therefore adding prebuilt portfolios in the form of target date funds, balanced funds, or managed accounts. But, in most cases, they are also leaving some or all of the old investment funds in place as choices for participants to build their own portfolios. Why?

One way to frame the issue is to ask: "Which is more likely to help participants reach their retirement goals, providing them with lots of investments to choose from so they have a wide variety, or providing them with a few prebuilt, professionally managed portfolios?" This question is framed with the exclusive benefit of the participant in mind. Another way to frame the issue is: "Which investment line-up is least likely to cause angst among plan participants (and possibly criticism or legal action against the plan fiduciaries)—lots of choice (everyone's favorite funds), or limited choice in the form of prebuilt, professionally managed portfolios?" This question is framed (cynically, we will admit) in the best interest of the plan fiduciaries and not for the exclusive benefit of plan participants.

That does not mean that plan fiduciaries consciously design their investment line-ups so they won't be criticized or sued by plan participants. But there is a reasonable possibility that they are a bit conflicted when making these decisions. It is reasonable, because it is accurate, to think that some participants will complain if the fund line-up is cut back substantially. And it is not just the rank-and-file who will complain; members of senior management will also have their say when you take away their favorite funds. So the pressure is there.

The fiduciary's duty is to frame the question in the right way. That does not predetermine the answer. There is always scope for different opinions—uncertainty and subjectivity are part of the terrain—but decisions are influenced by the way the questions are framed.

Our point is that DC plan governance is not as simple as it may appear on the surface, and that it changes as our knowledge and understanding about these issues change. In many ways, being a fiduciary of a DC plan is more difficult than being a fiduciary of a DB plan. Unlike with DB plans, DC plan fiduciaries are in partnership with the plan participants. The fiduciaries choose which choices to make available; the participant makes the final decision. DC plan fiduciaries must keep themselves from being influenced by others' opinions when they know those opinions will not lead to better outcomes for the participants. This is true even when that influence comes in the form of sharp (and possibly public) criticism.

Prudent Expert

DC plan fiduciaries are also held to a "prudent expert" standard. The term *prudent expert* does not appear anywhere in text of ERISA, but the term has become accepted as a convenient way to describe the standard.

The initial trustee standard was framed in a landmark court ruling in 1830, and became known as the "prudent man" standard. In the text of the ruling, Justice Samuel Putnam wrote, "All that can be required of a trustee to invest is that he shall conduct himself faithfully and exercise sound discretion. He is to observe how men of prudence, discretion and intelligence manage their own affairs. . . ."

This meant that a decision was acceptable if it followed a sensible process; it does not depend on the outcome. And that standard has stood the test of time, and still applies. But the authors of ERISA have raised the standard. Section 404(a)(1)(B) of ERISA requires a plan fiduciary "to act with the care, skill, prudence and diligence under the prevailing circumstances that a prudent person acting in a like capacity and familiar with such matters would use." The addition of the phrase "familiar with such matters" means that ERISA (and that includes DC) fiduciaries have to be both prudent and expert: Hence the standard is called the "prudent expert" standard. To the extent they are not familiar with such matters, they need to find someone who is, to help them in their decision making.

WHAT SHOULD A PRUDENT EXPERT KNOW—AND WHEN?

Notice that ERISA's words *prevailing circumstances* added another concept to the standard. That means you must make decisions based on the knowledge available at the time the decision is made. If new information becomes available later, you need to review your decision to see if it is still prudent in light of the new knowledge. But this raises the question: When is a piece of knowledge deemed to be something a prudent expert should know? Knowledge is dynamic. The understanding of new information is often gradual rather than instantaneous upon discovery. The emergence of evidence and the gradual strengthening of opinion on the dangers of smoking is an example.

An example relevant to DC plan governance is participant investment behavior. Chapter 10 is devoted to this topic, so we don't need to repeat it here. There was a time, though, when it seemed generally agreed that the best thing we could do for DC plan participants was to give them lots of investment choices along with education about how to be an expert investor, and then let them do their own thing. Today, it seems generally agreed that the best thing we can do for participants is build and manage their investment portfolio for them, rather than have them do it themselves. When did we cross the line? What day did this happen? Was it in the morning or afternoon of that day? Realistically, this is not a knowable piece of information, but DC fiduciaries across America have a decision to make. When they believe they have new information that requires them to update their plan governance decisions, they have a responsibility to act. That is why we are writing about DC plan governance. While the principles of good plan governance don't change much, the implementation of those principles does change over time.

NEW CHOICES BASED ON NEW KNOWLEDGE

Continuing with the presumption that participants are better served by having a choice of prebuilt portfolios rather than building portfolios themselves, how would plan fiduciaries modify their decisions? Two changes come to mind. First, they would make a portfolio type of investment the default investment option in their plan. Fortunately, U.S. regulations support the use of portfolio-type investments as plan defaults in their definition of qualified default investment alternatives (QDIAs).[6] Target date funds, balanced funds, and managed accounts are all approved QDIAs. Second, they would redirect their participant education efforts to encourage the use of prebuilt portfolios. The old message of "you, too, can be a successful investor" would be replaced with "leave it to the experts."

IN SUMMARY

Plan fiduciaries should have no trouble establishing a sensible model of governance for their plan. An entire industry of plan advisers and consultants are there waiting to help. Plan governance needs to be designed around clear plan objectives, and these objectives should be reaffirmed on a regular basis. As plan objectives change, plan governance should change with them. Fiduciaries must act in the sole interest of plan participants and leave their own interest aside when making plan decisions. Finally, as prudent experts, fiduciaries need to be aware of new and changing information that may affect their plan decisions, and revise their decisions when new information warrants it. If they do not have the expertise they need to execute their responsibilities as prudent experts, they must seek the help of someone who does have this expertise.

CHAPTER 20

Defined Contribution
Plan Effectiveness

Typically, you as the plan sponsor are concerned with reporting to your plan participants, who justifiably want to know how they are doing. It is much less common for sponsors to be concerned with metrics of the plan's aggregate effectiveness, but you should be. So this chapter deals with how to measure and track the effectiveness of a DC plan. It is part of sound plan governance to have clear objectives, to determine metrics for measuring your progress toward those objectives, to use those metrics on a regular basis, and to make adjustments to the plan based on these results.

Before we can develop metrics for plan effectiveness we must ask the question: effective at what? For the sake of this chapter, we are going to assume an overriding plan objective: to facilitate maximum retirement wealth accumulation for the participants.

This is not the same thing as ensuring an adequate postretirement income, for (at least) two reasons. First, most individuals are participants in a given plan for only a fraction of their overall working career. They will probably accumulate wealth in several other places and consolidate these wealth sources when they reach retirement. The goal, therefore, for these participants is to help them maximize their wealth accumulation while they are in your plan. That is your contribution to their income adequacy down the road. Second, society is still on the cusp of determining how much responsibility the plan sponsor should take for postretirement income adequacy. Facilitating maximum retirement wealth accumulation seems to be clearly within the scope of a DC plan, but once the plan has done this task, is it the plan's objective to take responsibility for the management of income distribution as well? If not (and the answer varies from one country to another), the plan sponsor can still facilitate sensible approaches to decumulation, as we will see in the next chapter. As version 2.0 truly takes over, it may also become an objective, in which case we will need to build metrics for that objective, too.

What about other plan objectives? For example, maximize tax deferred savings for key employees, create employee goodwill, effect high employee retention, satisfy a collective bargaining agreement requirement, or simply match what is an industry standard. These all may be objectives of specific DC plans. In some cases, these might even be the only objective of the plan. In these cases, the plan managers should determine metrics that match these unique objectives.

But, for now, we'll worry about wealth accumulation, and for this we will describe nine metrics.

The first two deal with plan participation:

- Participation rate
- Participation delay

The next three deal with inputs:

- Employee savings rate
- Employer contribution rate
- Match maximization

One deals with investing:

- Participant net investment return

And the last three deal with leakage:

- Hardship withdrawal usage
- Loans as distributions
- Early withdrawals

We'll explain each metric and why it is important, offer some suggested standards or benchmarks for each, and discuss ways in which a plan can improve its score for each metric.

We have been asked why we haven't combined these metrics into a single measurement to represent the plan's overall effectiveness. The answer is that improving plan effectiveness is a multifaceted problem, and we believe it requires a multifaceted solution. When combining metrics into a single measurement, there is the risk of a single high score in one metric masking the need for improvement in other areas.

PARTICIPATION RATE

This is simply the percentage of all company employees that are currently participating in the plan in some form. You may choose to measure this in terms of eligible employees. In that variation, you are removing from the denominator those employees who have not yet met the age and service requirements of the plan. Clearly, you cannot influence the participation of those employees who do not qualify for the plan. But you might consider easing eligibility standards (or removing them altogether) to allow for maximum participation from all company employees.

The most common concern we hear about doing this is that it can create unreasonable administrative cost and complexity, especially when the workforce has high turnover or is very young, and in these cases probably also lower paid, resulting in a lot of small account balances. This concern is understandable, and employers must make their own cost-benefit decision regarding eligibility requirements. Interestingly, it is often cited that McDonald's Corporation, with a large number of workers fitting this description, was one of the first employers in America to implement automatic enrollment in their 401(k) plan way back in 1984.[1] Subsequently in 2002, McDonald's eliminated the auto-enroll feature of their 401(k) plan.

The importance of the participation rate metric is obvious. Anyone who doesn't join the plan has no chance of accumulating wealth in the plan. The ultimate goal should be 100 percent participation.[2] One method for increasing participation is education. Employees need to be made aware of the enrollment process and deadlines, and education about the need to save can enhance participation. However, if you've read this far and didn't skip to this chapter, you know that we believe education will have only a small impact on participation rates. The real key to success here is automatic enrollment into the plan.

PARTICIPATION DELAY

This is the average length of time (we suggest measuring it in days) between an employee's hire date and the date they begin participation in the plan. Again, you may want to modify this to start measuring from the date the employee becomes eligible for participation. What this metric identifies is any inefficiency in getting people into the plan. The ideal value for this metric is zero, meaning everyone began their plan participation on their hire date (or eligibility date, if you are using that variation).

The importance of this metric is that you might have employees who, for whatever reason, delay their participation and therefore have a gap in their savings. Once employees get settled into a new job and routine, including getting used to exactly how much their regular take-home paycheck is, inertia or just plain forgetfulness works against their joining the plan at a later date. Some employers might find work-related reasons for chronic delay; for example, the nature of their work may make employees very busy with other distracting tasks during their first few months of employment.

This metric might be of particular interest to the human resource department: They might be able to build this into their orientation programs for new employees to improve the score. As with participation rates, a simple method for improving this metric is automatic enrollment.

EMPLOYEE SAVINGS RATE

The employee savings rate is the average of the percentages of employee annual pay that are contributed to the plan. This should be measured by counting both pretax and aftertax contributions to the plan. There are two variables that you will need to decide on with this metric. First, whether to measure all eligible employees or just those that are actively participating. Second, whether to use only plan-eligible compensation or total compensation in your calculation. Whatever you decide for these variables, keep them consistent year after year so you have a proper baseline for measuring your progress in subsequent years. The most inclusive variation of this metric, counting all eligible employees and using their total compensation, will give you the clearest picture of your employees' savings rate.

The importance of this metric is that contributions are the raw material for wealth accumulation. As we saw in the 10/30/60 rule, contributions represent ten percent of the ultimate benefits. You might conclude that contributions are therefore only one tenth as important as investment earnings. We offer another perspective: Think of contributions as having the potential for being multiplied tenfold in a well-run retirement program. For every dollar put in, your employees can ultimately take out 10! Seen this way, you might be better able to motivate them to contribute more.

How can you improve your score? Education? Yes, but let's not rely on this too much. Rather, use automatic enrollment. When implementing automatic enrollment you must choose a contribution rate for those automatically enrolled. It has been the practice in America to begin new participants at a fairly low rate such as 3 percent and escalate them a little bit each year (often 1 percent) until they reach a maximum contribution rate. There are three variables here: the initial contribution rate, the rate of acceleration, and the maximum contribution rate. All can be adjusted by you to nudge employee contribution rates higher (within any statutory contribution limits). You can consider starting participants at higher contribution rates, accelerating them quickly, and raising the maximum, where you think it is sensible. The participants can always opt out and reduce their contribution rates if they feel they cannot afford the automatic rate.

Unlike some of the other metrics we describe, there is no clear target to use as a benchmark for this metric. You know high is good, but how high you want to go is not clear. Two useful points of comparison do exist, however. One is the level of contribution at specific competitors or at other plans in general (surveys are published from time to time on this subject). The other is to track changes over time: Is the pattern of saving trending up, down, or flat?

EMPLOYER CONTRIBUTION RATE

Similar to the employee contribution rate, the employer contribution rate is measured as a percentage of aggregate participant compensation. Include all employer contributions, whether they are matching or universal (such as a profit-sharing contribution). And where the sponsor pays investment management fees, that, too, is in effect a sponsor contribution.

All the same logic applies to these contributions as to employee contributions; the greater the contributions, the greater the wealth potential. There are regulatory limits and affordability constraints that influence the employer's contribution rate.

MATCH MAXIMIZATION

This applies only to plans that have an employer matching contribution. The match maximization metric is the percentage of employees who contribute enough to the plan to receive the maximum employer matching contribution.

A matching contribution is basically free money to the participant. Sometimes the match is dollar-for-dollar, meaning that for every dollar the employee contributes to the plan the employer will contribute a dollar. In other cases, the match is a lower percentage of the employee's contribution; for example, the employer will contribute an amount equal to 50 percent of the employee's contribution. Most employer matching contributions have a ceiling. The most popular matching formula in America seems to be a 50 percent match of the first 6 percent of salary contributed by the employee, meaning that if the participant contributes 6 percent of salary, then the employer will contribute 3 percent of salary.

A 2006 study by Hewitt Associates covering over 1.3 million U.S. DC participants revealed that 21.8 percent of the participants in the study were not contributing enough to receive the maximum employer matching contribution.[3] Converting this result to our match maximization metric would put the industry at 78 percent. It is really hard to argue why this metric should be less than somewhere in the high 90 percent range.

How to raise the score? One way is to set the automatic enrollment contribution rate to a level that receives the maximum match. Education is again a fallback. We have to believe that education can be an effective tactic to raise this metric. Simple posters placed in commonly visited work areas with big bold print that say "Want Free Money?," and then a brief description of how to get the maximum employer match, should have some impact.

This assumes that you want all participants to receive the maximum employer match. We have heard from some plan sponsors that they are most interested in helping employees who are helping themselves (by contributing their own money to the plan), so these plan sponsors are not particularly concerned by those who are not maximizing the match. In addition, some employers may have budget constraints that would cause them to lower their match formula if everyone received the maximum. These are certainly practical considerations. But whether your goal is 100 percent of employees to match at the maximum or something less than that, it is still worth tracking the actual number who do.

PARTICIPANT NET INVESTMENT RETURN

Most plan sponsors measure investment returns on a fund-by-fund basis. When a fund is not performing well, they may take action such as putting the fund on a watch list or eventually replacing it if poor performance persists. What isn't tracked as often is participant-level investment performance. A plan may have the best funds available, but if participants use these funds inappropriately, their individual account investment performance could be poor. This is why a metric should be put in place to measure the net investment performance of the participant's accounts.[4] We say net because that is what matters, the net return the account experiences after fees are taken into consideration.

Participant net investment returns should be measured by age cohort. We explained in Chapter 8 why the risk tolerance of the average participant is related to the distance from retirement, decreasing as retirement approaches, and age is a good proxy for that. (And, in fact, in most plans the actual risk profile follows this pattern.) Measuring the average performance across all participants destroys the notion of a changing risk profile, and allows demographic changes over time to confuse the interpretation of the metric.

An age-appropriate benchmark could be related to the asset allocation in your target date approach, passively implemented. It would probably start at 100 percent in a combination of equity indices for the young, moving gradually (probably in 5-year or 10-year age ranges) to something that has more in fixed-income indices than in equity indices. While we see no sign yet of benchmarks accepted by the DC community for comparing and evaluating target date allocations, they may develop in time, in which case performance relative to industry standard benchmarks would also be useful.

This set of metrics then shows how your participants' accounts performed against an age-appropriate benchmark, unaffected by the fact that when equity markets are up, younger participants will tend to outperform older participants. These performance measures should be looked at for various time periods: 1, 5, and 10 years, for instance.

What should you do if these metrics show that your plan is falling behind? You probably need to dig a little deeper. Here are some secondary metrics that you can look at, for clues to what might be causing low performance:

- Percent of participants invested in asset-allocated types of investments (such as target date, target risk, balanced funds, and managed accounts): A low number may be a sign that this is what lies behind the performance problem. A high percentage is good.
- Percent of plan assets in asset-allocated types of investments: A high percentage is good.
- Percent of monthly cash flow being invested in asset-allocated types of investment: A high percentage is good.
- Percent of participants investing 100 percent of their account in (or percent of monthly cash flow going into) a single asset-allocated fund: A high number is good.
- Number of investment changes per participant in a single year (excluding rebalancing transactions): A low number is good.
- Fund-level investment returns (each fund should have its own benchmark): A return above the appropriate benchmark is good.
- Fund management fees: Fees lower than the fees of like alternatives are good.

A look at these metrics will usually identify what is going wrong, if something is. And you will recognize that our observations on whether high or low numbers are good are based on behavioral evidence on ways in which participants' own inexpertise tends to hurt them.

At this point, we should say a little more about fees. A plan can have investment-related fees and non-investment-related fees. All fees should be reviewed on a regular basis to make sure the plan (and each participant) is getting reasonable value for the fee being paid. The more commodity-like the aspect that you are paying for, the more focus you should put on paying the lowest possible fee. However, when it comes to aspects that are less commodity-like, where there are meaningful qualitative differences between the available choices, fees should be only a part of the evaluation process.

We have deliberately avoided listing fees as a metric in their own right. That is because, as we described in Chapter 9, it is often worth paying more for better (whether better investment, better record keeping, whatever). So the bottom line that you should look to is the net-of-fees performance. If you focus too much on fees as a goal in and of themselves, you may make decisions that are ultimately harmful. Think of fees as the defense on a basketball team—the fewer points you concede, the more likely you are to win. But if you make the reduction of points conceded your sole objective, you may build a team with no offense and lose every game. So the management of fees in a DC plan—like defense in basketball—is part of the way to succeed, but not an objective for its own sake. That said, among the attribution elements we have just listed, fees do have a special place, and it unquestionably makes sense to track them as part of the attribution of performance.

HARDSHIP WITHDRAWAL USAGE

This is the percent of assets leaving the plan each year in the form of hardship distributions. Ideally, this percentage would be zero. For the sake of context, Vanguard reported in April 2008 that hardship distributions from its 401(k) plans were running at a low rate, although rising over the two most recent years: Roughly 1.5 percent of accounts recorded a hardship withdrawal in 2007, and the total dollar amount of all withdrawals (average size: a little higher than $6,000) represented about one tenth of 1 percent of total record-keeping assets.[5] Other institutions also report an increase in hardship withdrawals in 2008, despite the 10 percent tax penalty that participants have to pay: 14 percent up on the previous year in the first eight months of 2008, according to T. Rowe Price Group, 7 percent according to Fidelity Investments.[6] Not that point-in-time statistics are important, but these figures show that in a time of serious economic downturn, some participants have higher priorities than saving for retirement.

It has been suggested that the availability of hardship withdrawals (and loans) in a 401(k) plan increases participation. But as plans move more toward an automatic environment, we suspect that this may cease to be true. It is certainly worth periodically reviewing the benefits and the cost of these features.

One way to reduce hardship distributions is to ensure that the process for validating hardship conditions is followed before the distribution is allowed. In addition, you may want to require a plan participant to meet with a financial counselor prior to allowing a hardship distribution. The purpose of this meeting would be to help the participant think through other financial options prior to taking the distribution: There may be other ways to meet the need, or to reduce the size of the necessary distribution. The real benefit of this process may simply be that participants are aware that you are paying attention to the hardships and are going to remain vigilant in holding people to a firm standard for hardship approval. That alone may reduce the number of hardship applications.

LOANS AS DISTRIBUTIONS

Plan loans also have the potential to be a serious form of leakage from the plan. When loans are taken and paid back in full, they have the potential to represent secondary leakage, in that over the long term loan interest rates tend to be lower than the forsaken investment returns. But our focus here is on loans that are not paid back and are taken as a distribution on termination of service (or payment default). We have not been able to find data on loans taken as a distribution. As a data point regarding loans themselves, the federal Thrift Savings Plan reported that, as of May 2008, among their 3.9 million participants, they had a total of 762,860 outstanding loans. The average size was a little higher than $8,000, and loans represented less than 3 percent of total plan assets.[7] As with hardship withdrawals, the use of the loan facility increases in times of economic stress. For example, T. Rowe Price Group reports an 11 percent increase in aggregate loans in each of 2006 and 2007, for the 1.6 million participants in its plans, with a further increase of 7 percent in the first two months of 2008, compared with the same months in 2007.[8]

The metric expresses loans taken as a distribution in terms of a percentage of plan assets. From the perspective of maximizing retirement wealth accumulation, ideally this number should be zero each year. Ways to improve on this metric mirror those mentioned in the hardship withdrawal section: Adhere to stated plan procedures for approval and consider requiring a financial consultation prior to application approval.

EARLY WITHDRAWALS

The early withdrawals category covers withdrawals from the plan prior to retirement age or termination of service. This primarily involves participants who are still working but are over age $59\frac{1}{2}$ and choose to take some or all of their money out of the plan. This could also involve participants over age 55 who are taking what regulations call "substantially equal installment payments" from the plan.

This metric is measured by the percentage of plan assets leaving each year in the form of early withdrawals. It is a useful metric because one of the factors that affects the sustainability of a decumulation program is the length of retirement. While we can't do much to control when our retirement ends, we can affect when it begins. Taking a distribution from a DC plan, even a partial withdrawal, constitutes a beginning of this decumulation period. So you want to be sure that participants do not begin withdrawing from their plans before they need to. That means making sure they understand decumulation sustainability and how it is affected by early retirement.

CONCLUSION

Sponsors, whether of DB or DC plans, typically take great pains in designing their governance processes to evaluate suppliers of service. They rarely judge the efficacy of their own decisions in the same way. But that is just as useful. The idea is not the negative one of searching hard for ways in which you fall short of perfection. It is the positive one of monitoring what is going on and seeing where you can become even more effective. The governance cycle consists of planning, then doing, and finally reviewing; and the purpose of the review is to understand things better, so that the next cycle will be more effective. These nine metrics, we think, make up a sensible set for determining your plan's effectiveness at maximizing retirement wealth accumulation.

CHAPTER 21

The Defined Contribution Plan Sponsor's Role in Decumulation

In most countries, defined contribution (DC) plan sponsors have no fiduciary responsibility to provide their participants with assistance in the decumulation phase of their retirement (beyond the basic fiduciary responsibilities they have to all participants, retired or not).[1] However, as we learned in Chapter 4, 60 percent of the benefits paid out of a typical DC account could, if the benefit is taken in the form of a life income, come from investment earnings after retirement. So the risk to participants' wealth from financial mismanagement after retirement is real. What a waste for a plan sponsor to devote time, money, and energy to building a strong program for the working years of their employees, only to see the benefit that might have been achieved squandered through neglecting the postretirement years.

We have seen how many of the steps that can be—and are being—taken to improve the accumulation phase are steps that lean on the sponsor, and reduce the burden placed on the participants. If the system continues to regard the participants as being on their own for the decumulation phase, the principles behind those solutions cannot be applied also to that critical phase, and we will not end up with the better system that this book is devoted to.

In addition, even though there may be no fiduciary responsibility, there are business considerations that make it worthwhile for a sponsor to consider assisting retired employees. They may be off the payroll, but retirees often stay in touch with their former colleagues and form part of the same community. Current employees can see whether the retirement plan served their friends well or poorly, and that observation helps to create the sponsor's reputation in the community. Some employers will respond to this incentive to enhance their reputation and give themselves an advantage in recruiting and keeping good workers.

It's not so much whether to help in the decumulation years, then, as how to help, that becomes the issue. That's the subject of this chapter. There are two forms of assistance. One is education, the other is providing access to financial products.

PROVIDING EDUCATION

Under the Employee Retirement Income Security Act of 1974 (ERISA), fiduciaries have a duty to prudently select and monitor the providers of education, and if plan sponsors provide the education themselves, they have a duty to provide it prudently. The person or entity providing education does not become a fiduciary merely by providing education (although they may be a fiduciary for other reasons). In the United States, there is a distinction drawn between education and advice. Advice incurs a fiduciary responsibility. While advice can start with education, the dividing line is that education opens doors to new thinking but does not recommend a particular door as the most appropriate one to open.

The size of the employer, and the extent of the desire to educate, will determine the time and resources devoted to this effort. The possibilities range from educational pamphlets written and distributed by providers of financial products, through internal programs and seminars, to subsidized access to external financial planners.

The ideal time to start educating employees is of course before they retire; and not just before they retire, but long before they do so, because their savings program is what makes retirement financially feasible. The financial aspect of retirement is only one aspect, arguably not as important as the psychological aspect. But getting the financial side right certainly helps enormously to make the retirement years happy ones.

We have mentioned elsewhere in the book the topics that financial (as contrasted with investment) education should cover. Financial literacy starts with budgeting, making choices, affordability—and those are every bit as important after retirement as they are during a worker's career. We have described extensively the interaction in the decumulation years across spending, investing, and length (and uncertainty) of life span. Those are added topics that workers should learn about before they retire.

Customization is always nice, but typically expensive. This holds for financial education, too. We leave it to financial planners to give customized advice. For more general workforce education, simplicity gives a concept its best chance of being understood and acted upon. Yes, there is always the danger of oversimplification. But, occasionally, there are concepts that aren't dangerously oversimplified, yet help to fix ideas in the mind.

One we have found appealing, for example, is the notion of the $20 bill. As we explained in the chapter on sustainable spending rates, withdrawal rates not exceeding 5 percent of one's assets each year have a good chance of lasting a lifetime. It is easy to grasp the idea that for every $20 bill that their assets represent, retirees can take $1 a year for the rest of their lives and have a good chance of not outliving their savings. Yes, that depends on assumptions and (even more) on actual investment choices and experiences; and the $20 bill probably becomes a $25 bill if the withdrawal is to have a really high chance of success. The point we are making is that the rule of the $20 bill is easy to understand and remember, and not too far (in most cases) from being useful; and a retiree who remembers this rule will have a better chance of adopting a sensible withdrawal rate in the retirement years.

PROVIDING ACCESS TO FINANCIAL PRODUCTS: IN-PLAN OR OUT-OF-PLAN

A sponsor that provides access to financial products within a DC plan takes the usual fiduciary responsibility for the selection and oversight of the products that are offered. We covered that in the chapter on DC plan governance. Any financial product has some chance that it will provide a disappointing outcome. It is not the fiduciary's job to ensure that no outcome ever disappoints; that would be impossible. But a standard way to reduce the probability of this happening is to diversify across products. This reduces the impact of a disappointing outcome from any one product.

In the decumulation phase, as we have seen, longevity risk becomes a potentially very important factor—a risk that is absent in the accumulation phase. Therefore, most fiduciaries, focused only on accumulation principles, do not have to consider it, and most have probably never done so. It brings a new dimension to the expertise required of a fiduciary. For example, it is no longer unthinkable that an insurance company offering a lifetime annuity might expire before an annuitant does. Reducing the impact of this risk by diversifying across annuity providers is a very modern approach, not one that would have been considered necessary a generation ago.

Similarly, the new generation of decumulation-oriented financial products, some of which underwrite longevity while others don't, creates a new field of required expertise.

Being so new, all of these things give fiduciaries less confidence in the way they will deal with them than the tried-and-tested field of accumulation products. And therefore the fiduciary's understandable first instinct is to avoid bringing these products into the ambit of their fiduciary responsibility.

That means that, for the near future, until experience builds up, any assistance to prospective retirees as regards financial products in decumulation is more likely to take place outside the DC plan (an "out-of-plan" solution) rather than via an in-plan solution.

Outside the plan, the sponsor can learn about financial products, decide that some merit consideration for the average worker, educate (but not advise) workers about those products, and arrange for a fee basis that reflects the employer's bulk purchasing power rather than the individual's nonexistent purchasing power.

Our discussion now considers design features that the sponsor can arrange and product features that the sponsor can look for.

DESIGN FEATURES

We identify six ideal features that a sponsor can try to incorporate into the design of an arrangement that helps retired employees to decumulate successfully. We are under no illusions that these are all achievable today.

1. *Optional.* It almost goes without saying that participation in the arrangement should be optional. Participants should not be forced or defaulted into it. This is consistent with our belief that postretirement plans should be customized. For example, not all retirees need longevity guarantees, even if some do and even if the risk averse want them; to force every participant to have some longevity guarantee would be to force risk aversion on them unnecessarily. This is similar to saying that not everyone should be forced or defaulted into a money market fund, even if it is suitable for some and particularly for the risk averse.

2. *Multiple carriers.* If there are longevity guarantees, counterparty risk can be reduced by having multiple insurance companies to underwrite each participant's longevity. (This is similar to using a multimanager investment structure to reduce the impact of one manager performing poorly.) At the time of writing we are not aware of any arrangements with this feature, but we do know of at least one insurance company that has contemplated this type of product structure.

3. *Potential replacement of product providers.* Just as investment arrangements permit the replacement of one manager with another, ideally, a longevity arrangement would also permit the replacement of one carrier with another. Negotiating in advance the terms of the disengagement will be difficult, and for an insurer to accept this possibility is itself bound to lead to a price premium to cover its own risk.

4. *Portability.* If the participant wants to move the arrangement into his or her individual account, that should be possible. Again, this is the equivalent of moving a DC plan balance into an individual retirement account. And again, it is reasonable to expect product fees to rise when converted from a group arrangement to an individual arrangement.

5. *Group fees.* Underlying our comments about fees increasing to accommodate certain features is the notion that the sponsor can negotiate group fees that are lower than the retail fees that individuals would have to pay on their own.

6. *Fee transparency and reasonableness.* Whether or not group fees are charged, there is a separate aspect that deserves mention. In keeping with the long-term trend toward greater transparency of fees in American DC plans (fueled by multiple sources from lawmakers through consultants to plan sponsors and participants, and well documented by the media), distribution products with bundled features (such as investment management and guaranteed withdrawal) should be held to the same standard of fee disclosure. Plan sponsors need enough information to understand not only the total fees embedded in these products but the cost of each of the features. As an example, within a guaranteed withdrawal product, sponsors should know what is being charged for asset management separate from the withdrawal guarantee charge; and if separate entities are providing these features, whether one entity is subsidizing the others. And when we mention reasonableness as a desirable feature, it is only with complete transparency that reasonableness can be determined.

PRODUCT FEATURES

Though we discussed products and their features and uses in Chapters 17 and 18, and we are firm believers in customization of postretirement arrangements, we identify here four features that may appeal to many retirees, particularly those without financial advisers.

1. *Dynamic asset allocation.* Just as plans change when circumstances change, it makes sense for the risk exposure represented by an individual's asset allocation to change when investment circumstances change. These changes are not tactical changes predicated on a manager's forecast of future market movements; they are strategic changes meant as a reaction to past market movements, predicated on the ability of participants to take higher risk after a series of good returns and to want risk reduction after market downturns.

2. *Defensible fund management arrangements.* Either passive management or multimanager active management would be easier to defend than arrangements under which an asset class is actively managed by one manager. This is exactly parallel to the accumulation phase.
3. *Longevity insurance.* For those who want longevity guarantees, offer a guaranteed minimum withdrawal benefits (GMWB) or advanced life deferred annuity (ALDA) product (see Chapter 18).
4. *Multiple choices of longevity guarantee.* Those who want longevity guarantees should be able to select either single-life or joint-and-survivor arrangements.

SIMPLICITY

We are very conscious of the fact that even listing a few features of desirable postretirement arrangements and of products can result in a search for a single product that ends up too complex or expensive to be practical in the real world. The marketplace will no doubt go through a period of trial and error to determine the combination of functions, features, and prices that meets the needs of the stakeholders. So we emphasize that there is one feature that we believe must be present in a successful distribution product: simplicity. The product must be simple to understand, simple to buy, simple to own, and simple to explain. If there is one thing we have learned through our decades of DC experience, it is that complexity creates anxiety and anxiety causes suboptimal behavior. If the products chosen by the sponsor are too complex, they stand less of a chance of catching on and being adopted by the mass of retiring employees.

PARTING THOUGHT

And there we end our tale. Perhaps simplicity and clear thinking are appropriate ways to sum up our message. DC has taken over from DB as a pillar of the system for funding postretirement income. It can fulfill its promise if it is made more efficient in the accumulation stage, if its output is focused more on lifetime income than on lump sums, and if the interaction of spending, longevity protection, and investing are better understood in the decumulation phase. There is no unique best way to do all of this; there are many ways. We hope that you, the reader, will do whatever you can to make it happen.

Notes

Preface

1. According to Financial Research Corporation's *Lifecycle Funds Quarterly Report,* First Quarter 2008, Fidelity, Vanguard, and T. Rowe Price owned the three largest market shares of target date mutual funds in the United States.
2. For the 12-month period ending December 31, 2008, the Russell Global Index showed a return of −42.79% (in U.S. dollars).
3. Bob Collie and Don Ezra, *Resist the Amygdala!* (Russell Investment Group, March 2007). Also Jason Zweig, *Your Money and Your Brain* (New York: Simon & Schuster, 2007).

INTRODUCTION   The Great American Retirement System?

1. But not in a collective DC plan, as we will explain in Chapter 14.
2. See note 1.

CHAPTER 1   DC Version 2.0

1. This chapter is based on Bob Collie, "401(k)s: The Launch of Version 2.0." *Russell Retirement Report 2008* (Russell Investments, 2007).
2. Or 401(a), 403(b), 457, and so on—but we refer to them collectively as DC or 401(k), for simplicity.
3. Department of Labor, Cerulli Associates, reported in Cerulli Quantitative Update: Retirement Markets 2006. We talk of version 2.0 of 401(k)s, but 401(k)s were themselves, in a sense, V2.0 of DC provision. Profit-sharing plans and money-purchase plans did not prove as popular as 401(k)s among corporations moving from DB to DC. These plans still exist, but according to the same study they represent less than 15 percent of total DC assets.
4. Investment Company Institute, Investment Company Fact Book, 48th ed. (2008).
5. Not that policy makers saw the wisdom of the changes instantly and by themselves. For example, McDonald's Corporation used auto-enrollment years

before PPA and even before Treasury guidance saying it was acceptable. Alicia Munnell (see note 7) and others proposed many of the changes we call DC Version 2.0 before PPA, and certainly influenced the legislation.

6. Nancy Webman, "Dawning of the DC Plan Age." pionline.com (October 2, 2006). We observe that some in Washington still do not accept it; but virtually everyone acknowledges it, even if reluctantly.

7. Alicia Munnell and Annika Sunden, *Coming Up Short: The Challenge of 401(k) Plans* (Washington, DC: Brookings Institution, 2004).

8. Alicia Munnell and Annika Sunden, "401(k) Plans Are Still Coming Up Short." (Center for Retirement Research at Boston College, 2006).

9. For more details of the impact of Enron's collapse on the retirement plans of its employees, see, for example, Christine Dugas, "Energy Giant's Disaster Devastates 401(k) Plans." *USA Today*, November 30, 2001.

10. Ted Benna, *The Day I Designed the First 401(k) Savings Plan*. At malvern401(k).net. Benna was not the only one wanting to make use of section 401(k)'s provisions at that time. See Herbert A. Whitehouse, "Toward a More Complete History: Johnson & Johnson's 401(k) Nursery." *EBRI Notes* 24(12), 2003, in which Whitehouse mentions several companies independently working to use section 401(k) after it was introduced in 1978, but before proposed regulations were issued in 1981.

11. The language we refer to is the common use of these terms. But ERISA's language has always been inclusive: "pension" accommodates both DB and DC, in ERISA.

12. Ruth Helman, Jack VanDerhei, and Craig Copeland, *The 2008 Retirement Confidence Survey* (Employee Benefit Research Institute: Issue Brief No. 316, 2008).

CHAPTER 2   More than You Ever Wanted to Know about Life Expectancy

1. National Vital Statistics Reports, 51(3): Table 11. Department of Health and Human Services, December 19, 2002.

2. Further subdivisions are possible. For example, by health (those currently in good health are expected to live longer, on average, than those in poor health); by region; by race; by habit (such as smoking, as anyone knows who has purchased life insurance; insurance companies ask about habits that they know affect life expectancy); and in many other ways.

3. We have since done the same exercise with larger groups, with similar findings. People don't know how uncertain a future life span is.

4. Why did we switch suddenly from the census-based population longevity table? Because the IRS table is probably more appropriate for the working population, in two ways. One is that the working population tends to display slightly greater longevity than the population as a whole. Another is that the IRS table contains projections of improvements in longevity, which is also appropriate. Someone who is 60 today will, on reaching 80, experience longevity that will probably be

higher than today's 80-year-old will experience. But a population table doesn't contain this projection. It's based on deaths of 80-year-olds around the time the census was taken, not the probably lower rate of mortality that 80-year-olds will face in 20 years.

5. The Society of Actuaries (the professional body for the American actuarial profession) publishes what it calls 1996 U.S. Annuity 2000 Male & Female Tables, appropriate for those buying lifetime income annuities. These tables use even longer life spans. According to them, a male/female couple aged 65 has a 50 percent chance that one of the couple will survive past age 92.

6. DB plans used to take away the problem of uncertain longevity, as far as the individual member was concerned, in the same way that insurance companies do when they sell lifetime annuities: by pooling all the people and funding for a little more than the average life expectancy of the group. More on this pooling mechanism in Chapter 16.

7. Bryan Appleyard, *How to Live Forever or Die Trying* (New York: Simon & Schuster, 2007).

CHAPTER 3   Retirement Is Expensive

1. According to Hewitt Associates ("Trends and Experience in 401(k) Plans in 2007," Hewitt Associates, 2007), for those who participate in such plans the average pretax contribution is 6.9 percent of earnings, say 7 percent. With the most common employer match formula being a 50 percent match up to the first 6 percent of earnings contributed, that implies an employer 3 percent contribution and a total 10 percent contribution. Of course, this is an oversimplification of an extremely complex set of numbers. In Vanguard, "How America Saves 2008: A Report on Vanguard 2007 Defined Contribution Plan Data," The Vanguard Group, Inc., 2008, the median contributions are 6 percent from participants and 3 percent from employers.

2. Aon Consulting. 2008 Replacement Ratio Study™, www.aon.com/retire.

3. As pay increases the overall required ratio rises, to 88 percent when current pay is $250,000; and Social Security replaces much less.

4. It is not only volatile investment returns that cause funding volatility, of course. The plethora of maxima and minima in U.S. funding regulations play as large a part.

5. Where do these numbers come from? We assume 3 percent annual inflation, so that the annual pay increase is 1.75 percent after inflation. We assume a safe long-term fixed income return of inflation plus 2.5 percent (from Treasury Inflation Protected Securities, for example), and an equity risk premium of a further 4 percent beyond that, implying a long-term average annual equity return of inflation plus 6.5 percent. The traditional asset allocation of 60 percent equities and 40 percent fixed-income then implies an average annual return of 4.9 percent above inflation, or 7.9 percent in absolute terms. Allow for some investment expenses, and we use 7.5 percent. But this assumption is so important

that we need to test what happens if we use different numbers—and we'll do that later in this chapter and the next.

6. Not all of the 12.4 percent is for retirement. A small portion is for survivor and disability benefits.

7. Moreover, for many years the trustees of the U.S. Social Security system have consistently said that the system will not be self-sustaining if it follows the path outlined in the central set of their annual projections.

8. Going back to the earlier issue of integration with Social Security, it is now clear that American workers face two forms of uncertainty. The DC plan exposes them to investment market uncertainty, and that is what this book focuses on. Social Security exposes workers to political uncertainty because they don't know how the system's benefits and contributions will change in the future. An individual still has the same four basic choices to adapt to either form of uncertainty.

9. Incidentally, this does not always work the other way around. Sometimes higher risk does not carry a higher expected return.

CHAPTER 4   Investment Returns Are All-Important

1. D. Don Ezra, "A Model of Pension Fund Growth," Russell Research Commentary. Russell Investments, June 1989; and Keith P. Ambachtsheer and D. Don Ezra, *Pension Fund Excellence* (New York: John Wiley & Sons, 1998).

2. These figures, and subsequent figures, do not necessarily total 100 percent, due to the effects of rounding. It is also worth noting that, in this case, the distributions from the plan are significantly lower than in the base case—the 5 percent return assumption produces retirement income of only 46 percent of that produced by the 7.5 percent base case assumption.

3. The distributions from the plan in this case are 77 percent of those produced by the 7.5 percent base case assumption. An increasingly popular choice of investment strategy is a target date fund, which gradually adopts a more cautious strategy as retirement approaches. This might be modeled by assuming a declining return (e.g., an initial 8 percent return that starts to fall by 0.1 percent a year from age 40 to reach a level of 5.5 percent by age 65). Using this return assumption, the 10/30/60 result turns into 15/36/49.

4. Morningstar. 2008 Ibbotson® SBBI® Classic Yearbook. We are grateful to Shailesh Kshatriya for compiling the data in the form shown in Figures 4.1, 4.2, and 4.3 and Tables 4.2, 4.3, and 4.4.

5. The reason has to do with the ability to deduct a capital loss from one's taxable income. That's why, in those days, some were willing to accept a small negative return before tax.

6. As well as the slim possibility of cash as an asset class delivering a negative return, there is also the possibility of a particular cash investment delivering a negative return, even if the broader asset class does not. It is rare for money market funds to "break the buck," but it has happened on occasion.

CHAPTER 5   Sustainable Spending

1. The authors greatly appreciate the efforts of their Russell Investment colleagues Yuan-An Fan, Richard Fullmer, and Grant Gardner for their work in simulating these results.
2. See note 1.
3. At the time of writing, the authors only know of one company offering this type of product, which is Vanguard.
4. The actual calculation is a little more complicated, but this is close enough for a first approximation, which is all that this appendix tries to achieve.
5. See, for example, Jeffrey R. Brown, Olivia S. Mitchell, and James M. Poterba, "The Role of Real Annuities and Indexed Bonds in an Individual Accounts Retirement Program," Working Paper 99-18. The Wharton Financial Institutions Center, 1999.

CHAPTER 6   Save More

1. Government Accountability Office. "Private Pensions: Low Defined Contribution Plan Savings May Pose Challenges to Retirement Security, Especially for Many Low-Income Workers," 2008.
2. And that is only the tip of the iceberg. The American Benefits Council on June 26, 2008, made available to its members a chart created by Davis & Harman LLP comparing features of ten different proposals to expand retirement savings coverage via DC-type arrangements.
3. This is the brainchild of J. Mark Ivry and David C. John, "Pursuing Universal Retirement Security through Automatic IRAs." The Retirement Security Project, www.retirementsecurityproject.org.
4. But, as we shall also see, Australia mandates coverage.
5. In Vanguard's database of 1,800 plan sponsors and 3,000,000 participants, the average participation rate across plans was 75 percent in 2007. Participation rates were generally lower in large plans; considering all employees in Vanguard-administered plans as if they were in a single plan, the 2007 participation rate falls to 66 percent. Both of these measures are basically unchanged since 2000. From "How America Saves 2008" (Valley Forge, PA: The Vanguard Group, Inc.).
6. James J. Choi, David Laibson, Brigitte C. Madrian, and Andrew Metrick, "Defined Contribution Pensions: Plan Rules, Participant Decisions, and the Path of Least Resistance." *Tax Policy and the Economy* 16. MIT Press, 2001. Revised in 2004 to include additional data and analysis.
7. Sarah Holden and Jack VanDerhei, "The Influence of Automatic Enrollment, Catch-up and IRA Contributions on 401(k) Accumulations at Retirement," EBRI Issue Brief No. 283. Employee Benefit Research Institute and Investment Company Institute, July 2005.
8. Franco Modigliani and Richard Brumberg, "Utility Analysis and the Consumption Function," in K. K. Kurihara (Ed.), *Post-Keynesian Economics* (London:

George Allen and Unwin, 1955); and Milton Friedman, *A Theory of the Consumption Function* (Princeton, NJ: Princeton University Press, 1957).

9. "MetLife Retirement Income IQ Study: A Survey of Pre-retirement Knowledge of Financial Retirement Issues," June 2008, www.MatureMarketInstitute.com.

10. But public-sector workers frequently contribute to their DB plans.

11. Many economists would argue that the difference is illusory in that employers pay a total compensation, which is divided between cash wages and other benefits, so that an employee in a defined benefit plan would receive, other things being equal, a lower cash wage than the precontribution wage of an employee in a 401(k) plan. There is certainly an important difference in terms of perception, however.

CHAPTER 7 Limit Leakage

1. Government Accountability Office. "Private Pensions: Low Defined Contribution Plan Savings May Pose Challenges to Retirement Security, Especially for Many Low-Income Workers," 2008.

2. See "Lump Sum Distributions," *EBRI Notes* 26(12) (December 2005).

3. Profit Sharing Council of America, "49th Annual Survey of Profit Sharing and 401(k) Plans Reflecting the 2005 Plan Experience," 2006; and Jack VanDerhei, Sarah Holden, Craig Copeland, and Luis Alonso, "401(k) Plan Asset Allocation, Account Balances, and Loan Activity in 2006," EBRI Issue Brief No. 308, Employee Benefit Research Institute, August 2007. Cited in GAO (2008), see note 1.

CHAPTER 8 Invest Better

1. Hewitt Associates, "Trends and Experience in 401(k) Plans (Hewitt Associates, 2007), p. 16. Fifty-six percent of surveyed plans used a money market or stable value fund as their default investment option. By 2007 this had declined to 17%.

2. John Hancock Financial Services (2002). "Insight into Participant Investment Knowledge and Behavior." Eighth defined contribution plan survey.

3. Greenwich Associates, "United States Investment Management Market Dynamics Report 2006," 2007.

4. Or, at any rate, if they are not experts, they typically seek input from experts. The American pension law, the Employee Retirement Income Security Act of 1974 (ERISA), requires investment fiduciaries not only to be procedurally prudent but also to bring expertise to their decisions.

5. Munnell, A., Soto, M., Libby, J., & Prinzavalli, J. "Investment Returns: Defined Benefit vs. 401(k) Plans": Issue Brief #52. Center for Retirement Studies at Boston College, September 2006.

6. Watson Wyatt Insider, "Defined Benefit vs 401(k) Plans: Investment Returns for 2003–2006," June 2008, www.watsonwyatt.com/us/pubs/insider.

7. Burgess and Associates, study performed for John Hancock, covering 2001–2005, www.johnhancock.com/about/news/news_aug1406.jsp.

8. See, for example, Vanguard, "How America Saves 2008: A Report on Vanguard 2007 Defined Contribution Plan Data," (The Vanguard Group, Inc., 2008), 35.
9. According to Peter Bernstein, Daniel Bernoulli introduced the concept of human capital in the eighteenth century; see Peter L. Bernstein, *Against the Gods* (New York: John Wiley & Sons, 1996). The authors also found useful the description of human and financial capital as it relates to total wealth in Roger G. Ibbotson, Moshe A. Milevsky, Peng Chen, and Kevin X. Zhu, *Lifetime Financial Advice: Human Capital, Asset Allocation, and Insurance* (New York: Research Foundation of CFA Institute, 2007).
10. Actually, there is, and many of us use it. We borrow against our human capital to obtain a mortgage, which we then invest in real estate. That's one way to convert bondlike human capital to equity-like financial capital. But we do this outside the 401(k) plan—indeed, it would be illegal to do it within the plan.
11. That, at any rate, is the principle. In the United States, the qualified default investment alternative (QDIA) regulations require all default options to be diversified, with the result that one does not see 100 percent equity exposure at the highest point of the glide path.
12. Throughout the book, we refer to the very best practices when we speak of fiduciary standards. These often go far beyond the minimum fiduciary standards required by the law. It is therefore quite feasible for fiduciaries not to do the things we mention and still be on the right side of the law. This is, in our experience, an important consideration, particularly with fiduciaries of small plans.
13. Shlomo Benartzi and Richard H. Thaler, "How Much Is Investor Autonomy Worth?," March 2001. AFA 2002 Atlanta Meetings. Available at SSRN: http://ssrn.com/abstract=394857.

CHAPTER 9   Reduce Fees

1. This is an example of what is referred to by some as the agency dilemma and by others as the agent-principal problem: That the incentives of those making the decisions are not necessarily exactly the same as those whom the decisions most affect.
2. Government Accountability Office, "Private Pensions: Changes Needed to Provide 401(k) Plan Participants and the Department of Labor Better Information on Fees," GAO-07-21.
3. This analysis depends on the assumption that the market return—or something very close to it—can be achieved by passive managers. This is not necessarily true in all markets.
4. Other experts disagree with us. One sees the record keepers as having very little pricing power, viewing their record-keeping business as a low-margin business that can feed money into their higher-margin investment and distribution products. The advice resulting from this perspective is for sponsors to recognize that record keepers will make the economics work one way or another, and to go into the relationship with eyes open as they seek to drive down costs.

CHAPTER 10   Why the Waste? Because We're
Only Human

1. Daniel Kahneman, Eugene Higgins, and Mark W. Riepe, "Aspects of Investor Psychology," *Journal of Portfolio Management* 24(4) (1998).
2. Dennis Dittrich, Werner Guth, and Boris Maciejovsky, "Overconfidence in Investment Decisions: An Experimental Approach," CESifo Working Paper Series No. 626, 2001. Available at SSRN: http://ssrn.com/abstract=296246.
3. J. Edward Russo and Paul J. H. Schoemaker, *Decision Traps: Ten Barriers to Brilliant Decision Making and How to Overcome Them* (New York: Simon & Schuster, 1989).
4. Ruth Helman, Jack VanDerhei, and Craig Copeland, *The 2008 Retirement Confidence Survey* (Employee Benefit Research Institute: Issue Brief No. 316, 2008).
5. Theodore S. Geisel, *Oh, the Places You'll Go!* (New York: Random House, 1990).
6. www.nobelprize.org.
7. David Laibson, "Golden Eggs and Hyperbolic Discounting," *Quarterly Journal of Economics*, May 1997.
8. Samuel M. McLure, David I. Laibson, George Leowenstein, and Jonathan D. Cohen, "Separate Neural Systems Value Immediate and Delayed Monetary Rewards," *Science* 306 (October 15, 2004).
9. Cass R. Sunstein and Richard H. Thaler, "Libertarian Paternalism Is Not an Oxymoron," *University of Chicago Law Review* 70(4) (2003).
10. Cerulli Associates, "Quantitative Update, Retirement Markets 2006," Exhibit 1.61.
11. Sheena S. Iyengar and Mark R. Lepper, "When Choice Is Demotivating: Can One Desire Too Much of a Good Thing?" *Journal of Personality and Social Psychology* 79 (2000).
12. Sheena S. Iyengar, Wei Jinag, and Gur Huberman, "How Much Choice Is Too Much? Contributions to 401(k) Retirement Plans." Pension Research Council Working Paper: 2003-10. The Wharton School, University of Pennsylvania, 2003.
13. Now, DB plan decision making is also frequently heuristic driven rather than entirely rational, but that is a different story altogether.
14. Terry Odean, "Do Investors Trade Too Much?" *The American Economic Review*, December 1999.
15. Terry Odean and Brad Barber, "The Courage of Misguided Convictions: The Trading Behavior of Individual Investors," *Financial Analysts Journal*, November/December 1999, pp. 41–55.
16. See, for example, Travis Sapp and Ashish Tiwari, "Stock Return Momentum and Investor Fund Choices," *Journal of Investment Management* 4(3) (3rd quarter 2006); or Morningstar Investor Return Methodology (March 2008).
17. Steven L. Beach and Clarence C. Rose, "Does Portfolio Rebalancing Help Investors Avoid Common Mistakes?" *Journal of Financial Planning*, May 2005.

CHAPTER 11   Financial Education

1. Jeffrey R. Brown, Marcus D. Casey, and Olivia S. Mitchell, "Who Values the Social Security Annuity? New Evidence on the Annuity Puzzle," NBER Working Paper No. 13800, February 2008. Available at SSRN: http://ssrn.com/abstract=1092850.

2. The correct answer to the Lottery Split question is $400,000. Either $240 or $242 would be considered acceptable as the correct response to the Interest question.

3. Organized by AARP and the Securities Industry and Financial Markets Association, New York, NY, on April 4, 2008.

4. Financial Literacy Foundation, "Financial Literacy: Australians Understanding Money," 2007, p. xii.

5. Presentation at the CITI-FT Financial Education Summit, New Delhi, December 2007.

6. *The Economist*, April 5, 2008.

7. These simple examples are taken from Jump$tart's "2007 12 Principles Calendar: 12 Principles that Every Young Person Should Know."

8. Copyright © by The Curators of the University of Missouri. Sponsored by Citi Office of Financial Education, Department of the Treasury, Jump$tart Coalition for Personal Financial Literacy, and University of Missouri–St Louis. Used here with permission.

9. Elizabeth Johnson, "From Financial Literacy to Financial Capability among Youth." *Journal of Sociology and Social Welfare*, September 2007.

10. Ibid.; see note 7.

11. This paragraph is based on Clive R. Belfield and Henry M. Levin, "Should High School Economics Course Be Compulsory?" *Economics of Education Review*, 2004.

12. Quoted in *The Economist*, see note 6. For an elaboration of these views see Richard H. Thaler and Cass R. Sunstein, *Nudge: Improving Decisions about Health, Wealth and Happiness* (New Haven, CT: Yale University Press, 2008).

CHAPTER 12   Case Study—Australia

1. Accurate, consistently reported, and complete numbers are, to the best of our knowledge, impossible to get. No single source gave us what we were looking for. The Organisation for Economic Co-operation and Development (OECD) publishes aggregate assets in funded pension arrangements, in absolute amounts and as a proportion of GDP, in "Pension Markets in Focus" (© 2007, November 2007, Issue 4), but in private correspondence we learned that the amounts for DC (exclusive of insured or book reserve or individual retirement account [IRA]-type) arrangements are only available for nine countries (and Australia is not among them). So we applied the DC proportions of total pension assets reported in Watson Wyatt's 2008 Global Pension Asset

Survey (available at watsonwyatt.com). We did not use Watson Wyatt as the source for all data because their reported assets for the United States included IRAs. As far as the OECD numbers themselves are concerned, they seem very low for Australia when compared, for example, with those reported by the Australian Prudential Regulation Authority (APRA). APRA reports total super assets of A$918 billion at June 30, 2006, equivalent to US$677 at that time, so that Australian DC assets would have been close to US$600 billion. With its rapid growth, Australia has by now probably overtaken the UK into second place in absolute terms, and extended its lead over second place as a proportion of GDP. Also, the OECD's figure for U.S. DC assets seems high, and we think it may include IRA assets. For comparison, the Federal Reserve Board's *Flow of Funds Accounts of the United States* reports $3,321 billion in private trusteed DC assets in 2006. Using this instead of $5,444 billion gives a figure of 25 percent for the United States' DC assets as a proportion of GDP.

2. We are grateful to our colleague Steven Schubert for making available to us a wealth of information and insight, including extracts from an unpublished paper he prepared for his students in a postgraduate course in Melbourne, Australia, and a presentation entitled "The Age of Partnership: Lessons from Around the World" prepared for Russell's global clients in 2008. Unless otherwise identified, Australian statistics quoted come from APRA.

3. The effective tax rate on investment returns is typically lower than 15 percent, particularly for equities. Realized capital gains are generally taxed at 10 percent. And dividends received from companies are deemed to have already been taxed at the corporation tax rate of 30 percent, so these dividends actually generate a tax refund in order to get to the stated 15 percent super fund tax rate.

4. But the social security safety net isn't available until age 65.

5. This also has a counterpart in the United States, where "designated Roth contributions" can be made (subject to much lower ceilings) from after-tax pay, and the proceeds of the separately tracked "designated Roth account" emerge tax free under conditions defining "qualified distributions," one of which is the attainment of age $59\frac{1}{2}$.

6. See note 4.

7. In another change, money can now be left in super indefinitely. But in that case, investment earnings continue to be taxed at 15 percent.

8. And, of course, who should pay for any increase.

9. Roughly half of Australian DC accounts are in retail funds, but those participants typically have an investment adviser, so they have access to expertise.

10. Do-it-yourself funds by their nature don't have a default option. They also have a wide dispersion of asset allocations, with the average having some very unusual characteristics: 57 percent in equities (but less than 1 percent overseas); a very high 22 percent in cash; 11 percent in real estate; less than 1 percent in bonds; and 10 percent in other assets.

11. We have been told that the main reason is probably that, having achieved the benefit of moving from stable value to target risk, the benefit

of a further move to target date is not as substantial or obvious to Australians.

CHAPTER 14   Collective Defined Contribution

1. Most Canadian DC plans follow the traditional route of using individual accounts for each participant. Collective DC is used only in multiemployer plans; some commentators call them "target benefit" plans.
2. In the United States, these plans are known as Taft-Hartley plans, named for the 1947 Act from which they originate. Advocates of these plans point to DC contributions, DB benefits (as long as a prudent margin is preserved), and low cost. They have argued that such plans could have a broader participation base, becoming omnibus pension systems across multiple unions that would compete broadly for employer participation, generating greater scale and even lower costs.
3. Incidentally, the Dutch seem very keen on longevity protection. Even their individual DC plans typically result in an annuity purchased at retirement.
4. We emphasize *individual* longevity protection, because the plan attempts to pay postretirement income for as long as its members live. But if the plan as a whole experiences far greater longevity than the actuary projects, this protection may require increased contributions or benefit reductions. This could be a particular problem for a plan in a declining industry, with retirees greatly outnumbering active members.
5. But they do need to understand the nature of the "promise" underlying the benefit level in their collective DC plan, and how it is different from the promise in a DB plan. That requires a different form of education.
6. Justin Fox, "Where Retirement Works," June 14, 2007. Available at www.time.com/printout/0,8816,1633069,00.html.
7. Thao Hua, "DC Conversions Have a Dutch Flavor," April 3, 2006. Available at www.pionline.com/apps/pbcs.dll/article?AID=/20060403/PRINTSUB/604030713/1031/TOC.
8. "Collective DC: Arcadis Pension Fund," published September 26, 2006. Available at www/epn-magazine.com/news/printpage.php/aid/1737/Collective_DC_Arcadis_pension_fund.html.
9. www.pensionrights.org/policy/international_pensions/netherlands_dc_plan.html.
10. The Dutch do not recognize collective DC as a third type of plan, as far as regulation is concerned. A plan is either DB or DC, for them. When the initial benefit is guaranteed, the plan is classified as DB, even though indexation remains conditional on having sufficient assets. When the contribution is fixed, the plan is DC, even though the benefit formula mimics DB—what we've called *collective DC* in this chapter.
11. Keith P. Ambachtsheer and D. Don Ezra, *Pension Fund Excellence* (New York: John Wiley & Sons, 1998).
12. Reported April 1, 2008, by CBC News. Available at www/cbc.ca/canada/toronto/story/2008/04/01/teachers-plan.html?ref=rss&loomia_si=t0:a3:g4:r5:c0.

CHAPTER 15   The First Dial: Your Personal Spending Policy

1. It's also an essential start for making a will. One thing that one of the authors learned many years ago about a will from his father-in-law, who was in the insurance business, is that everybody already has a will. A will is a document that says what will happen to your estate after you're gone. The law says what will happen, if you haven't written your own document. So think of the law as the will you're saddled with by default. That means everybody has a will—it just may be that someone else wrote it for you.
2. Bureau of Labor Statistics, Consumer Expediture Survey, 2006.
3. George Kinder, *The Seven Stages of Money Maturity* (New York: Dell Publishing, 2000).
4. Paul Fronstin, Dallas L. Sallisbury, and Jack VanDerhei, "Savings Needed to Fund Health Insurance and Health Care Expenses in Retirement: Findings from a Simulation Model," Employee Benefit Research Institute, Issue Brief No. 317, May 2008.
5. Donald R. Hoover, Stephen Crystal, Rizie Kumar, Usha Sambamoorthi, and Joel Cantor, "Medical Expenditures during the Last Year of Life: Findings from the 1992–1996 Medicare Current Beneficiary Survey," *Health Services Research* 37(6) (2002), 1625–1642.
6. Jane Li, Robert Del Col, Lisa Burns, and Jim Graves, "A Process-Centered Approach to Retirement Income," FundQuest Incorporated, 2007.
7. We ignore the fact that Social Security is unsustainable, in the sense that government projections show that its terms will have to be changed in some way for its benefits and its financing to be brought into balance over the long term.
8. Ruth Helman, Jack VanDerhei, and Craig Copeland, *The 2007 Retirement Confidence Survey*. Employee Benefit Research Institute: Issue Brief No. 304, 2007.
9. Ibid.
10. Ruth Helman, Jack VanDerhei, and Craig Copeland, *The 2008 Retirement Confidence Survey*. Employee Benefit Research Institute: Issue Brief No. 316, 2008.
11. McKinsey & Company (2006). "Cracking the Consumer Retirement Code."
12. Ibid.
13. See note 10. No doubt some had multiple reasons, accounting for the total exceeding 100 percent.

CHAPTER 16   The Second Dial: Your Longevity Protection Policy

1. In order to protect their solvency, insurance companies almost invariably invest the assets backing their annuity liabilities into fixed-income investments designed to generate cash flows exactly in line with the expected payments they will need to make—a so-called matched investment policy. This greatly reduces the risk that disappointing investment returns could leave them unable to meet their liabilities.

2. All 50 states, the District of Columbia, and Puerto Rico have life and health guaranty associations that provide some protection against insurer insolvency. For more information on this topic, we suggest visiting www.nolhga.com or www.naic.org.

3. Here's another way to think of the value of longevity protection. If he lives 40 years and draws his annuity for 40 years after paying only $12.04, the realized annualized internal rate of return on his transaction is 7.91 percent rather than the 6 percent on which the 22-year purchase price is based. This means that survival for two additional standard deviations generates an additional annual return of 1.91 percent for him; and if you believe that the equity premium is worth roughly 3 percent per annum, the annuity pays the long-lived annuity purchaser the equivalent of a 64 percent exposure to equities, without the volatility.

4. Jeffrey R. Brown, Olivia S. Mitchell, James M. Poterba, and Mark J. Warshawsky, *The Role of Annuity Markets in Financing Retirement* (Cambridge, MA: MIT Press, 2001).

5. Meir Statman, *What Do Investors Think? Risk-Aversion, Loss-Aversion and the Annuities Puzzle.* Presentation to the Retirement Income Industry Association, February 2007.

6. Moshe A. Milevsky and Virginia R. Young, "The Real Option to Delay Annuitization: It's Not Now-or-Never." York-Schulich-Finance Working Paper No. MM11-1, 2001.

CHAPTER 17   The Third Dial: Investment Policy

1. In clarifying the ideas expressed in this section, we found a very useful discussion in Peng Chen and Moshe A. Milevsky, "Merging Asset Allocation and Longevity Protection: An Optimal Perspective on Payout Annuities," *Journal of Financial Planning,* June 2003.

2. As always, we ignore credit risk here: the risk that the insurer might not survive as long as the purchaser.

3. One example is a variable immediate annuity sold by the Teachers Insurance and Annuity Association–College Retirement Equities Fund (TIAA-CREF).

4. Ruth Helman, Jack VanDerhei, and Craig Copeland, *The 2007 Retirement Confidence Survey.* Employee Benefit Research Institute: Issue Brief No. 304, 2007.

5. Wei Sun, Robert K. Triest, and Anthony Webb, "Optimal Retirement Decumulation Strategies: The Impact of Housing Wealth." Federal Reserve Bank of Boston Public Policy Discussion Paper No. 07-2, 2007.

6. We are conscious of the fact that we are suggesting a holistic approach—taking housing wealth into account—in decumulation, though we didn't do so in discussing accumulation. Is it more important in decumulation than in accumulation? Yes and no. Yes, because in decumulation housing wealth is something to draw on if you're in danger of outliving your wealth, a situation that doesn't have a counterpart in accumulation. No, to the extent that in the accumulation chapters we dealt only with the wealth building up in the DC plan; it was

beyond our scope to expand the discussion to all forms of wealth. But, in fact, in our accumulation years we tend intuitively to do what the target date glide path suggests: By taking out a mortgage and buying real estate, we are converting human capital into real property. This also enables us to get leverage, which we can't do with the glide path in the DC plan. So in our accumulation years many of us convert human capital into both real property and financial assets.

7. Greenwald Strategy Service 2007 Financial Advisor Survey, Mathew Greenwald & Associates, Inc., October 31, 2007 (a presentation to Russell Investment Group).

8. While Social Security payments are indexed to the cost of living, most DB pensions (at least in the private sector) are fixed dollar.

9. In the United States, this might take the form of Supplemental Security Income, paid to those over 65 and with low incomes. See www.sa.gov/pubs/11000html.

10. But see Chapter 18, where we describe new products that can guarantee you an income for life as well as potentially provide a death benefit if you die early.

11. See, for example, Richard K. Fullmer, "Modern Portfolio Decumulation: A New Strategy for Managing Retirement Income," *Journal of Financial Planning,* August 2007.

12. See note 6 in Chapter 16.

13. Quoted in Richard I. Kirkland, Jr., "Should You Leave It All to the Children?" *Fortune,* September 29, 1986.

14. Charles W. Collier, *Wealth in Families* (Cambridge, MA: Harvard University, 2006).

CHAPTER 18   Product Innovation with Decumulation in Mind

1. New design features are common not only because the features themselves are of interest, but also because they help the products to resist commoditization.

2. At the time of writing, we have not seen this product on the market. But its features have been discussed in investment literature.

CHAPTER 19   Defined Contribution Plan Governance

1. The observation that governance is about process is consistent with ERISA's fiduciary principles, which are also about process. For a more detailed analysis, see Bevis Longstreth, *Modern Investment Management and the Prudent Man Rule* (New York: Oxford University Press US, 1986), chap. 44.

2. "Responsible parties" are those who, by education or experience, have the abilities to fulfill their duties competently, or who can fulfill those duties through the selection and monitoring of consultants and experts.

3. 2007 Annual Social Security Statement, "Unless action is taken soon to strengthen Social Security, in just 10 years we will begin paying more in benefits

than we collect in taxes. Without changes, by 2040 the Social Security Trust Fund will be exhausted."

4. Nor, for that matter, should the interests of the employer affect the fiduciary's decision. But we do not discuss that aspect in our example.
5. The Vanguard Group, *How America Saves, 2007.*
6. "Default Investment Alternatives under Participant Directed Individual Account Plans; Final Rule," Department of Labor, Employee Benefits Security Administration, 29 CFR Parts 2550, *Federal Register,* October 24, 2007.

CHAPTER 20   Defined Contribution Plan Effectiveness

1. John Beshears, James Choi, David Laibson, Brigitte Madrian, and Brian Weller. "Public Policy and Saving for Retirement: The 'Autosave' Features of the Pension Protection Act of 2006," in *Better Living through Economics,* 2007, p. 8.
2. Unless, of course, you believe, as we discussed in Chapter 6, that low-paid employees have valid reasons for not participating.
3. 2006 Hewitt Universe Benchmarks. "How Well Are Employees Saving and Investing in 401(k) Plans?"
4. There are certainly sponsors who feel, "It's not my role to second-guess what my participants do; my role is to give them good choices and good defaults and to make sure they understand that decisions have consequences." Fair enough. Our metric is aimed at sponsors who want to reduce the waste factor that their own contributions are subjected to when participants make the sort of poor decisions we highlighted in Chapter 10.
5. William E. Nessmith and Stephen P. Utkus, "Hardship Withdrawals and the Mortgage Crisis," Vanguard Research Note, Vanguard Institutional Investor Group, April 2008.
6. Jennifer Levitz, "Investors Pull Money Out of their 401(k)s," September 23, 2008, http://wsj.com/article/SB122212664298765183.html#.
7. Federal Thrift Investment Board, Board Member Meeting Minutes, www.frtib.gov/FOIA/minutes.html. June 2008 Minutes, see page one of Attachment 1. Thrift Savings Fund Statistics.
8. Sue Asci, "Consumers Increasingly Take Loans from Retirement Plans," *Investment News,* April 14, 2008, www.investmentnews.com/apps/pbcs.dll/article?AID=/20080414/REG/702355424/-1/Topic&template=printart.

CHAPTER 21   The Defined Contribution Plan Sponsor's Role in Decumulation

1. That is because a lump sum is an acceptable form of benefit. An exception is the United Kingdom, where a lifetime annuity is the compulsory form of exit from a DC plan (though even there up to 25 percent of the benefit can be taken in a lump sum).

About the Authors

Don Ezra is Global Director, Investment Strategy for Russell Investments. He is a widely published author, and has won a Graham and Dodd Award from the *Financial Analysts Journal* and the Roger Murray Prize from the Q Group in the United States. He was a delegate to the National Summit on Retirement Savings in 2002 and 2006 and to the White House Conference on Aging in 2006. In 2004 he was given the Lillywhite Award of the Employee Benefit Research Institute "for extraordinary life contributions to Americans' economic security."

Bob Collie has been working with defined benefit and defined contribution plans in the United Kingdom and United States for more than 20 years, playing at different times the role of actuary, investment consultant, and strategist. He has written and presented extensively on many aspects of the pension challenge—both actuarial and investment-related over those years. He works for Russell Investments, based in Tacoma, Washington, in the beautiful Pacific Northwest.

Matthew X. Smith leads the defined contribution consulting practice in the United States for Aon Consulting. He has been involved with the design, implementation, administration, consulting to, and asset management of defined contribution plans for over 25 years. He has also written and spoken widely on topics involving defined contribution plans during his career. Matt lives and works in the Seattle, Washington, area.

Index